Jonathan Goodman has been described as 'the greatest living master of the true-crime literature' (Jacques Barzun) and 'the premier investigator of crimes past' (Julian Symons).

Once a theatre director and television producer, Jonathan Goodman then became managing director of a specialised publishing company. In 1970 his first true-crime book, *The Killing of Julia Wallace*, was published and since then, as a full-time writer on crime, he has published many true-crime accounts and novels. He is one of the few lay members of the British Academy of Forensic Sciences, a member of the Medico-Legal Society, and is on the committee of the Crimes Club. He lives in London.

Murder in
Low Places

Jonathan Goodman

HEADLINE

Murder in High Places was
for K (Mrs Robert F Hussey) with love –
and so is this.

First published in Great Britain in 1988
by Judy Piatkus (Publishers) Ltd

First published in paperback in 1989
by HEADLINE BOOK PUBLISHING PLC

ISBN 0 7472 3208 3

Printed and bound in Great Britain by
Collins, Glasgow

HEADLINE BOOK PUBLISHING PLC
Headline House
79 Great Titchfield Street
London W1P 7FN

Contents

Introduction

Once I had decided where to draw a dividing-line near the crown of a social scale, and another at the desirable end of a means table, choosing the contents of a book called 'Murder in *High* Places' was fairly simple: I did not have an over-abundance of cases to choose from; some of those cases would have been noticeably absent if I had left them out.

But for a book called 'Murder in *Low* Places', choosing has been difficult. In part, because the adjective will be expected to refer to locations of murder as well as to a lack of social standing or capital of the murderers or their victims; in part, because people or places considered low by some onlookers are viewed with envy by some others; in part, because most murders that have been committed in unequivocally low places by people who felt quite at home in them have been of the thud-and-blunder sort, and don't, it seems to me, deserve remembrance; in part, because – despite what I have just said – the stock of undoubtedly apt and worthy cases is so large that picking from it is as well done with a pin as thoughtfully.

But I have not used a pin. I have selected cases that are diverse – of period, of apparent motive, of means of murdering – and that, often long ago, I enjoyed discovering. It just so happens that the stories, between them, and to say nothing of other characters' killings mentioned in them incidentally, contain thirty legally-accepted murders; I have not done a further, more general count, but I guess that that number exceeds the previous entire tally of murders that I had written about. I have not changed my mind that, as a rule, mass-murderers (who used sometimes to be called 'multicides'; the term 'serial-killers' is now so much the rage that it must soon be out of date) are dull: the minute that murdering becomes a habit, the murderer, usually a nonentity to start with, usually becomes a caricature of a human being; a murder should be as especial an event to the murderer as it is to the victim. I can think of only a few exceptions to the rule; William Palmer (who gave lethal meaning to the betting term 'winning accumulator'): George Joseph Smith (he would deserve immortality even if he had not made his brides momentarily more blushing by entering the bathrooms while they were bathing); the mass-murderers in this collection, and perhaps a couple more. With the deepest respect to De Quincey, John Williams, the depopulator of Ratcliffe Highway, is not one of them.

I have noticed, as no doubt you have too, that sometimes, quite by chance, certain stories in a collection are linked by something that has nothing whatever to do with what the main title suggests is the link between all of them. An anthology that I compiled a few years ago, its title unfruity, turned out to have a number of apple-association tales – and *this* collection has some leather connections: one of the blunt instruments was a leather-dresser's hammer, one of the mass-murderers liked dressing up in leather clothes, and two others, a partnership, lived and smothered within smell of a tannery. Which, all in all, goes to show that – rather in the way that some eagerly-beavering Ripperologists rummage in their respective culprits' horoscopes, Masonic lodges' programmes for ladies nights, and entries in the *Wisden Cricketers' Almanack* for facts that can be made to support their choice, and pretend they haven't seen connected facts that can't – one could gather a job-lot of stories, and then, after a little tinkering with some of them, give the book a title relevant to at least a paragraph of every item. The title might have to be something like 'Murder by Men Wearing Three-Piece Suits' or 'Murder by Men Who Didn't Wear Three-Piece Suits', but never mind.

I believe that, for the sake of variety, one or two of the stories in any collection of stories should, as it were, take advantage of the collection's title. In an anthology called *The Seaside Murders* that I compiled, I included tales of murder that happened beside the sea but nowhere near a seaside resort. And in *this* book, one of the accounts is of two roughly concurrent murders, one committed in a subterraneously low place by a visitor there, the other in an upstairs bedroom by someone who dwelt below stairs.

Three of the shorter pieces first appeared, shorter still, as articles in the *Manchester Evening News* or the *Northern Echo* or *Sussex Life*. I am grateful for help I have had from David Allen, Albert Borowitz, Richard Boyd-Carpenter, Ivan Butler, Philip Chadwick, Joe Gaute, Dr Lewis Gavin, Peter Jackson, Henry Somake, Bill Waddell, Richard Whittington-Egan and Ian Will.

An Anatomy of Murders

Perhaps to some extent because some writers of social history are financially dependent upon patrons (usually, these days, state-funded research-subsidising councils or large companies that, needing to gloss their image, sponsor academic projects as well as snooker competitions), and so feel that they must try to elevate their trade above its proper purposes, few writers of social history take notice of the nine-days' wonders that occupied the minds of people who lived during them, leaving little or no room for interest in what was happening in parliament and other important places. But nine days can be a long time in social history; and if the writing of such history is to meet one of its purposes, which is to give an idea of how it *felt* to be a supernummerary member of the cast of a period, then the wonders – provoking oohs of abhorrence or ahs of admiration from the mass of men, their own deeds giving no cause for exclamation – must not be retrospectively shunned on account of a sort of snobbery.

Generally speaking, snobbery of the more usual sort lies behind the neglecting of scenes of *criminous* nine-days' wonders. The notion that it is not quite nice to express a fascination with celebrated crimes has resulted in some strange pretences – the strangest, it seems to me, in regard to 39 Hilldrop Crescent, an address which in the summer of 1910 became as famous as 10 Downing Street, and which still rings a bell in many people's memories. For the benefit of other people, let me explain that 39 Hilldrop Crescent, in the district of North London called Holloway, was where Dr Crippen murdered his wife, who was best known as Belle Elmore, her stage-name as a singer, his motive probably being that he wanted to be free to marry his mistress Ethel Le Neve; he, with Ethel (she dressed as a boy), sought to escape to his native America, and, for the first time, wireless

4

telegraphy was used in aid of catching a murderer. In the 1960s, hearing that the house, damaged by a bomb during the Second World War, was to be replaced by a block of council flats named after Margaret Bondfield, a trades-union politician, I wrote to the local mayor, suggesting that Margaret Bondfield should be given her due on some other council estate, thereby allowing the block in Hilldrop Crescent to be sensibly, appropriately designated: as Crippen Court, perhaps, or Le Neve's Folly, or – best of all, I considered – Elmore's End. The mayor politely turned down my suggestion; he made it clear, carefully without saying so, that the very idea of signifying the site of a murder appalled him. I did not pursue the matter – did not try to make him understand that the act of murder is rarely significant towards making a murder case celebrated; that, speaking of Crippen, his apparently inaugural use of the drug hyoscine as a means of murdering certainly made him notable to connoisseurs of crime – but that the Crippen *case* caught the public imagination, and had retained it, far more because of events preceding and following the murder than because of the murder itself.

It has since occurred to me that a virtually sure way, not merely of making snobs about murders cure their genteelness, but of inverting their snobbery, is to mention that our royal family considers that one murder at any rate – and that in a royal home – warrants efforts to keep it in mind. At the Palace of Holyroodhouse, in Edinburgh, men are employed to show visitors around the chambers and passages associated with the murder of Mary Stuart's friend, David Riccio.

Edinburgh has other criminous remembrances. In the High Street stretch of the Royal Mile to Holyroodhouse, granite blocks, embedded heart-shaped in the pavement, mark where the Tolbooth Gaol, demolished in 1817, was entered: publicists of the city declare that a custom of spitting on the heart survives, but I have seen no more spittle there than on undecorated parts of the pavement. Diagonally across the Mile, at the edge of the stretch called Lawnmarket, is a pub named after Deacon Brodie, who – a bourgeois by day, a burglar by night – gave Stevenson the idea for *Dr Jekyll and Mr Hyde*. And farther west in the Mile, in Grassmarket, a small garden has been made, intentionally where a scaffold stood till 1784. (Deacon Brodie, having been nocturnally successful till 1788, was hanged elsewhere, on gallows that he had over-optimistically paid the hangman to modify.)

A short distance on from the far-from-royal end of the Mile, where the mean thoroughfares of High Riggs and West Port meet, is a pub that till 1969 was the Main Point Bar. In the summer of that year it was vamped so as to become the Burke & Hare – a name reckoned to be apt because opposite, on the side of West Port sometimes almost shadowed by the Castle, is where Tanner's Close used to be: the site is part of the site of a present office-building. In 1972, I noted[1] that the Burke & Hare 'is like a psychedelic space-capsule; there are a few naive wall-paintings, and behind the bar are modern portraits, quite pretty but hardly lifelike, of the murderers'. Subsequently, so I'm told, the Burke & Hare was for a while a 'go-go pub' (meaning that some of the female employees served toplessly), and more recently, perhaps still, has been a 'live-music pub'. Its name-providers deserve, if not a better memorial, a more fitting one.

> Up the close and doun the stair,
> But and ben[2] with Burke and Hare;
> Burke's the butcher, Hare's the thief,
> Knox the boy that buys the beef.

The roles ascribed in that verse, the most abiding of many that commented on the affair in the last two months of 1828, fit the rum-ti-tum scansion better than they fit the facts that came to light in those months. Knox – who I think you will feel sorry for, sorrow about – enters the tale, unwittingly salient to it, after its beginning. Before that beginning, there are some things you should know about Burke and Hare.

Both were called William. They were born about the same time, the early 1790s, in different parts of Ireland – quite where, whether in Catholic or Protestant places, has become a matter of dispute, but is not important. In 1818, or thereabouts, they migrated to Scotland, still strangers to each other, and worked as

---

[1] *In* Bloody Versicles: The Rhymes of Crime, *Jonathan Goodman, David & Charles, 1971.*

[2] *Out and in.*

navvies, always far apart, on the cutting of the Union Canal between Edinburgh and Falkirk, a distance of twenty-five miles, which took till 1822. Meanwhile, Burke (who may have left a wife and children in Ireland) co-habited with an ugly Scotswoman, 'the upper half of her face out of proportion to the lower', who called herself Helen M'Dougal; the surname was that of a man she had lived with but never married. After being paid off as a navvy, Burke, with Helen M'Dougal accompanying and assisting him, peddled secondhand goods in and around Edinburgh; eventually, having picked up the rudiments of cobbling, boots and shoes were his main stock in trade. In the late summers, six in all, the couple helped farmers with the harvest, each earning more than they would have made from peddling.

Compared with Burke, Hare prospered. As a navvy, he had toadied to the leader of his gang, himself an Irishman, who was known as Log – probably the source or a shortening of 'Logue'. Once the canal was ready, its owners re-employed Log, now as an overseer of 'lumpers' of cargo ('stevedores' they would be called today, except by trades-unionists, who would insist on 'handlers'), and Log, in turn, re-employed Hare. From what one gathers of Log, he was not of the type to give favours generously, and so he may have extorted a tribute from Hare – a once-and-for-all slice of his first pay-packet or slighter acknowledgments regularly. Or perhaps, being subtle as to the remittance of returns from a favour, he persuaded Hare to rent bed-space in the doss-house which he and his wife Margaret kept, they themselves living there, in Tanner's Close – an alley so called because there was a tannery, its smell almost smothering residential ones, at the closed end. In any event, Hare became one of the Logs' lodgers. Since there is no reason to suppose that the house looked much different by the winter of 1828, one of the several descriptions of it printed then may be quoted here:

The entry from the street begins with a descent of a few steps, and is dark from the superincumbent land.[1] On proceeding downwards, you come to a smallish self-contained dwelling of one flat, and consisting of three apartments. One passing down the close might, with an observant eye, have seen into the front room;

[1] *In the particularly Scots sense, 'land' means a group of dwellings.*

a ticket, 'Beds to let', invited vagrants to enter. The outer
apartment was large, occupied all round by these structures called
beds, composed of knocked-up fir stumps, and covered with a few
grey sheets and brown blankets, among which the squalid
wanderer sought rest, and the profligate snored out his debauch
under the weight of nightmare. Another room opening from this
was also comparatively large, and furnished much in the same
manner. The door stood generally open, and, as we have said, the
windows were overlooked by the passengers up and down; but, as
the spider's web is spread open while his small keep is a secret
hole, so here there was a small apartment, or rather closet, the
window of which looked upon a pig-stye and a dead wall.

Hare's stay at the house long outlasted that of other lodgers,
and would have lasted longer but for a falling out with Log, who
ended the argument by ousting him. A reason will soon appear
either for the rumour or for crediting the rumour that the dis-
agreement arose from Log's suspicion that Hare was 'making
free' with Margaret Log. Supposing that Log *was* suspicious,
then he must also have doubted Margaret's fidelity, for no man
could have made free with her without her consent: unaccountably nicknamed 'Lucky', she was built like a present-day woman
shot-putter, that condition derived from her years of hard
labouring as a member of her husband's gang of canal-diggers.

It is reasonable to presume that Hare, as well as being ejected
from the lodging-house, was sacked from his job as a lumper.
There are only guesses as to where he lived and how he made a
living till some time in 1826, when, learning that Log had died,
he thoughtfully returned to Tanner's Close to console the
widow. Finding that a similarly thoughtful lodger was already
consoling her, he engineered the man's departure. Even while
the muscular Margaret was outwardly mournful, she and Hare
took up where, according to the uncharitable view, the late Log
had forced them to leave off; within months of Mrs Log's becoming a widow, she felt entitled, under a Scots secular law that
perceived living in sin as a marital state once it was engrained, to
call herself Mrs Hare. But though Hare could now make free
with her to her heart's content, he could not, she insisted, live
free of charge, slothful when out of her bed. And so he did odd
jobs; and in the first two late summers of his undocumented

marriage, left Margaret managing her main inheritance, which was still known as Log's lodging-house, while he harvested out of town – secondly, on a farm at Penicuik, a ten-mile walk away.

If Hare had ever met his countryman William Burke before (which is as some legends have it), neither had been much impressed by the other; but their toiling together at Penicuik, their carousing at night, and their sharing of a barn for sleep – Burke's woman, still passing as Helen M'Dougal, ever present – established a friendship; and at the end of the harvest-time, Hare, saying that he wished to prolong the friendship – perhaps thinking, too, of pleasing Margaret by bringing her custom – invited Burke, which meant Helen as well, to stay at 'his' lodging-house in Tanner's Close, an invitation that was accepted.

More than a year later, drawings and pen-portraits of Burke and of Hare, most of the efforts intended to conform with mind-pictures of human monsters rather than to be lifelike, made both men seem protean. Of the reporters' descriptions that I have read, the following strike me as being most likely the least inaccurate:

> Burke . . . is a man rather below the middle size, and stoutly made, and of a determined, though not peculiarly sinister, expression of countenance. The contour of his face, as well as the features, is decidedly Milesian.[1] It is round, with high cheek bones, grey eyes, a good deal sunk in the head, a short snubbish nose, and a round chin, but altogether of a small cast. His hair and whiskers, which are of a light sandy colour, comport well with the make of the head and complexion, which is nearly of the same hue. He has what is called in this country a *wauf* rather than a ferocious appearance, though there is a hardness about the features, mixed with an expression in the grey twinkling eyes, far from inviting.
>
> Hare's . . . eyes are watery, curiously shaped, and have certainly a peculiarity about them, which seems to hover betwixt leering and squinting; the forehead is low; combativeness is large – destructiveness middling;[2] the nose, mouth, and chin, very

---

[1] *Irish-looking. From Milesius, a mythical king of Spain; his sons and their followers are said to have seized Ireland.*

[2] *Both assertions according to phrenology, the so-called science of gauging a person's characteristics from bumps on his head, which was all the rage.*

vulgar and commonplace; and his countenance, on the whole, though it may betray more or less of what we may call a sinister dash of expression, indicates anything but intense ferociousness. Nothing can better describe his appearance than the common remark that 'he is a poor silly-looking body'; for though Hare is certainly no beauty, everyone has seen hundreds of uglier men. He can neither read nor write, and his mind, in other respects, is just as untutored as an Esquimaux Indian's. He is five feet six inches high and weighs 10 stones.

It has lately been suggested that the invention of the wheel arose from an attempt to make ear-rings. Though that suggestion is probably wrong, it is probably not far wrong. Many innovations arise unintendedly, as offshoots from purposes; others can be credited to or blamed upon a pure serendipity, away from any side-track: hardly any bright ideas arrive already pristine, not needing the slightest refinement. Looking at Burke and Hare as trail-blazing entrepreneurs, one sees, not just one or two, but all three of those facts exemplified.

Their business partnership can be said to have been founded on Thursday, 29 November 1827, a couple of months after they had laboured amid the alien corn of Penicuik. That day began miserably for the Hares, with the discovery that their longest-abiding lodger, an army-pensioner called Donald, his surname apparently unknown to anyone in the house, had died during the night. The Hares' misery was not from bereavement, nor even from the thought of inconveniences that Donald's dying on the premises would put them to – but from his having died just prior to when his pension was due, owing (so the story goes) four pounds. (The amount of his debt is open to question. Unless Margaret Hare had frequently lent cash to Donald, feeling secure that she would be repaid on his pension-day, the debt was the accumulation of threepences – that sum being what it cost to spend a night in Log's lodging-house. Four pounds of threepences – 240 pennies in the pound, remember – was the equivalent of 320 nights' lodging, and nothing that one knows of Margaret suggests that she would have allowed anyone increasing 'tick' for anywhere near as long as ten and a half months. *If* 'four pounds' is no exaggeration, then – accepting the subsequent reckoning that there were seven dossing beds, each meant for three occupants, and assuming that the house was full most nights – it was as if the Hares had lost a fortnight's receipts.)

Hare – Margaret too, perhaps – sought condolence from Burke – Helen M'Dougal too, perhaps. But Burke, rather than commiserating, remarked to the effect that the cloud cast by Donald's death might have a golden lining: maybe Donald's change of status, from pensioner to corpse, had increased his monetary value. Burke soon explained what he meant. I shall take longer.

Medical men had complained of a dearth of bodies for dissection since before anatomy was recognised as a medical science. The situation had been greatly improved early in the sixteenth century, while Henry VIII reigned in England, James V in Scotland, by Acts that allowed surgeons and barbers to have the bodies of executed felons for, so far as Henry was concerned, 'anatomies with out any further sute or labour to be made to the kynges highnes his heyres or successors for the same. And to make incision of the same deade bodies or otherwyse to order the same after their said discrecions at their pleasure for their further and better knowlage instruction in sight learnying & experience in the scyence or facultie of Surgery.' Since there were, roughly speaking, 2,000 executions per annum in Henry's name (and, though no one in Scotland seems to have tried to keep tally during James's near enough concurrent rule, surely an annual average there and then that measured up, per capita, to England's), the supply of fallen bodies fell not far short of the demand: in England, at any rate, may have come close to being sufficient during the supposed reign of Henry's juvenile son Edward, between 1547 and 1553, when the annual average of hangings at Tyburn alone was 560.

But over the next two centuries and a half, while the number of theoretically capital offences grew (to a neat peak of 222 in 1810), the number of offences that were in fact punished helpfully for anatomists dwindled to a couple of dozen, and they provided annually only a hundred or so 'subjects' (that was the anatomists' euphemism for corpses put to scientific ends). From about the middle of the eighteenth century, matters were made worse by the mushrooming growth of private schools only or especially of anatomy, each needing almost as frequent a supply of subjects as did the long-established colleges of surgeons and the medical faculties of universities.

All sorts of proposals were put forward, in parliament, in the press, and elsewhere, for reducing, even remedying, the short-fall: suicides of the discreet sort – who though they had not disfigured their bodies outwardly, were clearly careless of them – should be eligible; the remains of paupers should be dissected before being buried, still more higgledy-piggledy than at present, in communal graves (support for that proposal: 'returns obtained from 127 of the parishes situate in London, Westminster, and Southwark, or their immediate vicinity, show that out of 3,744 persons who died in the workhouses of these parishes in the year 1827, 3,103 were buried at the parish expense, and that of these about 1,108 were not attended to their graves by any relations'); all persons who came to their death by duelling, prize-fighting, or any other dangerous activity that warranted discouragement, ought to be offered – sight unseen, lest pernick-ety anatomists thought to pick and choose those tidily wounded from those that weren't; 'as prostitutes have, by their bodies during life, been engaged in corrupting mankind, it is only right that after death those bodies should be handed over to be dissec-ted for the public good'; all medical men should bequeath their own bodies. None of the notions was taken up.

And so (much as in the 1920s and early 30s, in the United States, the illegality of alcohol gave rise to illegality of a far worse kind, colloquially called bootlegging), the anatomists' insuffi-ciency of legally-proper subjects led to the creation of a black market: at first, a market solely in bodies from undertakers or kept absent from undertakings that, rather like Hamlet without the Prince, had coffins without occupants, that omission super-ficially repaired by the inclusion of ballast to about the right body-weight. But before long, as anatomists outbid one another for legally-improper subjects, and thus pushed up the recom-mended retail price, and as once-impeccable anatomists accepted that as they couldn't lick their body-buying rivals, they had to join them, the subjects-suppliers, their numbers growing too, looked for ways of ensuring an adequate stock, and, in many cases, looked downwards.

Auxiliary to the petty crime of corpse-selling, the crime of grave-robbing became almost as prevalent; it was only a bit more risky in terms of legal consequences in the event of apprehension, for, there being no property in a dead body, a prosecution for felony could not be brought unless some portion of the shroud or coffin could be proved to have been stolen with the body; even if such evidence existed (which was rarely: in 1828 the magistrate of a busy court reckoned that he had had no more than half a dozen cases of theft from burial grounds in as many years), defendants were usually cautioned or fined – hardly ever imprisoned. Grave-robbers were far more worried that they might be caught in or, while laden, after the act by relatives or friends of their plunder; when that happened, the consequences were often brutally severe, and sometimes fatal. One precaution against undisciplined citizens' arrest was the 'casing' of the site and environs of an intended dig, so as to ensure that there was no all-night sentry or regularly-visiting watchman; another, which might be in addition to the casing, was the posting of a menial, sharp of both sight and hearing, to keep cave while the work was in progress; yet another, most expensive but best of all, was the bribing of employed sentries or watchmen respectively to look the other way or to miss out the place of excavation from duty-rounds – such dereliction not only paid for but agreed to on the understanding that, following the emptying of the coffin, the soil that had been dug out would be shovelled back and patted, leaving the grave looking unspoiled, giving no reason for the guard's usual employers to question his conscientiousness.

The employment of guards was but one of the initiatives aimed at repelling or resisting the grave-robbers.[1] Most of the initiatives were intended to make the employment of guards unnecessary; few fulfilled that intention. In some burial-grounds, bijou lodges, not unlike Wendy houses but more secure, were built, their purpose being to store bodies till they were too putrid to serve as subjects. (One such lodge survives in the burial-ground in the village of Crail, on the coast of Fife, north-east of Edinburgh.) A report published about 1810 in a Scots paper speaks of a bereaved father whose determination to

---

[1] I shall stick to calling them that because each of the several nicknames for them – for instance, sack-'em-up-men, body-snatchers, and, the loveliest, resurrectionists – was particular to a part of the country.

keep the body of his son safe from dissection was greater than his desire that the body should remain intact:

> Curiosity drew together a crowd of people on Monday, at Dundee, to witness the funeral of a child, which was consigned to the grave in a novel manner. The father . . . had caused a small box, inclosing some deathful apparatus, communicating by means of wires, with the four corners, to be fastened on top of the coffin. Immediately before it was lowered into the earth, a large quantity of gunpowder was poured into the box, and the hidden machinery put into a state of readiness for execution. The common opinion was that if anyone attempted to raise the body he would be blown up. The sexton seemed to dread an immediate explosion, for he started back in alarm after throwing in the first shovelful of earth.

Iron-founders and blacksmiths did a brisk trade in mort-safes, cages that fitted snugly over and around tombstones (some still to be seen in Greyfriars Churchyard, Edinburgh); often more decorative than the tombstones they protected, mort-safes were not a sure protection of what lay beneath the stones: certain grave-robbers, most likely ex-miners, were able to reach their quarry, irrespective of mort-safe, simply by burrowing diagonally rather than digging vertically. Another use of iron towards keeping remains secure – one that must have required a doubling of the customary number of pall-bearers – was as a material for coffins. Going by an advertisement in *Wooler's British Gazette* for 13 October 1822, a Mr Edward Lillie Bridgman, who traded in funerary equipment from premises on Fish Street Hill, close to London Bridge, seems to have believed that iron coffins were his prerogative:

> Many hundred dead bodies will be dragged from their wooden coffins this winter, for the anatomical lectures (which have just commenced), the articulators, and for those who deal in the dead for the supply of the country practitioner and the Scotch schools . . . Those undertakers who have IRON COFFINS must divide the profits of the funeral with EDWARD LILLIE BRIDGMAN. TEN GUINEAS reward will be paid on the conviction of any Parish Officer demanding an extra fee, whereby

I shall lose the sale of a coffin. The violation of the sanctity of the grave is said to be needful, for the instruction of the medical pupil, but let each one about to inter a mother, husband, child, or friend, say shall I devote this object of my affection to such a purpose; if not, the only safe coffin is Bridgman's PATENT WROUGHT-IRON ONE, charged the same price as a wooden one, and is a superior substitute for lead.

One cannot make out whether the extent of grave-robbing came near what Mr Bridgman and his competitors did their copy-writing best to alarm the public into believing that it was. Facts and figures are few and, geographically, far between: nearly all of them are in regard to happenings in and around one or other of the main seats of medical learning, Edinburgh and London. Rough counts that were occasionally made in those cities were dependent upon the market researchers' sly quizzing of the anatomists' porters and students, most of whom at first gave equally sly replies, and then, when fuddled by the drink provided coaxingly by the researchers, said whatever the researchers wanted them to say. The counts, inefficient in any case, were deficient of data that had nothing to do with dissection – a skewing omission, because some graves were robbed in aid of unscientific practices, either necrophilic or, as the following cutting from the *Universal Spectator* of 20 May 1732 instances, commercial:

> John Loftas, the Grave Digger, committed to prison for robbing of dead corpses, has confess'd to the plunder of above fifty, not only of their coffins and burial cloaths, but of their fat, where bodies afforded any, which he retail'd at a high price to certain people[1] . . .

---

[1] *Candle-makers, perhaps: a line of the ballad 'The Surgeon's Warning' by Robert Southey (1774–1843) has the repentant eponym admitting 'I have made candles of infants' fat'. Or maybe Loftas's retail was of suet or, cooking beforehand, dripping – possibilities that remind one of the domestic servant Kate Webster, who in 1879, at Richmond, Surrey, having murdered her mistress, chopped up the body, boiled scraps of it, and soon afterwards, possibly irrelevantly, touted two large pots of dripping to a fellow-frequenter of her local pub.*

James Blake Bailey[1] refers to 'a statement by the police in 1828 that the number of persons who, in London, lived regularly on the profits of exhumation, did not exceed ten; there were, in addition to these, about two hundred who were occasionally employed'. But by no means all of the bodies dissected in Edinburgh and London, or intended to be, were of Edinburghians[2] and Londoners – a fact exemplified by an incident at Liverpool, an account of which was printed as a broadsheet:[3]

Discovery of thirty-three Human Bodies, in Casks, about to be shipped from Liverpool for Edinburgh, on Monday last, October 9, 1826.

Yesterday afternoon, a carter took down to one of our quays three casks, to be shipped on board the Carron Company's vessel, the *Latona*, addressed to 'Mr G. Ironson, Edinburgh'. The casks remained on the quay all night, and this morning, previous to their being put on board, a horrible stench was experienced by the mate of the *Latona* and other persons, whose duty it was to ship them. This caused some suspicion that their contents did not agree with their superscription, which was 'Bitter Salts,' and which the shipping note described they contained. The mate communicated his suspicions to the agent of the Carron Company, and that gentleman very promptly communicated the circumstances to the police.

Socket, a constable, was sent to the Quay, and he caused the casks to be opened, when Eleven Dead Bodies were found therein, salted and pickled.

The casks were detained, and George Leech, the cartman, readily went with the officer to the cellar whence he carted them, which was situated under the school of Dr McGowan, at the back

[1] *Librarian of the Royal College of Surgeons of England, in his book* The Diary of a Resurrection, *Swan Sonnenschein, London, 1896.*

[2] *That term preferable, surely, to the proper 'Edinburgher,' which sounds like a haggis in a bun.*

[3] *Readers familiar with broadsheets will know that it is wise to be wary of what any of them say; generally, truth is not allowed to mar a sensational tale. But most of the statements made on* this *broadsheet are verified by reports published subsequently in the* Liverpool Mercury.

of his house in Hope Street; the cellar was padlocked, but, by the aid of a crow-bar, Boughey, a police officer, succeeded in forcing an entrance, and, on searching therein, he found four casks, all containing human bodies, salted as the others were, and three sacks, each containing a dead body. . . . In this cellar were found twenty-two dead bodies, pickled and fresh, and in the casks on the quay, eleven, making in the whole thirty-three.

The carter described the persons who employed him as of very respectable appearance, but he did not know the names of any of them.

Information of the above circumstances was speedily communicated to his Worship, the Mayor, who sent for Dr McGowan. This gentleman is a reverend divine, and teacher of languages; he attended the Mayor immediately, and, in answer to the questions put to him, we understand he said that he let his cellar in January last to a person named Henderson, who, he understood, carried on the oil trade, and that he knew nothing about any dead bodies being there. . . .

Mr Thomas Wm. Dawes, surgeon, of St Paul's Square, deposed that he had examined the bodies, by the direction of the Coroner. In one cask he had found the bodies of two women and one man; in another, two women and two men; in the third, three men and one woman, and in the other casks and sacks he found 22 [*sic*] bodies, viz., nine men, five boys, and three girls; the bodies were all in a perfect state . . . There were no external marks of violence, but there was a thread tied round the toes of one of the women, which is usual for some families to do immediately after death. Witness had no reason but to believe that they had died in a natural way, and he had no doubt the bodies had all been disinterred. The Season for Lectures on Anatomy is about to commence in the capital of Scotland. . . .

The bodies, by the direction of the Coroner, were buried this morning in the parish cemetery, in casks, as they were found. . . .

A good many of the bodies dissected in Edinburgh hailed from Dublin – for, contrary to the legend of Scots meanness, Irish grave-robbers could get better prices from the anatomists of Edinburgh, who also paid shipping costs, than from those of Dublin. Indeed, the respective prices were so far apart that some

Irish middlemen, having bought bodies ostensibly for home use, made profit from them by despatching them to Edinburgh. In January 1828, Irish nationalists, irked by the discovery that a porter at the Royal College of Surgeons in Ireland was engaged in such unpatriotic export, murdered him; whether his body was donated to his employers or, to the financial good of a cause, travelled elsewhere, one cannot tell.

Enough has been said, I think, to show that, by the time that the pensioner known only as Donald died in the later Log's lodging-house in Tanner's Close, a quite considerable cottage – or, usually, churchyard – industry served anatomists' purposes; and that Edinburgh (which had recently become two-faced: part of the city to the north of its Castle so beautiful that its dubbing as 'the Athens of the North' was a sort of flattery to Athens; part of the city to the south of its Castle ugly as sin and so kippered by smoke as to be called Auld Reekie) was the perfect place in Great Britain, in the world, for setting up a business specialising in the supply of fresh corpses.

But the firm of Burke & Hare was not considered by either of the partners to be one at its outset; the selling of Donald's body was meant to be a one-off transaction, a means of reimbursement of his debt, no more than that.

As several persons already knew of Donald's death (foremost among them, presumably, the two surviving occupants of his death-bed), and were already spreading the knowledge around West Port, it was necessary to dissemble his interment. And so an undertaker was called in, he arriving, unconcerned about measurements, with a coffin in tow; and the minute he had fitted the body into the coffin and hurried away to Greyfriars churchyard, there to make a booking for space in the next available paupers' pit, Burke used his cobbling jemmy carefully to lift the coffin-lid; then he and Hare lumbered the body into the small back room (the window of which, you will remember, looked upon a pig-stye and a dead wall), then both men – hurrying, for fear that the undertaker might induce the Greyfriars sexton to cramp a ready-dug pit, and return importunately – filled the coffin with an apt amount of tree-rind filched from the pile of it that the nearby tanner used towards turning skin into leather; then Burke banged the lid back on while Hare swept dropped bits of tree-rind out of sight; and then they rested.

Briefly, though. Knowing not even the basic formalities of what they had to do next, they set off long before they should have done to find a buyer. It was still daylight when they headed east, unloaded, making for Surgeons' Square[1]. Reaching South Bridge (which was, is, adjunct to the North Bridge, a viaduct spanning a deep hollow between the New and Old Town), they encountered a young man somehow or other acquainted with Burke. The encounter made the story of them very different from how it should have turned out.

The young man was a student of medicine. Knowing that, Burke told him that he himself and Hare were on their way to 2 Surgeons' Square, the off-campus premises in which Alexander Monro III, professor of anatomy at Edinburgh University, dissected, usually lecturing the while, and explained – on the qt, of course – what they hoped to accomplish there.

The young man was studying anatomy under Robert Knox. He may, just making conversation, have mentioned that Knox – known behind his back as 'Old Cyclops' because an attack of smallpox soon after his birth in 1793 had blinded one of his eyes – was reckoned, except by rivals, to be the most informed and informative anatomist in the city; that his school, which had become his alone two years before, following the death of its founder, John Barclay, who had taught and eventually employed him, was far and away the most successful of the private schools of anatomy; that there was no comparison between Knox and the third of the Alexander Monros, who was more butcher than anatomist, a professor only because his father and grandfather had each, in turn, graced the same Chair – and whose lectures demonstrated his dependence on his grandfather's notes, which he parroted, with the inclusion even of phrases like 'When I was a student in Leyden in 1719'.

Getting to his point, the student advised Burke and Hare to amend their destination in Surgeons' Square from No. 2 to No. 10 – Dr Knox's Rooms for Practical Anatomy and Operative Surgery – and they said that they would do so.

---

[1] *Which was subsequently erased; it was a hundred yards or so east of South Bridge, roughly where Infirmary Street curves into High School Yards.*

And, momentously to the outcome of the story, they did so –
only to be shooed by an uppity doorman to the tradesmen's
entrance; and there, once their shy mutterings were com-
prehended, only to be told that such dealings were done after
dark: they could return that night if they so wished – no appointment was needed, since someone was always on duty to take
delivery and to negotiate a price.

They traipsed away.

There was still a chance that Robert Knox would not be
ruined; that some more expendable anatomist would be
sacrificed.

However, rather than seeking a daytime buyer, they returned
to Tanner's Close, and there whiled away the time till dusk –
when, having thought to wrap Donald's body, they took it
(Burke, the burlier, sometimes allowing Hare respite by carrying
it piggyback) to 10 Surgeons' Square: a distance of about a mile,
twice as far as Greyfriars, which they passed on their right.

They arrived so early in the dark as to be met, not only by the
head porter, David Paterson, but also by three students of such
seniority and promise that Knox either waived their fees or even
paid them a little something for assisting him. Their names were
William Fergusson, Thomas Wharton Jones, and Alexander
Miller: all three would achieve fame and fortune from surgery –
especially Fergusson, who in 1866 was knighted by Queen Victoria, and in the following year became Her sergeant-surgeon.
The first thing that Burke and Hare were told was that it was best
for all concerned if they kept their surnames to themselves; and
so they were merely 'John and William' when, at Paterson's
bidding, they carried their load upstairs to the lecture-room,
deposited it on a slab which, when Knox was demonstrating,
made a frame for the focus of as many as three hundred pairs of
studying eyes, slid away the sacking and then the shirt, and stood
aside while Fergusson, Jones and Miller appraised – certainly
noting the freshness and the absence of signs of burial, putting
those twos together to make four, but, the need for subjects being
what it was, keeping the joint conclusion to themselves. Words
were whispered to Paterson – words that he translated in his
mind into a price: £10 – about the average. Nudging the clearly-
novice John and William further aside, away from earshot of the
students, he offered £7.10s. Take it or leave it, he said. And they,

believing that hesitation might cause him to lower the offer, surely not to be more generous, said, as with one voice, *done*.

£7.10s. Giving that sum meaning is hard. Government reckonings of inflation do not go so far back; even if they did, one would trust them no more than one trusts today's. It is sensible, I think, to see that sum in relation to the threepence a night that the Hares charged for lodging – that, so far as Burke was concerned, taking Helen M'Dougal into account, was sixpence. Presently, no doss-house – not even one with as few mod cons as the Hares' – provides accommodation for under a couple of pounds a night. But let us say a pound. Again reminding you that there were 240 pennies in the pound till we were decimalised, simple arithmetic – too simple, you may think – shows that as there were 80 threepences in the pound, and as one of those threepences bought a night's stay in Log's lodging-house, threepence then would be worth at least a pound now; ergo, 7½ of Burke's and Hare's pound would amount, at least, to our £600.

No wonder, then, that Burke and Hare were happy. Hare was so taken aback by the happiness that, without thinking of what Margaret would say, he split the proceeds fairly: £4.5s. retained (which, if the extent of Donald's debt to Margaret is believed, left Hare with a Crown), and £3.5s. for Burke (who, after all, had initiated the venture, and had done the lion's share of the labour). It would be nice to say that Burke, who for the first time in his life could afford munificence, insisted upon covering the overhead expenses associated with the undertaking of the rind-filled coffin; but there is no evidence that he did.

Between one and three weeks went by. That is as accurate as it is possible to be; the Christmas of 1827 was coming. Meanwhile, one of the Hares' lodgers began to look sickly. Whereas we know three things about the subject-matter of Burke and Hare's first transaction at 10 Surgeons' Square – that his first name was Donald, that he was a retired soldier, and that, therefore, he had reached a decent age – only two things are known about his immediate successor: his first name, which was Joseph, and his trade, which was corn-milling. The minute Joseph began to look sickly, both Burke and Hare expressed concern – though, so they subsequently insisted, for different reasons, Hare's being that if it turned out that Joseph was suffering from typhoid, cholera, or some other contagious disease, the lodging-house would have to be closed for a time, and Burke's being that he might catch whatever it was that Joseph was suffering from. Each for his own reason, they agreed upon euthanasia. Telling Joseph of the medicinal worth of whisky, which he was only too glad to believe, they dosed him into unconsciousness, thus making redundant Hare's spread-eagling of himself over Joseph while Burke pressed a pillow on the latter's face. There were no undertaking expenses: if anyone enquired as to Joseph's whereabouts, they could reply that he had gone away – which in no time at all was a truth. Whoever accepted the body on behalf of Robert Knox cannot have observed the merest anything suggesting that death might, just might, have resulted from a contagious disease; he or they must have caught a whiff of the whisky, but, perhaps, was or were so entranced by a scent quite different from the anticipated kind as to be uninquisitive of it. Joseph's body being a better prospective subject than Donald's had been, David Paterson was told to pay more for it – and did, delighting John and William by giving them ten of the sovereigns that since 1817 had been valued at a pound apiece.

Delighted them: encouraged them, too. From now on, in the absence of corpses that had become so through natural causes or of lodgers whose smothering could, with a little creative thought, be justified as humane, Burke and Hare manufactured death. They were helped in that trade, on a part-time, beck-and-call basis, by their women and one or two of Burke's immigrant kin.

The striking difference between their story and those of the majority of other persons known to have committed 'serial killings' is that, while they were busy, no one influential had the slightest idea that a serial of killings was in progress: most of their victims, whether lured or conveniently present, had flitted about too frequently to be noticeable by their absence; a problem that taxes the ingenuity of lots of murderers, that of doing away with a body, was no problem at all for the Edinburgh partnership, whose creations were *intended* for destruction in aid of a science. (Just think what an immense advantage that was to Burke and Hare – of how the depriving of it from such latterday serial killers as the same-initialled Brady and Hindley, Henry 'Big H'

McKenny, and Dennis Nilsen, put them to far more work after their killings than beforehand.)

Perhaps to mislead any eavesdroppers on their shop-talk, Burke and Hare used jargon for some nouns of their trade: the things that were jargonised as subjects by the men of Surgeons' Square were, to them, 'shots', and their acts of murder were 'tricks'. Though the jargon was subsequently translated and utilised by reporters of their activities, none of it caught on with the public (but one reporter's turning of Burke's name into a verb was accepted so widely as to earn entry into English dictionaries, the present best of which retain it – '**burke,** *v.t.* to murder, esp. by stifling: hence (*fig.*) to put an end to quietly').

The exact number of persons murdered by Burke and Hare, or by one or other of them, was never established, each of them admitted, in effect, to having lost count. The minimum number, inclusive of Joseph the miller, is sixteen.

A little was left of 1827 when Hare – perhaps taking an unintending stroll rather than prowling for prey – met and made conversation with an old woman, Abigail Simpson; her complaint of footsoreness was his cue to ask her to the lodging-house to rest awhile. As she had done once a week for years, since her retirement from the domestic service of a rich man, she had walked from her cottage at Gilmerton, five miles south-east of Edinburgh, specially to present herself at the kitchen-door of the rich man's house in the New Town and to receive from one of his present servants her pension of eighteen pence and from another a can of broth. She was on her way home when Hare met her; and so the encounter must have been on South Bridge, part of the straightest route to Gilmerton – and so, as that place was about a mile from Tanner's Close, Hare must have enveigled her by more than the promise of a nap. Probably by the promise of whisky. In any event, having been ushered into the small back room, she was made more drowsy by Hare's hospitality. Burke, joining them, showed off his tenor singing voice: not ostentatiously, for people were sleeping in other rooms, but with the sincerity that always watered his eyes when he sang Irish sentimental songs, which made up his whole repertoire. A lullaby did the trick – or rather, made the 'trick' opportune. The moment Abigail snored, she was smothered. Burke wiped his eyes. Alexander Leighton, a chronicler of the partnership[1] and, of all its chroniclers, the most observant of equivocations in it, would enquire in regard to Burke's musicalness on this occasion and on some similar ones:

> Could that man have had any sense of the beautiful in the sentiments of the lyrics which, it was said, he sang with feeling, if not pathos? Can it be possible that such a sense can be consistent with a demoralisation such as his? We suspect that it is. We are led to expect its impossibility by a reference to opposite, if not antagonistic, feelings: we cannot love and hate the same object. This is true, and would seem to disprove our proposition *à priori*. We can reconcile the contradiction only by having recourse to the different faculties of the imagination and the sense. The poet who has ravished his readers by a description of the beauty of female virtue and innocence has been found in a brothel. One of the most touching religious poems in the world has been sung by one who, among brawling revellers, maligned religion and its votaries. The praises of temperance have been enchantingly poured forth by a bacchanal. The oppressor of the poor has wept at a representation of affecting generosity. Anyone may fill up the list without perhaps including a hypocrite. The imagination has its emotions, and the sense its feelings, or, perhaps, no feelings. The why and the wherefore touch the ultimate, and we are lost; but the fact remains, as proved by evidence, that William Burke could, in song, be pathetic.

Abigail Simpson's body, carefully made anonymous, was the first that John and William presented to Robert Knox in person; his only comment to them, framed unquestioningly, was that the body was fresh. The trick produced a gross profit of £10.1s.6d – the small change of that amount being the pension-payment that the old woman had travelled so far to collect. No doubt the eighteen pennies were claimed by Hare as reimbursement for the single overhead, his spiritual means of making Abigail ready for the pillow. As was to be so for all but one of the subsequent deals, the disbursement from Knox was divided one half to Hare,

---

[1] The Court of Cacus, Alexander Leighton, *Houlston & Wright, London and Edinburgh, 1961.*

two-fifths to Burke, and a tenth to Margaret – she having insisted that she was entitled to that share as proprietor of the murder-scene. (Though some of the later tricks were done elsewhere, she still took her tenth – perhaps, without saying so, considering it as danger-money, for by the time of the first murder on other premises, she and the unpercentaged Helen M'Dougal had overheard their men, both drunk, mutually moaning that opportunities were scarce, and discussing the possibility of producing a related subject, which in Hare's case, he having no true relatives in Edinburgh, could only have meant Margaret.)

Neither of the next victims was known by any name to those who profited from them. First, an Englishman who sold matches on street-corners came to the lodging-house, meaning to sleep there; so weak was he that Hare did not waste even a night-cap on him, and merely stood by while Burke, not bothering with a pillow, pinched his nose with one hand and barred his mouth with the other. The body was barely away when the Hares alone, and quite as arrogantly, made another: Margaret enticed an old woman in, and plied her with whisky till she was unconscious; Hare, told of the catch when he returned for supper, entered the small back room, arranged the bed-tick so as to impede the old woman's breathing, went back and ate the meal that his wife had meanwhile dished up, and later checked that, partial undressing apart, a delivery was ready for 10 Surgeons' Square.

Unlike those murders, both done with a casual efficiency, the next was about as organised as a tossed salad. I shall tell of it in collaboration with the anonymous compiler of one of the first books on the entire case,[1] sometimes altering his tense and always putting his contributions in italic.

On the night of Tuesday, 8 April, a pair of prostitutes, Janet Brown and Mary Paterson, neither more than twenty, were apprehended for some offence other than prostitution, probably for being drunk and quarrelsome, and lodged in the watch-house of Canongate, the final stretch of the Royal Mile to the Palace of Holyroodhouse. It would be as well for you to get your bearings: Canongate runs east from High Street, which, at its centre, cuts across the Bridges and separates them as North and South; as

[1]West Port Murders, *Thomas Ireland Jnr, Edinburgh, 1829.*

you know, Tanner's Close was about a mile west of the Bridges – therefore, well over a mile west of Canongate.

Janet, *though a girl of the town, seems to have been possessed of a considerable intelligence.* She was pretty; petite. Mary was altogether beautiful – of tresses, features, form. *Well educated, she had lost in youth the guiding care of a mother. Her beauty was a snare to her, and her perverse will, though accompanied but not modified by a kind heart, greatly tended to accomplish her downfall.*

They were released from custody before daybreak on the Wednesday. Without having to walk far, they went to the house of a Mrs Laurie, *where they had formerly lodged* – and which was certainly either a brothel or a sort of specialising temps agency. Mary, already thinking of making up for the night's work she had lost, put her hair in paper curlers. She was still wearing them when, at about 7 a.m., she and Janet left Mrs Laurie's and sauntered back to Canongate – to an ever-open spirits shop run by a man named Swanston. *They had there a gill of whisky, and while drinking it, they observed Burke, who, in company with Swanston, was drinking rum and bitters.*

Now what Burke was doing out, and in Swanston's, at that time of the morning cannot be surely explained. Some authors have suggested – no: stated – that he was reconnoitring for prey; but other possible explanations appear more likely – among them, that he had sought sexual pleasure from Helen M'Dougal at a time of the night or month that seemed inconvenient to her, and, angry at her rebuff as well as being still keen for satisfaction, had flounced out, chiefly to emphasise his anger but also in the hope of picking up an insomniac prostitute in Swanston's, which, despite its proximity to a watch-house, was a public house of ill repute.

He entered into conversation with the girls Brown and Paterson, and affected to be much taken with them, and three gills of rum and bitters were drunk at his expense. He wished them to accompany him to his lodgings, which he said were in the neighbourhood, and upon Brown expressing reluctance, was very urgent that she should go, saying that he had a pension and could keep her handsomely, and make her comfortable for life, and that he would stand between them and harm from the people in the house. This particular attention to her she supposed to be in consequence of finding her more shy and backward than Paterson, who was always of a forward fearless disposition. They consented to go along with him, and he promised them breakfast when they reached the house. He purchased, before leaving Swanston's, two bottles of whisky, and gave one to each of the girls to carry.

As has been indicated, Burke was not the only one of his family to have emigrated to Scotland. His brother Constantine, who was properly married and conventionally employed (as a scavenger, or street-cleaner, by the Edinburgh council), dwelt in a house in Gibb's Close, a dark alley off Canongate. It was to that house that Burke took the girls – surprisingly to Constantine and his wife, Elizabeth, who were in bed. Now acting his lie that he lodged in the house, *Burke swore and abused the woman* (Elizabeth) *for her negligence at not having the fire lighted* – and neither she nor Constantine undermined his lie.

The fire was lighted up, and breakfast, consisting of tea, bread, eggs, and Finnan haddocks, prepared; but during this process, the two bottles of whisky were produced and partly drunk by Burke, Constantine, his wife, and the two girls. Constantine partook only of part of it, having in the meantime left the house to his work as a scavenger. Before the whisky was finished, however, Burke requested Brown to leave the house along with him. He accompanied her to a neighbouring public house (not Swanston's), *where he gave her two bottles of porter which he also partook of, and a pie.*

It appears that Constantine had delayed his scavenging or gone to it by a roundabout route, taking in Tanner's Close, for while Burke and Janet Brown were at the pub, a matter of fifteen minutes or so, Helen M'Dougal turned up at Constantine's house. She seemed calm when they returned. She had not introduced herself, or been introduced, to Mary Paterson, who was by now showing signs that she had drunk quite a lot of rum and whisky; and she did not introduce herself to Janet. Burke made no introductions. Embarrassed by those omissions of social etiquette, *Constantine's wife whispered to the girls that the woman lately arrived was Burke's 'wife'. Upon Helen M'Dougal's upbraiding him for his conduct, Brown apologised for being in his company, mentioning that they did not know him to be a married man, otherwise they would not have come, and proposed then to*

*leave the house. M'Dougal replied that she did not blame them,
but that it was his constant practice to desert her and spend his
money upon loose women. She requested them to sit still, and
seemed anxious that they should not go away.* Burke must then
have piped up, saying something in his defence, and Helen
M'Dougal must have made a more provocative remark, thus
starting a quarrel between them. *It got more violent, and she took
up the eggs which had been set down for breakfast and threw them
into the fire. Upon this, Burke took up a dram glass and flung it at
her; it hit her forehead above the eye and cut it.*

*At the commencement of the uproar, Constantine's wife ran out
of the house, as Brown subsequently supposed for the purpose of
bringing Hare; indeed, as she saw no other person dispatched
anywhere, it is difficult to account otherwise for this vampire's
speedy appearance. Burke then succeeded in turning Helen
M'Dougal out of the house, locking the door upon her. By this time
Paterson was lying across the bed in a state nearly approaching
to insensibility. Burke pressed Brown to go along with him into
bed; but, as she herself subsequently observed, much as she might
have been disposed to yield to his wishes, she could scarcely have
done so after the brawl she had so recently witnessed, and while
M'Dougal was still making a noise at the door and knocking for
admittance, and she peremptorily refused. She persisted in her
wish to be allowed to depart, promising to return in a quarter of
an hour. Upon this promise she was suffered to depart, and Burke
at her request conducted her past M'Dougal, who was still upon
the stair-head apparently much enraged.*

*She went straight to Mrs Laurie's, and jestingly told her that
she had got fine lodgings now; but after informing Mrs L. of the
circumstances, she agreed to go back along with Mrs L.'s servant,
and endeavour to get Paterson removed. Upon her return she did
not recollect perfectly the close in which the house was situated,
and applied at Swanston's for a direction to the residence of the
man who left his public house with herself and Paterson. She was
told, among other things, that she would probably find him in his
brother's in Gibb's Close. Even after getting into the close and the
stair, she did not recognise the house, and entered that of a decent
woman, enquiring if it was there she was before. She was
informed that they kept company with no such people, but it
would likely be in the house upstairs. They proceeded up accord-*

ingly, and found there M'Dougal and Hare and his wife. Mrs Hare ran forward to strike Brown, but was prevented. Between her leaving Burke's and returning, there was only about an interval of twenty minutes.

During those twenty minutes, Mary Paterson was smothered to death, and her body tucked out of sight, probably beneath the bed. It was extraordinarily stupid, doing a murder then and there – but that reproving comment should be viewed in the light of a general statement, which is that stupid murderers are less likely to be caught than are studious ones. Supposing that I had to choose between allying myself in a murderous way with a couple like Burke and Hare or with a pair of geniuses like Leopold and Loeb, I should choose the former alliance without thinking twice. Stupid acts are hard for sensible people to credit, difficult for them to understand. Private murders that the murderers try to *keep* private are usually suspected, detected, through logic of some sort; if those murderers are illogical, then anyone with a flow-charting mind (which is what detectives are supposed to have) is likely to be baffled by them. Had Burke and Hare and their women possessed, between them, as much intelligence as did Janet Brown, the murder of Mary Paterson would have been the final instalment of the serial.

When Janet asked where her colleague was, the Hares and Helen M'Dougal *alleged that she had gone out with Burke, and added that they expected them back soon, and invited her to take a glass of whisky with them. She did so, in the hope that Paterson might quickly return. Mrs L.'s servant then left them, and M'Dougal commenced a narration of her grievances from Burke's bad conduct, and railed at him for going away with the girl. In a short time the servant returned for Brown, Mrs L. having become alarmed at her report. No attempt was made to detain Brown; but she was invited to return, which she promised to do.*

In the afternoon she did go back, and was informed by Constantine Burke's wife that Burke and the girl had not returned. (One gathers, then, that the woman of the house had it to herself. If she had done any tidying, no more even than making up the bed and emptying the potty, she can hardly have failed to notice that her brother-in-law and his friends had left something behind. Either she had done no tidying or she was a wonderfully calm liar.)

Some time before six in the evening, when it was getting dark, Burke and Hare – the former having slept his hangover away – came to collect their belonging. They did not take long to undress it of all but a chemise (ungratefully, or because Constantine's wife had OS measurements, Burke called back in a day or so for the other garments) and to put it in a canal-boat sack that one of them had thought to bring. Though, as Closes went, Gibb's was much handier than Tanner's to Surgeons' Square, the route through back-doubles was crowded with children who had nowhere safer to play; and a group of them, eager for diversion from hop-scotch, followed Burke and Hare and made them hurry by chanting, presumably in fun, 'They're heaving a corpse.'

Arrived, panting, at No. 10, they were met by William Fergusson (he who would become surgeon to the Queen) and a less tutored student: 'a tall lad' is the sole description of him, but he should, he really should, have made his name from the fact that, from a single glance at the dead face of Mary Paterson, he thought that it was as like that of a girl he had perused in Canongate a few nights before 'as one pea is like another'. And he said as much, forcing Fergusson – who also had recognised the body – to ask 'John' for its provenance. Burke replied that he and William had bought the body from an old woman, a stranger to them, at the back of Canongate. No other question was asked. For a reason that can only be surmised, Fergusson told one of the suppliers to cut off the beautiful tresses, paper curlers and all, and gave him a pair of surgeon's clippers to do so. Perhaps as a tacit way of expressing his disquiet, Fergusson offered only eight pounds for the finest subject that John and William had yet provided. They did not dare to haggle.

Days later, another of Knox's students saw the body – and was more disturbed by it than either Fergusson or the tall lad had been. For he had known Mary Paterson intimately, paying for that right. That none of the three students – nor any of those that two of them gossiped with – spoke warningly to Knox is proved by what he did. Rather than dissecting the body when its turn became due, he, delighted by its beauty, had it preserved to illustrate his lectures on muscular development for the next three months; whisky, which had so greatly contributed towards Mary Paterson's death, was the agent of her corpse's salvation. Knox shared his delight with artistic friends, by arranging private viewings; and he allowed two artists to draw portraits of the submerged still-life.

Meanwhile, Janet Brown pestered Constantine. *Whenever she saw him, which she frequently did at his work early in the morning, she enquired after her friend. His answers were always very surly; on two occasions saying, 'How the h—ll can I tell about you sort of people; you are here today and away tomorrow;' and on another, 'I am often out upon my lawful business, and how can I answer for all that takes place in my house in my absence.' It was pretended that Paterson had gone off to Glasgow with a packman; but this reply did not satisfy Brown, as she knew that Paterson was a well-educated girl, and could write sufficiently well to send an account to her friends if she had left Edinburgh. No more satisfactory intelligence, however, could be obtained.* Janet must have wondered whether Mary was dead. But if the idea of murder entered her mind, it was dispelled as far-fetched.

Before summer, when all of the anatomists reduced the prices they paid for subjects, Burke and Hare made two further sales, having killed – perhaps vice versa – an old Irishwoman named Effie who had survived by selling oddments discarded by people in the New Town to people in the Old Town who could make use of them (bits of leather, for instance: Burke, when cobbling, had often bought them from her, and that was how she had got to know him well enough to make her enticement easy); and a woman of whom nothing is known other than that she too was old. When Burke first spotted her, in West Port, she was so drunk – and therefore ready primed for the intention that had brought him out – that she would surely have keeled over but for the flanking support of two constables, whose occupation he considered no hindrance to his now-specific intention; speaking to one of them, Andrew Williamson, with whom he was on good terms, having given him titbits of information about local ne'er-do-wells, he offered to relieve him and his fellow-officer of their burden, thus freeing them for less onerous duties, and Williamson was much obliged.

On a day early in June, Burke found an embarrassment of opportunities. While making his way to Log's with a man whose drunkenness was almost the equal to that of the woman he had accepted from the constables, he was intercepted by yet another old woman. She was accompanied by a boy of about twelve – he was her grandchild; he was a deaf mute. Both were tired, for they had walked from Glasgow, meaning to stay with friends in Edinburgh. She told Burke the friends' address, and asked if he could direct her to it. Burke knew that the address was close by; but he hummed and hawed while deciding between a bird in the hand and two in the bush. Then, the decision made, probably on the basis that the drunken man would be available, just as drunk, some other time, he sat him in the gutter, and, turning to the old woman from Glasgow, told her that her friends lived some distance away – but in the direction of his lodgings, where she and her grandson were welcome to bide awhile, refreshing themselves until he pointed them towards their journey's end. At Log's, she was introduced to the others; and they – Margaret, who was noticeably pregnant, especially – made a fuss of the boy, and every so often expressed sadness at his afflictions, speaking softly though he could not hear. Then Margaret, saying that the boy was safe with her, told the old woman to follow the men into the small back room. The old woman, expecting the promised refreshment, did so. Eventually, the men returned. And some time later, the boy, frightened but unable to scream, was murdered too.

The partners may have been considering a 'double event' for weeks – ever since Burke had bought a horse and cart, both decrepit, or before that transaction, he in that case thinking of it as a solution to additional haulage problems. But though they had, or thought they had, transport sufficient for concurrent deliveries, they felt that they required a single container for more than one body. A herring barrel was acquired. The bodies of the Glaswegian woman and her grandson were contorted into it. The barrel was humped on to the cart. Burke had learned soon after his purchase that the ancient horse could not cope with heavy loads, and so he and Hare walked beside the cart once the horse was ambling, and put their shoulders behind it on rising ground. Having laboured as far as the Meal Market, the horse took a 'dour fit', refusing to go farther. Efforts to make it obedient failed – but drew a crowd. Burke, more furious than worried, engaged a porter with a 'hurley-barrow', and the barrel was transferred.

The porter, it was afterwards nicely said, 'had fewer scruples than the horse', and dragged his vehicle to Surgeons' Square. Burke followed; Hare stayed behind, to make arrangements regarding the horse and cart – which, according to the writer just quoted (and I must tell animal-lovers to skip to the next paragraph), amounted to having both towed to a neighbouring tanyard, 'where it was found that the poor beast had two large dried-up sores on his back, which had been stuffed with cotton, and covered over with a piece of another horse's skin'.

Meanwhile, Burke, having paid off the porter, was experiencing difficulties associated with the barrel, the contents of which, pliable when inserted, had stiffened, making them hard to extract. The help of several students was required before assessment could be carried out by William Fergusson.

It would not be surprising if – despite the sixteen pounds realised from the sales – Burke, depressed by the loss of his horse and cart, and Hare, petulant at the troubles they had put him to, had a row. That would have been one of several between them at about this time. As a counterpoint to their disharmony, Margaret was using her pregnant state as the excuse for being more snappy than usual. Helen M'Dougal, made miserable by all of this, was accused by the others of casting gloom, and was sometimes smacked by Burke on that account. There is a tale that Margaret broached the idea to Burke that, as Helen was such a drag, he might be advised to take her away somewhere, murder her (whether or not with the extra motive of financial profit was up to him), send back word of her passing for the Hares to pass around, and return long enough later as to have obviated the need to buy mourning dress. Burke and Helen did go away at the end of June, to stay with relatives of hers at Maddiston, near Falkirk, but they both returned to the city at the end of July – not, however, to Log's, but to a house in an unnamed close, separated from Tanner's by the eastward Weaver's Close. They sub-rented a room in the house from John Broggan, whose wife was a cousin of Burke's. Some four months from the start of their tenancy, a reporter noted that,

in approaching Burke's you enter a respectable looking land from the street, and proceed along a passage and then descend a stair, and turning to the right a passage leads to the [front] door, which is almost opposite to the house of Mrs Law [of whom further mention will be made shortly after this quotation]; a dark passage within the door leads to Burke's room. The room is small, and of an oblong form; the miserable bed occupied nearly one end of it (that next the door). Everything presented a disgusting picture of squalid wretchedness; rags and straw, mingled with implements of shoemaking, and old shoes and boots, in such quantities as Burke's nominal profession of a cobbler could never account for. A pot full of boiled potatoes was a prominent object. The bed was a coarse wooden frame, without posts or curtains, and filled with old straw and rags. At the foot of it and near the wall was [a] heap of straw. The window looks into a small court, closed in by a wall. At the top of the stairs leading down to the room is a back entrance from a piece of waste ground. There are several outlets from it.

The breach between the partners was widened: chiefly by Burke, who at first suspected, and then established through enquiries at 10 Surgeons' Square, that Hare had done a deal while he, Burke, was at Maddiston – and partly by Hare, who at first felt cut to the quick, and then, ignoring the outcome of Burke's inquiries, took umbrage at the fact that Burke was so distrustful of him as to have made them. But eventually, each recognising that he needed the other – or that if he tried to go it alone, he would be up against fierce competition – they resolved their differences; or made out that they had. The business recovered.

August and September comprised the slack season; they were the months of vacation for all of the schools of anatomy (Knox's impending term, commencing on Monday, 6 October, meanwhile being advertised on handbills: 'FEE for the First Course, £3, 5s; Second Course, £2, 4s.; Perpetual [till the end of July 1829: any of the parents or guardians who paid the undiscounted lump-sum would wish that they had opted for the instalments arrangement], £5, 9s. N.B. – *An Additional Fee of Three Guineas includes Subjects*. Arrangements have been made to secure as usual an ample supply of Anatomical Subjects.'); prior to the respective re-openings, subjects were required only for lecturers' private use and for their crammings of promising students or poor ones who were rich enough to be able to afford bespoke tuition. Even so, Burke and Hare did four tricks – at least four – during that period:

Item. Since the death of her husband in 1826, a Mrs Hostler had eked out a living by doing other people's washing. As she had no mangle of her own, a friend, Mrs Janet Law, had allowed her the use of hers, and so she had become a regular visitor to the unnamed close, arriving from her home in Grassmarket with a basketful of wet and rumpled linen, cranking the load between the wooden rollers of Mrs Law's mangle, panting out gossip (for she was a busy-body) as she did so, relaxedly telling further tales while sharing her whisky-flask with Mrs Law (who was taciturn compared with her but equally fond of a dram), and then departing with a basketful of damp and folded linen. In the weeks round about the arrival of Burke and Helen M'Dougal in the house across the close, she often amended the routine of her trip by popping into that house to give pre-natal counselling, founded on her own experiences long ago, to Mrs Broggan, who may not have wanted but certainly needed it; and when the baby was born, she gate-crashed the celebration, which, almost as rowdy as a wake, was also attended by the Broggans' new tenants and two friends of theirs from Tanner's Close. One can believe Burke's subsequent recollection that Mrs Broggan was not at the party; but his statement, made almost in the same breath, that her husband was absent too seems to have been a kindly lie – though why he should have lied (Hare was prevented from telling the truth by his insistence that he wasn't at the party either) is hard to fathom, considering that, while all but one of those who were at the party were still recovering from it, Broggan borrowed £1.10s. from Burke, and the same sum from Hare, and straightway absconded. While the party was in full swing, Mrs Hostler, who had been the life and soul of it, left the room with Burke. She was singing her favourite song, 'Home, Sweet Home'. It was the last that was heard of her. The total of three pounds that Broggan got from Burke and Hare came from the eight that the body of Mrs Hostler fetched.

Item. During their month in the country, Burke and Helen M'Dougal had stayed with relatives of her former 'husband'. Before leaving, Burke had told one of them, Ann M'Dougal, who seems to have been much the same age as Helen, that he would like to repay her favours by putting her up in Edinburgh. Almost certainly, he did not then regard her prospectively, as raw material for his trade; nor when she wrote from Maddiston, accepting the invitation; nor during the first weeks of a stay that he had imagined would last a few days. But anyone who has suffered from providing indeterminable hospitality will understand his eventual cracking under a pressure made more pressing by Hare. It is not known whether Helen was openly understanding. He, pricked by remorse at the ending of a 'distant relative', insisted that Hare had to do the actual smothering – but nonetheless expected his accustomed share of the proceeds. Though Ann had meant to stay longer, only a short time passed before her real relatives in Maddiston grew concerned at her continued absence. Some of them travelled to Edinburgh, hoping to learn what had become of her. Perhaps they did not know Burke's still-new address; if they called at Log's, they would not have been directed. They finished up at Constantine's – where, quite by chance, they found Helen. She was very drunk. When they explained the purpose of their trip, she said that they need not have troubled themselves, as Ann was murdered and sold long before. Thinking that she was joking in the worst possible taste, they smiled politely and left, returning to Maddiston without having made further inquiries.

Items. Mary Haldane, a prostitute long past her prime, was delighted when Hare, observing her on her beat in Grassmarket, indicated that she was to follow him to Tanner's Close. Her delight was short-lived. She left three daughters, they subsequently enumerated as follows: 'One was married to a tinsmith named Clark, carrying on business in the High Street of Edinburgh; the second was serving a sentence of fourteen years' transportation for some offence; while the third was simply following the unfortunate example of one who should have sheltered her from evil influences.' The third, whose name was Peggy, was not left for long. Becoming anxious at her mother's disappearance, she asked around, and received information from several people, all of whom had known 'Mistress Mary' at least by sight, for though she had been but one of many prostitutes of the Grassmarket, she had been the one least used and so most often on display – and made still more conspicuous by the fact that her smile, intended to be enticing, had revealed that she was left with only a single central tooth. Hearing from David Rymer, a grocer in West Port, that her mother had gone with Hare, Peggy went to Tanner's Close. Margaret Hare, perhaps post-natally depressed, flew into a tantrum at the very idea that her husband had consorted with a loose woman – but instead of ordering Peggy out, invited her in. Hare, returning, instantly slipped away to summon Burke. Shortly afterwards, the bed in the small back room, still cold from the body of Mary Haldane, accommodated her daughter's.

In the week when October began, the week in which the anatomists of Edinburgh stocked up for their new terms, revising their rates upwards, Burke and Hare killed James Wilson – who, being mentally retarded in relation to his age, which was eighteen, was known to many people in the Old Town, and not just behind his back, as 'Daft Jamie'. After his disappearance was explained, a pamphlet devoted to him alone described his manners, partly as follows:

> His father died when he was about twelve years of age; and his mother being a hawker, he was left, during her absence, pretty much to his own devices. He generally wandered about the streets, getting a meal here and a few pence there. He was one of those wandering naturals known to everybody, and being a lad who, while deficient in intellect, was kind at heart, he was a universal favourite, only the very small and the very impudent boys troubling him. He was such a simpleton that he would not fight to defend himself. Little boys, about the age of five or six, have frequently been observed by the citizens of Edinburgh going before him holding up their fists, squaring, and saying they would fight him; Jamie would have stood up like a knotless thread, and said, with tears in his eyes, that he would not fight, for it was only bad boys who fought; the boys would then give him a blow, and Jamie would have run off, saying, 'That wiz nae sair, man, ye canna catch me.' Then about a thousan' gets [brats] hardly out o' the egg-shell, would have taken flight after him, bauling out, 'Jamie, Jamie, Daft Jamie.' Sometimes he would have stopped and turned round to them, banging his brow, squinting his eyes, shooting out his lips (which was a sign of his being angry), saying, 'What way dae ye ca' me daft?' 'Ye *ir*,' the little gets would have bauled out. 'I'm no, though,' said Jamie, 'as sure's death; devil tak me, I'm no daft at a'.' 'Ye *ir*, ye *ir*,' the gets would have bauled out. He then would have held up his large fist, which was like a

Dorby's mell [stonemason's mallet], saying, 'If ye say I'm daft, I'll knock ye doun.' He would then have whirled round on his heels and ran off again, acting the race-horse.

Robert Kirkwood, another half-wit, was familiarly known as Boby Awl. Jamie and Boby were fast friends, and no one could get them to fight, though frequent attempts were made to do so. They seemed to have a fellow-feeling for each other, and each of them firmly believed that his companion, and not himself, was 'daft'.

When the activities of Burke and Hare were exposed, Daft Jamie was given more words than the rest of the victims put together. So many of the words make up obvious inventions as to raise a suspicion that many of the others make up subtle ones. Therefore, one may as well be content with an account that implicitly admits poetic licence:[1]

> ATTENDANCE give, whilst I relate
> How poor Daft Jamie met his fate;
> 'Twill make your hair stand on your head,
> As I unfold the horrid deed:–
>
> That hellish monster, William Burke,
> Like Reynard sneaking on the lurk,
> Coyduck'd his prey into his den,
> And then the woeful work began:–

[1] I shall leave out several stanzas of the 'Elegiac Lines on the Tragical Murder of Poor Daft Jamie', published as a single sheet by W. Smith, of 3 Bristo Port, Edinburgh, who also made a mint of 'thrip pences' from A Laconic Narrative of the Life and Death of Poor Jamie, and of shillings from An Authentic Narrative of the Life and Death of Robert Kirkwood – that work given its ending by the fact that Boby Awl had recently been killed by the kick of a donkey; his body went to Alexander Monro's dissecting room. Mr Smith's advertisement before publication of the latter booklet asserted that it would be 'very entertaining to any who might read it, though they never saw the Oaf. There will be nothing inserted to offend or corrupt the morals, so that an abbess or modest damsel may peruse it without blushing.' All of the 'Elegiac Lines' and the Laconic Narrative are reproduced, with many other pieces of ephemera, in Burke and Hare: The Resurrection Men, edited and with an introduction by Jacques Barzun (Scarecrow Press, New Jersey, 1974).

'Come, Jamie, drink a glass wi' me,
And I'll gang wi' ye in a wee,
To seek yer mither i' the town –
Come drink, man, drink, an' sit ye down.'

At last he took the fatal glass,
Not dreaming what would come to pass;
When once he drank, he wanted more –
Till drunk he fell upon the floor.

Like some unguarded gem he lies –
The vulture waits to seize its prize;
Nor does he dream he's in its power,
Till it has seized him to devour.

The ruffian dogs, – the hellish pair, –
The villain Burke, – the meagre Hare, –
Impatient were the prize to win,
So to their smothering pranks begin:–

Burke cast himself on Jamie's face,
And clasp'd him in his foul embrace,
But Jamie waking in surprise,
Writhed in an agony to rise.

But help was near – for it Burke cried,
And soon his friend was at his side;
Hare tripp'd up Jamie's heels, and o'er
He fell, alas! to rise no more!

No sooner done, than in a chest
They cramm'd this lately welcom'd guest,
And bore him into Surgeons' Square –
A subject fresh – a victim rare!

And soon he's on the table laid,
Expos'd to the dissecting blade;
But where his members now may lay
Is not for me – or you – to say.

But this I'll say – some thoughts *did* rise:
It fill'd the Students with surprise,
That so short time should intervene
Since Jamie on the streets was seen.

But though his body is destroy'd,
His soul can never be decoy'd
From that celestial state of rest,
Where he, I trust, is what the bless'd.

One to go.

Perhaps I suffer from an optical illusion, but my perception that Friday the Thirteenth appears more often than the law of averages insists that it should as the date of a murder or of a murderer's downfall makes me wonder whether the superstition of it arose from others' same perception or is a more reliable superstition than most. Burke and Hare did their last murder on a Friday that was not a Thirteenth. The next best date, however: the final day of October, which is Hallowe'en.

Whereas most of the earlier victims were short of names, the last victim had so many that the legally-required cataloguing of all of them whenever she was mentioned during the preliminaries of the trial must have accounted for a good five minutes of the proceedings: 'Madgy or Margery or Mary M'Gonegal or Duffie or Campbell or Docherty.' Ringing a further change, albeit slight, several of those employed to note the testimony verbatim preferred Dougherty to Docherty. I shall follow the subsequent majority minimisation, which left 'Mary Docherty'.

She was Irish. Having mislaid a grown-up legitimate son in Glasgow, she had found him there, only to mislay him again; failing this time to find him in Glasgow, she had reasoned that he must be in Edinburgh, and had come there in search of him. By the morning of Hallowe'en, her quest had brought her to David Rymer's shop, where spirits as well as groceries were on sale. It was there that Burke entered into conversation with her. Using the promise of a bowl of porridge as bait, he led her across West Port and through the unnamed close to his place.

It was already quite crowded, and every so often throughout the rest of the morning, it became more crowded still. Helen was invariably there; after dishing up the porridge for Mary Docherty, she poured her a dram or two – or more: sufficient, at any rate, to make her feel so at home that she took off, and washed, a red-and-white striped bed-gown that she wore like a petticoat. Also ever-present were two relatives of Helen's – James Gray and his wife, whose name, like that of a former relative of

Helen's, was Ann. The Grays were staying there while looking for permanent accommodation in or near the Grassmarket, which was James's birthplace: within a few days, he would be fêted, and everyone would know something about him – at the very least that, 'after an attempt to learn his trade as a jeweller, he enlisted in the Elgin Fencibles, transferring afterwards to the 72nd Regiment, and recently returned with his wife to Edinburgh after an absence of seventeen years'. Among those who popped in and out of the room were other tenants in the house and Mrs Law, from across the close. Burke himself left for a while, explaining to Mary Docherty that he had to fetch drinks for a party on the true eve of All-Hallows, which he hoped she would stay for. Actually, that was only one reason for his absence: while he was out, he found Hare and told him that he had 'a shot for the doctors'; and he obtained a tea-chest, free of charge, from Rymer's. Soon after his return, the Hares arrived and were introduced to Mary Docherty. They sized her up, comparing her with the tea-chest.

What with one thing and another, the morning passed quickly, and so did the afternoon, and it was dark before the partners got round to discussing their business matter. Mary Docherty was in a state fit for their purpose; but the trouble was that the party, begun earlier than was meant, was proving so successful that it looked like going on all through the night. In considering how to curtail the revelry without causing offence, Burke suddenly realised that, even if that could be accomplished, a problem would remain: *the Grays* – who, as house-guests, would remain when all the party-guests had gone. Forgetting his wish to be inoffensive, he shouted at the Grays above the others' din that they were making too much noise; they were to leave forthwith, he shouted – and when they asked where they could go, suggested Log's. With them out of the way, he turned his attention to the rest of the inconvenient crowd – most of whom, being slow to take offence, took their time before departing, the thickest-skinned of them not until eleven or so. Of course, he was not rude to Mary Docherty.

While Helen and Margaret waited in the passage, far less from a sense of delicacy than as a precaution in case an ejected party-goer wandered back, their men did the trick.

What Burke did shortly afterwards, at about midnight, makes

one wonder whether he and his partner had been *commissioned* to provide a subject promptly – and, supposing that they had, whether any of their previous tricks were done in fulfilment of an order rather than on spec. Leaving Hare to do some tidying, he hurried from the house, up the close, and along West Port – to No. 26. That was the home of David Paterson, Dr Knox's porter – a fact that indicates, if nothing else, that Paterson knew the identities of John and William. Paterson lived at 26 West Port with his mother and a teenaged sister, Elizabeth – who, answering Burke's knock, informed him that David was not yet back from work. Burke said that he would wait. Paterson arrived within a few minutes. According to his testimony at the trial: Burke 'told me he wanted me to go to his house'.

> Q. Did you go? A. Yes.
>
> Q. Did you find people there? A. I found Burke and another man and two women.
>
> Q. After you went in, what passed? A. [Burke] told me he had procured something for the doctor, pointing to the head of the bed, where there was some straw; he said it in an under-voice. I was near him at the time.
>
> Q. Was anything shewn to you at that time? A. Nothing.
>
> Q. What did you understand he meant? A. I understood him to mean a dead body, a subject.
>
> Q. What were his exact words? A. His words were, 'There is something for the doctor' (pointing to the straw) 'which will be ready tomorrow morning.'
>
> Q. Was there sufficient straw to cover the body? A. There was.
>
> Q. Was *that* woman [Helen M'Dougal] there? A. She was. . . .
>
> Q. Do you know these people? A. I know them by the name of Hare; they are the other persons that were at Burke's house that night. . . .
>
> Q. What did you say to him when he called on you? A. I told him if he had anything for Dr Knox, to go to himself and agree with him personally. I afterwards saw Burke and Hare in Dr Knox's rooms in Surgeons' Square, along with Dr [Thomas Wharton] Jones, one of Dr Knox's assistants. This was between twelve [midnight] and two.
>
> Q. Did anything pass there? A. Either Burke or Hare told Dr Knox they had a dead body for him, which they would deliver there

the next night; and I had orders from Dr Knox to be in the way to receive it, or any parcel that might come. . . .

Having quoted that testimony, I must say that I do not believe that Paterson told the whole truth. But I say that uncritically of him. The witness-oath is only slightly more frightening to religious persons than to irreligious ones, whose earthly fear of it is that it will be used against them if they are caught out in a salient lie and prosecuted for perjury. Anyone in a situation similar to Paterson's would be as sparing of the truth as he was.

The morning after the night before began surprisingly early, considering that Burke and Hare cannot have got to their respective beds much before three. By 9 a.m. on that first day of November, they, their women, three of the people who had stayed till near the end of the party, and the Grays, full of apologies for the rowdiness that Burke had used as an excuse for getting rid of them, were drinking in his place. The last-mentioned five of the company were unaware that the body of Mary Docherty lay beneath the straw. Which does not mean that none of them commented on her apparent absence. When Mrs Law enquired what had become of the 'little woman', Helen M'Dougal snapped that she had 'kicked the d——d b——h's backside out of the door', and, seeing that Mrs Law expected some explanation of that action, went on to say that Mary Docherty had become 'very fashous' (annoying) – 'asking for warm water, then cold water, and then asking for a flannel clout and soap to wash herself with, to make her white'. Perhaps thinking that that explanation sounded insufficient (or, more likely, that Mrs Law may have been awoken by Mary's protesting at the trick), Helen added that, after the party, Burke and Hare had 'begun a fighting', thereby causing Mary to 'roar out murder' – which, the last straw so far as she, Helen, was concerned, had resulted in Mary's being 'thrust out of the house, for an old Irish limmer [hussy]'.

Ann Gray (who, incidentally, had a year-old baby; where it was all this time is as unreported as are the whereabouts of Margaret Hare's even younger child) seems to have thought of getting back into her hosts' good books by doing some house-work: not a lot – 'I washed the floor and put a little sand on it.' But by noon the place was messier than previously, partly because Burke had thrown whisky about, explaining that he 'wanted to get quit of it to get more'. Feeling peckish, he told Ann Gray to cook a pan of potatoes. However, when she went close to the pile of straw, meaning to reach under the bed for the potatoes, he shouted at her 'to come out of that, as she might set the bed afire with her pipe'. That being the second time he had ordered her away from the proximity of the straw, she took notice of it; and began thinking that either her memory was at fault or the pile had grown since Hallowe'en; and, long before five in the afternoon, was convinced that her memory was perfectly all right. But, till then, she was never left alone long enough to satisfy her curiosity as to how a pile of straw – which should, if anything, have slumped – had swollen. The coast at last clear, she rummaged.

The minute her husband returned from wherever he had been, she indicated her find. Picking up their few belongings (the baby too, presumably), they hurried from the room – only to meet Helen in the passage.

James Gray:

> I asked what was that she had got in the house; and she said, what was it? and I said, I suppose you know very well what it is. She fell on her knees in a supplicating attitude, imploring that I would not inform of what I had seen. She offered me some money, five or six shillings, to put me over till Monday; and there never would be a week after that but that I might be worth ten pounds a week. I said my conscience would not allow me to do it. She followed us; and when we got out to the street, we met Mrs Hare, and she enquired what we were making a noise about – and said, can't we go into the house, and decide our matters there, and not make a noise about them here.

Compromising, the Grays went with Margaret and Helen to a pub. There is little doubt that if they had gone back to the house, neither of them would have emerged alive. In the pub, while Margaret was spendthrift in buying rounds, Helen repeated the better of her offers to James, and agreed wholeheartedly when Ann expressed concern at the disgrace that might fall upon their family. But after nearly an hour, James indicated to his wife that it was time to leave – to all three women that he had decided that he must do the right thing.

As the Grays headed east, towards the police office next to St Giles' Cathedral, Margaret and Helen scurried in search of their men. Burke, the first to be found, took immediate action: he too went east, hurriedly – to Allison's Close, off Cowgate, which was the home of a porter, John M'Culloch. He got M'Culloch to follow him back to the unnamed close. Hare had been found by the time they arrived. The three of them lifted the body from the straw and wedged it into the tea-chest; M'Culloch, the heaviest, sat on the lid to press it down; ropes were tied round the chest; Burke and Hare heaved it on to M'Culloch's shoulders. He set off. He did not need to be told his destination. Either the women did not want to let the partners out of their sight, or the partners felt that the women should not be left on their own to try and fool the police: whichever, all four hurried out of the close and followed the lumbering M'Culloch, catching up with him before he reached the end of West Port and crossed into Cowgate.

As that group continued on their way, just to the north of them, in the parallel High Street, a smaller group – made up of the Grays and a constable, John Findlay – set off in the direction of West Port.

The arrival of the latter group at Burke's place was observed by a young girl who helped Mrs Law about her house. She told Constable Findlay of the recent comings and goings, mentioning in particular the final exodus, begun by a strange man carrying an obviously heavy tea-chest. Findlay may have accepted the Grays' theory that the body they claimed to have seen had been removed in the chest – but still, he was perplexed as to what he should do next. In the end, he decided to do nothing other than 'provide a police presence' until a superior officer turned up and told him what to do.

Meantime, the impromptu cortège reached 10 Surgeons' Square. The women waited outside while M'Culloch, at David Paterson's bidding, took his load to the basement, and Burke and Hare (no longer mere 'John and William') learned from Paterson that they had a good reason to have an argument with him, and did so. The good reason was that Paterson, quite forgetting that they had made an appointment, had neglected to consider their cash-on-delivery requirement, and, its being a Saturday night, hardly ever a transacting time, was not carrying a float. M'Culloch, returning to ground-level, discerned what the argument was about, heard from Burke or Hare that they could not pay him, and joined in. Paterson said, well, then, he would have to inconvenience Dr Knox at his home. He set off there, the three incommoded men following him, the two tut-tutting women following them: quite a journey – south from South Bridge, along Nicholson Street, along Clerk Street, and halfway down Newington to Newington Place, next to a cemetery larger than that of Greyfriars. He went into the doctor's house. Soon afterwards emerging, he told the suppliers that the doctor had had, or could only spare, five pounds – which they would have to accept on account of the ten they were owed. He led the way to a local, bought drinks for himself and the retinue out of the fiver, and handed over the change – five shillings of which went to M'Culloch. The peculiar amount left must have needed complicated arithmetic so as to work out its three-way split; and, probably, the landlord's help in dividing the cash into its percentages of 50, 40 and 10 – unless, of course, Margaret Hare for once fore went a share, and her husband, not wishing to display his difficulty with figure-work in so large a company, agreed to an easy 50–50.

Paterson went back to Surgeons' Square, M'Culloch left the others in Cowgate, the Hares bade adieu to Burke and Helen at the entrance to Tanner's Close, and the latter couple walked the few further steps to their home. The time, by then, was close to eight.

Shortly before, Constable Findlay had been reinforced by a superior officer, Sergeant-Major John Fisher, who had only acknowledged his salute, not told him what to do, as he, the sergeant-major, was intent on hearing what the Grays had to say.

He was still listening when the residents returned.

Sergeant-Major Fisher:

I asked Burke what had become of his lodgers, and he said that there was one of them, pointing to James Gray, and that he had turned out him and his wife for their bad conduct. I then asked him what had become of the little woman that had been there on the Friday, the day before, and he said that she was away. And I asked, when did she leave the house, and he said, about seven o'clock in the morning. He said William Hare saw her go away.

Then I asked, was there any other person saw her go away, and he said, in an insolent tone of voice, there were a number more.

I then looked to see if I could see any marks on the bed, and I saw the marks of blood on a number of things there; and I asked Helen M'Dougal how they came there, and she said that a woman had lain in there about a fortnight before, and the bed had not been washed since. She said, the little woman can be found, she lives in the Pleasance; and she said she had seen her that night in the Vennel, and that she had apologised to her for her bad conduct the night previous. I asked her then, what time the woman had left the house, and she said, seven o'clock at night.

Burke and Helen had not got their story straight enough. Burke: '. . . seven o'clock in the morning' – Helen: '. . . seven o'clock at night'. Noting that discrepancy, the sergeant-major reckoned that he had cause to take them to the police office; but he was most polite in saying so, telling them 'that it was all personal spite [on the part of the Grays] – that he must take them to the office, as he had been sent down'.

And so, on this evening that had already seen the making of several pedestrian groups, yet another was made, its composition representative of all of its predecessors: two policemen (the junior one of whom should have been told by the other to stay on guard, even if that had meant the impolite use of both of their sets of handcuffs), the accusing Grays, and the couple who, if only one of them during their tale-tallying had considered that seven o'clock struck twice a day, might well have fooled the senior policeman away from a decision to make the group. Burke, though, swaggered to the police office, for he was confident of the fable that a murder charge depends upon the finding of a body; and Helen, taken in by her man's panache, did her best to swagger too.

At the police office, the couple were interviewed by a superintendent. The sergeant-major listened to the first few minutes of the exchange, and then strolled back to Burke's place. Before he was joined there by the superintendent and a police surgeon, Dr Black, he talked with Mrs Law, she having come from across the close to suggest that he should. At one point, she altered the course of their conversation, for her gaze had been caught by something on the bed that, strangely enough, no one seems to have noticed till then: a red-and-white striped bed-gown. Mrs Law was convinced that it was the little woman's. The sergeant-major agreed with Mrs Law – and, later, the superintendent agreed with the sergeant-major – that if the little woman had gone of her own volition, whether at 7 a.m. or at 7 p.m., the recent continuously chilly weather would have reminded her not to leave her bed-gown behind.

The official version of two important events that occurred early next morning, which was Sunday, keeps them separate and in this order:

First, a crowd of policemen entered 10 Surgeons' Square, and some of them went to the basement, unroped a tea-chest, and emptied it of the body of a little woman (subsequently recognised as Mary Docherty by several people, Mrs Law among them).

Second – at eight o'clock – fewer policemen entered Log's lodging-house, roused the Hares (who, once fully awake and informed of the reason for the call, acted astonishment), got them to put on the rest of their clothes, and took them to the police office, where they were lodged in separate cells, away from the separate cells of Burke and Helen M'Dougal.

Now, I believe that the officially-second event occurred before the officially-first event. And I believe that there was a cause-and-effect relationship between them – that something said by one or both of the Hares led to the apparently-warrantless raiding of 10 Surgeons' Square. Why else should the police have picked on that place, one among dozens of schools of anatomy? Indeed, why should the police have picked on *any* school of anatomy? All that they are officially said to have known prior to the raid is that a little woman had disappeared in mysterious, probably sinister, circumstances; that if she was dead, her body had probably been carried away in a tea-chest; that Burke and his woman had probably made lying statements; that Hare – referred to by Burke simply as a witness to the truthfulness of the same part of each of his statements (the first to the sergeant-major, the second to the superintendent), and by Helen M'Dougal similarly, though only in her statement to the superintendent – was prob-ably guilty of *some*thing if Burke and his woman were guilty of *any*thing; that if Mrs Law's juvenile helpmate had observed efficiently, *both* of the Hares, Burke, and Helen M'Dougal had left the close soon after an unknown man carrying a now-suspicious chest had set off for an unknown destination. The police had not yet identified the carrier as John M'Culloch – and so had not learned the destination from him. Mrs Law knew nothing of the Burke & Hare business partnership – and so had not given the sergeant-major any clue pointing even in an eeny-meeny-miney-mo fashion to the schools of anatomy, let alone directly to Dr Knox's establishment.

Yet that was where the policemen chose to call. Maybe those policemen had no connection with the policemen at the St Giles office: it has happened (most notably in recent times towards the downfall of the mass-murdering 'Black Panther', Donald Neilson) that policemen working on one case have stumbled upon evidence vital to the solution of another case that they knew little or nothing about. Excepting such serendipity, Dr Knox's establishment was raided because of something said by one or both of the Hares.

Edinburgh, as well as being a centre of anatomical excellence, was renowned for the study and practice of other medical disciplines: pathology was one – its fairly recent offshoot, *forensic* pathology, another. A simple but sure way of telling whether a forensic pathologist is good or suspect lies in the fact that good forensic pathologists are sometimes unable to arrive at the firm conclusions that their employers would like. Robert Christison, Professor of Medical Jurisprudence at Edinburgh University, who 'minutely examined' the body of Mary Docherty at the St Giles' police office, starting on the Sunday and continuing the next day, found many signs suggesting that she had been murdered – but none that permitted him to go farther than saying that murder was a 'probability'.

The reports of the case in Monday's papers failed to live up to their headlines. In the *Edinburgh Evening Courant*, for instance, 'EXTRAORDINARY OCCURRENCE' was followed by a report so replete with innuendo that most people who read it must have read it again in the forlorn hope of fathoming what made the occurrence extraordinary.

But never mind – the public's mystification encouraged and assisted rumour-mongers, and long before the day was out, people were turning up at police offices – not just in Edinburgh, though mainly there, but throughout Scotland, even south of the border – either to give accounts of their own miraculous escapes from the murderers of West Port or to explain why they were convinced of the fate of missing friends or relatives. Most of those people went away dissatisfied with their reception. There were at least two, however, whose information was seized upon.

Janet Brown, who can never have imagined that she would enter a police office of her own accord, told of the disappearance of her friend and colleague, Mary Paterson. She impressed whoever it was she told by giving the names and addresses of the women associated with her profession who could corroborate parts of her narrative. Taken, first, to Constantine Burke's house, the interior of which she had already described, she accused both Constantine and his wife of having provided the scene of a crime (they, like several other of the partners' occasional helpers, were arrested on suspicion); and taken, second, to William Burke's place, she sorted from a mess of old clothes a number of items that she said were Mary's.

The mother of Daft Jamie Wilson appears to have suggested that he was a victim after lots of persons unrelated to him had made the same suggestion: perhaps, if she had been more prompt, arriving before her son's nickname was scribbled on many police memos, no one would have paid much attention to her. Taken to Burke's place – which, by then, was awkward to reach, for West Port was clogged with sightseers – she picked out some garments which she thought were Jamie's, and a snuff-spoon that she was sure was his.

During the first fortnight of the investigation, Burke and Helen M'Dougal each fell into the trap of agreeing to make far longer and more detailed statements than the slight ones they had made just before and shortly after their arrest. There had been only one discrepancy between their slight statements, but the more they talked, the more the discrepancies grew. The Hares also made further statements during this period – but, for a reason that will instantly appear, what they said was never publicly divulged.

During the second fortnight, the Hares received word from the Lord Advocate, the law officer who had the final say as to whether or not prosecutions were to be brought, that *if* they agreed to 'peach' against the other couple, they would be granted immunity from prosecution – would get off scot-free. (Though the 'proposal' was put to Hare alone, it obviously applied to his wife as well.) I believe that the *if* was a legal fiction – that the Hares had been peaching (or, to use the present-day expression, singing) for quite some time, probably from when, if my previous belief is correct, one or both of them said something that sent the police to 10 Surgeons' Square. Subsequently, spokesmen for the Lord Advocate tried to gloss his decision to let the Hares turn King's Evidence by saying that he was faced with a 'some-or-none' predicament: there was insufficient evidence against the Hares to guarantee their conviction, and without their evidence against Burke and Helen M'Dougal, both of *them* might be acquitted. One can punch so many holes into that excuse that it finishes up as water-tight as a cullender. Unfortunately, one cannot be astonished at the most gaping of the holes, punched with the fact that the combined weight of the Hares' guilt was greater than the combined weight of the guilt of Burke and Helen M'Dougal – for though the Hares certainly deserve to be called The First of the 'Supergrasses', they were no more super than many of their present-day successors, whose 'songs' are about people they hired to help with crimes that came unstuck.

Whether by accident (caused by a logjam in the High Court of Justiciary's calendar) or by design (prompted by a desire to have things over and done with before the festive season, thus giving a sort of present to the populace), the trial began at 10.15 a.m. on Christmas Eve, a Wednesday, the intention being to have verdicts before the day was out. Those in charge feared that rowdies might take the law into their unskilled hands, and so, the night before, three hundred policemen were brought into Edinburgh from constabularies round about; leave was stopped for infantrymen at the Castle and cavalrymen at the barracks of Piershill; the defendants and the two protected witnesses were transported – each in a separate covered wagon, each wagon flanked by armed outriders – from Calton Gaol, at the east of the New Town, to the venue of the trial, Parliament House, behind St Giles' Cathedral.

A reporter would write, not once with tongue in cheek, that it was not so much to the accounts published in the newspapers, which merely embodied and gave greater currency to the statements circulating in society, as to the extraordinary, nay, unparalleled circumstances of the case, that the strong excitement of the public mind ought to be ascribed, These were without any precedent in the records of our criminal practice, and, in fact, amounted to the realisation of a nursery tale.

The recent deplorable increase of crime has made us familiar with several new atrocities. Poisoning is now, it seems, rendered subsidiary to the commission of theft: stabbings, and attempts at assassination, are matters of almost everyday occurrence: and murder has grown so familiar to us that it has almost ceased to be viewed with that instinctive and inexpressible dread which the commission of the greatest crime against the laws of God and society used to excite.[1]

But the present was the first instance of murder alleged to have been perpetrated with the aforethought purpose and intent of selling the murdered body as a subject for dissection to anatomists: it was a new species of assassination, or murder for hire: and as such, no less than from the general horror felt by the people of this country at the process, from ministering to which the murderers expected their reward, it was certainly calculated to make a deep impression on the public mind, and to awaken feelings of strong and appalling interest in the issue of the trial.

Of the extent of the impression thus produced, and the feelings thus awakened, it was easy to judge from what was everywhere observable on Monday and Tuesday. The approaching trial formed the universal topic of conversation, and all sorts of speculations and conjectures were afloat as to the circumstances likely

[1] *Did that sentence appeal to Thomas De Quincey (who was then living in Edinburgh) and prompt him towards his famous comments: 'If once a man indulges himself in murder, very soon he comes to think little of robbing; and from robbing he comes next to drinking and Sabbath-breaking, and from that to incivility and procrastination. Once begin upon this downward path, you never know where you are to stop. Many a man has dated his ruin from some murder or other that perhaps he thought little of at the time.'? Those comments appear in the 'Supplementary Paper on Murder, Considered as One of the Fine Arts', which was published in* Blackwood's Magazine *(Edinburgh) of November 1839, and which speaks nostalgically of 'the sublime epoch of Burkism and Harism'.*

to be disclosed in the course of it, and the various results to which it would eventually lead. As the day drew near, the interest deepened; and it was easy to see that the common people shared strongly in the general excitement. The coming trial, they expected, was to disclose something which they had often dreamed of, or imagined, or heard recounted around an evening's fire, like a tale of horror, or a raw-head-and-bloody-bones story, but which they never, in their sober judgment, either feared or believed to be possible; and hence, they looked forward to it with corresponding but indescribable emotions. In short, all classes participated more or less in a common feeling respecting the case of this unhappy man and his associate; all expected fearful disclosures; none, we are convinced, wished for anything but justice. . . .

So early as seven o'clock in the morning of Wednesday, a considerable crowd had assembled in the Parliament Square and around the doors of the Court; and numerous applications for admission were made to the different subordinate functionaries, but in vain. The individuals connected with the press were conducted to the seats provided for them a little before eight o'clock; the members of the Faculty[1] and of the Society of Writers to the Signet[2] were admitted precisely at nine; and thus, with the jurymen impannelled, and a few individuals who had obtained the *entrée* in virtue of orders from the Judges, the Court became at once crowded in every part.

About twenty minutes before ten o'clock, the prisoners were placed at the bar. The male prisoner was dressed in a shabby blue surtout, buttoned close to the throat, a striped cotton waistcoat, and dark-coloured small clothes. The female prisoner was miserably dressed in a small stone-coloured silk bonnet, very much the worse for the wear, a printed cotton shawl, and a cotton gown. Both prisoners, especially Burke, entered the Court without any visible sign of perturbation, and both seemed to attend very closely to the proceedings which soon after commenced.

The Judges present were the Right Honourable the Lord Justice Clerk [Lord Boyle] and Lords Pitmilly, Meadowbank,

---

[1] *The Faculty of Advocates in Scotland.*

[2] *The oldest body of law practitioners in Scotland, their duties correspond to those of solicitors in England.*

and Mackenzie. Their Lordships having taken their seats, and the instance having been called, the Lord Justice Clerk said – William Burke, and Helen M'Dougal, pay attention to the indictment that is now to be read against you.

But that was the cue for the first delay. Patrick Robertson, one of Burke's four counsel (all instructed by an Agent for the Poor), objected to the reading of the indictment, explaining: 'It contains charges which I hope to be able to show your Lordships are incompetent, and the reading of the whole of the libel must tend materially to prejudice the prisoners at the bar.' Henry Cockburn,[1] the senior counsel of Helen M'Dougal's four (also instructed by the aforementioned Agent), made a similar objection. Both were turned down by Lord Meadowbank, who growled that he was 'against novelties' – whereupon the Clerk of Court read an indictment which charged both prisoners with the murder of Mary Docherty, and Burke alone with the murders of Mary Paterson and Daft Jamie Wilson.

That over, Patrick Robertson presented defences against the indictment – a task in which he was eventually assisted by his leader, Sir James Moncrieff, the Dean of Faculty.[2] The defences were that Burke ought not to be tried on one occasion for three 'unconnected' murders, and that his trial ought not to be combined with that of Helen M'Dougal, 'who was not even

---

[1] *The greatest Scots lawyer of his time – some would say of all time – Cockburn was near fifty when he defended Helen M'Dougal. For the past fifteen years, he had appeared as counsel for prisoners – most of them of his own Whig persuasion – who were accused of political offences. In 1834 he was appointed, as Lord Cockburn, a judge of the court of session, and three years later became a lord of justiciary. He contributed many articles to magazines, particularly the* Edinburgh Review; *his journals were published posthumously – as* Memorials of His Time *(A & C Black, Edinburgh, 1856),* Journals of Henry Cockburn *(2 volumes; Edmonston & Douglas, Edinburgh, 1874), and* Circuit Journeys *(Davis Douglas, Edinburgh, 1889), which is the wonderfully entertaining record of his judicial travels from the autumn of 1837 till a few days before his death in the spring of 1854. A one-man show presented at the 1969 Edinburgh Festival had Russell Hunter as the eponymous* Cocky.

[2] *President of the Faculty of Advocates in Scotland.*

alleged to have any concern with two of the offences of which he was accused.' The second of those defences against the indictment was echoed by Henry Cockburn – his ground being that 'the accumulation of panels [Scots for 'defendants'] and of offences . . . exposed his client to intolerable prejudice'.

The Lord Advocate, Sir William Rae – he who had authorised immunity for the Hares, and who now led three Advocates-Depute for the prosecution[1] – fought long and hard to keep the indictment intact; but the judges decided that, though the precedents he quoted were as good as those quoted on behalf of the prisoners, the prosecution should be restricted to one charge: if the jury failed to convict on that, the Lord Advocate could 'proceed *seriatim* on the other acts that were not that day to be tried'. Not managing to hide his anger, Sir William said that as he was 'tied down to proceed with the trial of one of the crimes', he would choose 'the third case libelled' (Mary Docherty): 'On that footing, there seems nothing to prevent my proceeding against the woman as well as against the man. She can suffer no prejudice in now being brought to trial for the single act on which she is charged as art and part guilty along with Burke.'

The deal struck with the Hares had become a very poor one from the Lord Advocate's bureaucratic point of view; and, since he was supposed to be a guardian of justice as well as a tactician of the law, an even worse deal so far as the people of Scotland were concerned. In the case of the murder of Mary Docherty, there was very nearly as much evidence against William Hare as there was against his ex-partner – more evidence against William Hare than there was against Helen M'Dougal – about the same amount of evidence against Helen M'Dougal as there was against Margaret Hare. The inequities were apparent. They would be turned to the benefit of one of the defendants.

The judges' diminishing of the indictment, unaccompanied by a single understanding word as to the practical problems that raised for the lesser members of the prosecution team, must have sent those members into a frenzy of activity while a jury (the

---

[1] *And who, by the way, was an intimate friend of Sir Walter Scott; he is referred to as 'Dear loved Rae' in the introduction to the fourth canto of* Marmion.

Scottish fifteen) was being selected from among the forty-five
men ordered to be available as representatives of the various
areas within the judicial region – the City of Edinburgh, the
Town of Leith, the Counties of Edinburgh, Linlithgow and
Haddington. The occupations of the selected jurymen were as
follows: agent, banker, builder (two such), brewer, cooper,
engraver, grocer (three), ironmonger, manager of the Hercules
Insurance Company, merchant (three – one of them being John
M'fie, of Leith, who was chosen as chancellor: in most other
English-speaking countries he would have been called the fore-
man of the jury).

In the expectation of three counts to the indictment, the
prosecution had arranged for fifty-five witnesses to be on hand –
including six associated with 10 Surgeons' Square: Robert
Knox, three of his graduates who had stayed on as assistants
(Thomas Wharton Jones, William Fergusson, Alexander
Miller), a student (James Evans – was he the 'tall lad' who
recognised Mary Paterson?), and David Paterson. The winnow-
ing of the become-irrelevant witnesses left eighteen, of whom
only one, David Paterson, was associated with 10 Surgeons'
Square.

Though that drastic reduction meant a shortening of the
testimonial part of the proceedings, that part had been delayed
for two hours by the legal argument that had resulted in the
reduction – and so the judges were concerned that if they didn't
keep things moving, virtually uninterrupted by adjournments,
they might still be on the bench when they were supposed to be in
their pews for the Christmas Morning service at St Giles'. With
no breaks for airings of the courtroom, its atmosphere soon
became stagnant – prompting the Lord Justice Clerk to order the
opening of a large window, an act that alleviated the stench at
the expense of warmth; spectating advocates and Writers to the
Signet wrapped their gowns round their heads – 'giving to the
visages that were enshrouded under them,' it occurred to a
reporter, 'such a grim and grisly aspect as assimilated them to a
college of Monks or Inquisitors, or characters imagined in tales
of romance.' At four in the afternoon, no refreshments having
been provided, 'Burke asked when he would get dinner, and
being informed it would be about six, begged that he might have
a biscuit or two, as he would lose his appetite before that time.

Both panels ate bread and soup heartily; and although they displayed no external marks of inward emotion, they frequently, especially the woman, took copious draughts of water' – which presumably means that some kind of latrine was discreet within the dock.

It may be that, though the panels must really have been hungry and thirsty, they exaggerated their relief with the intention of showing their contempt for the witnessing Hares and in the hope of putting them off their respective strokes. The judges' disregard of normal meal-times – as well as of most normal meals – means that one has little help towards the assessment of when particular witnesses were called. Hare was the fifteenth witness, his wife the sixteenth. The previous witnesses were, in order of appearance, a surveyor (who proved his plans of the unnamed close), a woman with whom Mary Docherty had stayed on the night before Hallowe'en, and a man who was a lodger in the same house on the same night (both the landlady and the lodger had subsequently identified the body), David Rymer's shop-boy, three residents of the unnamed close, David Paterson's sister, Paterson himself, another resident of the unnamed close, Ann and James Gray, John M'Culloch (who, lacking immunity, was carefully laconic regarding his porterage of the body), Sergeant-Major John Fisher. Going only by the fact that the number of transcript pages devoted to the evidence of those fourteen witnesses is about the same as the number of pages that report questions, answers, and legal arguments during Hare's turning of King's Evidence, it seems likely that he took the stand late in the afternoon.

His entrance produce a great sensation in the Court.

LORD JUSTICE CLERK: You understand that it is only with regard to [Mary Docherty] that you are now to speak? *To this question the witness replied by asking, 'T'ould woman, Sir?'*
LORD JUSTICE CLERK:Yes.

LORD ADVOCATE: You are a native of Ireland, Hare? *A.* Yes.

How long have you been in this country? *A.* Ten years.

LORD JUSTICE CLERK: Are you a Roman Catholic? *A.* Yes.

Do you wish to be sworn in any other way than that now

administered by my brother?   *A.* I never was sworn before, Sir,
and I am no judge of that.

(*The New Testament was handed to the witness.*)

LORD MEADOWBANK: Now, you will observe that there
is a representation of the Cross on the book of the New
Testament; lay your right hand upon the Cross, and repeat the
words of the oath after me.

(*The witness was sworn in this manner.*)

The examination-in-chief went pretty well as the Lord Advocate had hoped and planned. But he sat down without relief, alert
to every question from Henry Cockburn, every answer from
Hare. Cockburn began the cross-examination most politely, pre-
fixing the first question 'Mr Hare'. That question and the following four were to do with Hare's legitimate occupations since his
arrival in Scotland. The sixth, 'Have you been engaged in
supplying bodies to the doctors?', was answered 'Yes'. The
seventh, put just as politely – perhaps intentionally phrased
confusingly – was:

'Have you been connected in supplying the doctors with subjects
upon other occasions than those you have not spoken to yet?'

According to some reports of the trial, Hare replied, 'No –
than what I have mentioned'; according to others, he had no
chance to reply before the Lord Advocate, speaking as he jumped
to his feet, said: 'I object to this course of examination.'

At Cockburn's request, the witness was withdrawn. Then
Cockburn fought against the objection: 'I may as well explain at
once that I hold myself entitled to ask this gentleman to reveal his
whole life. In particular, I mean to ask him this specific question:
"Have you ever been concerned in murders beside this one?" I
am ready to admit that he is not bound to answer; but I am
entitled to put that question, let him answer it or not as he
pleases. It will be for the jury to judge of the credit due to him
after seeing how he treats it.'

For half an hour, Cockburn – with Burke's Sir James Moncrieff joining in – argued one way, the Lord Advocate the other.
And the judges argued between themselves. The point at issue
was made nicer by the fact that the judges had already agreed that
Burke should not be prejudiced by being tried on one occasion
for more than one murder. Cockburn won.

The witness was recalled.

COCKBURN: Hare [no 'Mr' now, or ever afterwards], you mentioned when last here that you were concerned in supplying the medical lecturers with subjects. Did you assist in taking the body of the old woman to Surgeons' Square? *A.* Yes.

Were you ever concerned in carrying any other body to any surgeon? *A.* I never was concerned in furnishing none, but I saw them do it.

LORD JUSTICE CLERK: You are not bound to answer the question about to be put.

COCKBURN: Hare, I am going to put a very few questions to you, and you need not answer them unless you please . . . Now, Hare, you told me a little ago that you had been concerned in furnishing one subject to the doctors, and you had seen them doing it. How often have you seen them doing it? (*The witness said nothing.*) Do you decline answering that question? *A.* Yes.

Now, sir, I am going to ask this question, which you need not answer unless you please – Was that of the old woman the first murder that you had been concerned in? (*The witness said nothing.*) Do you choose to answer or not to answer? *A.* Not to answer.

I am going to ask another question which you need not answer unless you like – Was there murder committed in your house in the last October? (*The witness said nothing.*) Do you choose to answer that or not? *A.* Not answer that.

You mentioned that Burke came and told you that he had got a 'shot' for the doctors, and that you understood that that meant that he intended to murder that woman or somebody? *A.* That was his meaning.

How did you understand that? Was that a common phrase amongst you? *A.* Amongst him.

And so it went on. Cockburn was happier when Hare refused to answer then when he did. The silences added up to a loud admission of guilt. Reading the full transcript of the cross-examination of Hare, one is struck by a feeling of *déjà vu*, for it seems like a trial-run for the presently-familiar exhibitions given by witnesses before United States House Committees who have been granted only partial immunity from prosecution or who make the monotonous most of the one thing they respect about the Constitution, which is that there is a Fifth Amendment to it.

A moment after Hare was led from the court by an usher (in Scots legal parlance, a macer), another usher led his wife to the witness-box. There being no crèche in Parliament House, she held her baby daughter in her arms. The child had whooping cough – brought on, probably, by the dampness of Calton Gaol – and, according to Henry Cockburn, 'its every paroxysm fired her [Margaret] with intenser anger and impatience'; others, however, suspected that she initiated some of the crowing, by slyly tweaking the child under cover of its swaddling-clothes, either to give herself a noisy time in which to consider awkward questions or to hinder the jury's hearing of answers of hers that she was not altogether happy with. The Lord Advocate may occasionally have wished that he had a remote-control tweaker: for instance, when, in answer to a question he posed as to what had gone through her mind when, late on Hallowe'en, she – and Helen – returned to the room and saw no sign of Mary Docherty, she replied, 'I had a supposition that the old woman had been murdered' – *and added*: 'I have seen such tricks before.'

Apparently it had been arranged between the two sets of defenders that Cockburn should do the whole of the cross-examination of Hare, Moncrieff the whole cross-examination of his wife. Although Moncrieff was almost up to Cockburn's standard as a speech-maker, he lacked the agility of mind that went towards Cockburn's brilliance as a questioner: he had prepared a script of what Margaret Hare had to be asked, and, ignoring opportunities she gave for improvisation, stuck to it. She agreed with him that she had said, in examination-in-chief, that when she and Hare first went to Burke's place on the night of the murder, Mary Docherty was there. Then:

> Was Burke not in when you went in there? *A.* I am not sure.
> Did he go in a little after? *A.* I do not recollect whether he was in, or whether he came in or not. I have a very bad memory.

Think what Cockburn would have done with that last comment! If Moncrieff, doing the very least, raised his eyebrows at it, the movement was not noticed by any of the reporters who peered through the gloaming of the courtroom to catch something visual to write about. The only thing they noted was that Moncrieff, asking no further questions, sat down. All in all, Margaret Hare – and the Lord Advocate – got off far more lightly than was deserved.

Just two more witnesses, both doctors: Alexander Black, the police surgeon, and Robert Christison, the forensic pathologist. Then the statements of each of the panels, admitted by their respective counsel, were read aloud.

That ended the case for the prosecution.

You may need to be reminded that, in those days, defendants were not allowed to speak for themselves. As neither Burke nor Helen M'Dougal brought forward 'exculpatory evidence', the Lord Advocate straightway began his closing speech. About an hour before, across the yard from Parliament House, the bellmen of St Giles's Cathedral had rung in Christmas.

Rae devoted the centre of his speech to his decision to let the Hares turn King's Evidence, saying, *inter alia*,

> It is naturally revolting to see such criminals escape even the punishment of human laws; but this must be borne, in order to avoid greater evils; and it may form some consolation to reflect that such an example of treachery, by a *socius criminis*, must tend to excite universal distrust among men concerned in similar crimes, if any such should hereafter exist. Fortunately for the safety of life, a crime of this nature cannot, in all its details, be accomplished without assistance; and nothing can be more calculated to deter men from its commission than the probability of the perpetrators readily betraying each other.

Rae finished soon after three in the morning.

Now it was Moncrieff's turn.

Speaking loudly, in the hope of keeping the jurymen awake, he apologised to them in advance for the length of his address. 'We have been sitting here, gentlemen, about seventeen hours. . . . But when you consider that the lives of these prisoners are in your hands, I am sure I need say nothing more to entitle me to your utmost indulgence while I submit to you the observations which appear to me to be material on behalf of the prisoner Burke.' Meaning to swerve their minds from the rumours they must have heard since All-Hallows, he spoke to them as if confident that, by a kind of magic, their taking of the juror's oath had made them, each and as a group, more critical of conjecture than most other Scotsmen and groups of Scotsmen. And he tried to persuade them that there was nothing very special about the charge:

> Gentlemen, this case may be represented as anomalous and unprecedented in some views of it; but I must beg your attention . . . to this plain view of the matter – that the thing of which this prisoner is accused is simply and singly *murder*. There is no aggravation, and no other crime or offence charged; and when, therefore, it is supposed that this case is of an extraordinary and unprecedented nature, this can only refer to the motive by which it is said the prisoners were actuated in committing the murder. But what does that amount to but that the motive was a miserable *gain*? There is surely nothing anomalous or unprecedented in that. A vast proportion of murders of which we hear are committed from the same motive of gain – to conceal robbery, or escape in housebreaking. And what difference does it make to the crime of wilful murder, whether the motive be to rob a man of his watch or a few shillings, or to sell his body for a few pounds?

Rae had done his best to give credence to the Hares' testimony; Moncrieff had the easier task of discrediting it:

> What is there to restrain them from telling the most deliberate series of falsehoods? . . . Hare is a person who tells you that, for the paltry object of a few pounds, he was leagued with another to destroy a fellow creature; and when he is asked if he had ever committed other murders, *declines to answer the question*. That is the person that comes before you this day – and he comes, not with the motive of a few shillings or pounds, but the tremendous motive of saving himself from an ignominious death, which the law would inflict upon him if he did commit these horrible crimes . . . Just change the position of the parties, and suppose that Mr Hare was at the bar, and Burke in the witness box. I do not know what case you might get from Burke or M'Dougal; but nothing could hinder them from making as clear a case against Hare and his wife, totally transposing the fact, and exhibiting the transaction as altogether the reverse of what Hare says it is.

Moncrieff finished about five in the morning.

It would not be surprising if some members of the jury, desperate for sleep, for refreshment, for relief from the cramping and numbing, had cried out in anguish at the sight of Henry Cockburn pulling himself to his feet – at being reminded, or realising, that the two conflicting speeches they had survived were to be followed by a third, presumably not much different from the second. Maybe there were some muted wails – causing Cockburn to begin by saying, 'Considering the hour, I will not hasten, but hurry over, the facts and the views upon which I feel the firmest conviction that you can pronounce no verdict, so far as the female prisoner is concerned, but one that will declare that the charge against her has not been proven.'

Till now, the two sets of defenders had worked in concert, their respective spokesmen trying to avoid saying anything that they knew the others preferred to be said only by the speaking prosecutors. When Cockburn departed from the arrangement, he did so discreetly, inserting a remark that Moncrieff must have appreciated, and making it seem that he was not so much deserting Burke's defenders as welcoming the prosecutors to his side:

> In stating these facts and views, I shall assume – though in the face of the admirable address which you have just heard, I cannot admit – first, that there was a murder committed, and second, that it was committed by the prisoner Burke. Still I maintain that there is not sufficient credible evidence to convict this woman. And if you know how to interpret the pleadings of counsel as well as we do, you would have seen perfectly well that the Lord Advocate himself feels that there is a most material difference between the cases of the two panels.

After quoting authorities on what did and did not make a person accessory to a crime, Cockburn ingeniously drew conclusions from certain facts. No doubt he would have been less daringly ingenious if the jury, the judges and the prosecutors had been more alert. Certainly, he would not have risked a particularly audacious theory, which went as follows: one of the neighbour-witnesses had spoken of hearing, late on Hallowe'en, a woman's shouts of 'Murder!' and 'Police!' – they intermingled with sounds like 'the stifled moans of an animal suffocating'; the intermingling, said Cockburn, showed that the shouting woman was not the moaning woman – ergo, said Cockburn, the shouting woman was none other than Helen M'Dougal, she doing her utmost either to prevent a murder or to broadcast the news that murder was being done.

Cockburn exhausted was a better advocate than his closest rival just back from holiday. Anyone else, after twenty hours of thought and talk and questioning and acting, would surely have started to search for words, to stumble over them: he became stronger still – began to rage, but was always in control of the rage.

I believe, gentlemen, that if you will ransack both your notes and your memories, you will find no material circumstances, independently of those mentioned by the accomplices, against the female prisoner. Before coming to the testimony of the accomplices, I should wish you to ask yourselves whether these circumstances form sufficient evidence against her. I apprehend that they not only don't form *sufficient* evidence, but that they form absolutely no evidence at all. . . . Accordingly, the prosecutor *concurs* with us in thinking that, without the accomplices, he has no case. His Lordship has pretended, indeed, to argue otherwise. But his own conduct establishes what his real conviction is. It is always the duty of the public prosecutor to bring the guilty to trial when he can. He has no right to take culprits from the bar and place them in the box unnecessarily; and, therefore, the very fact that an accomplice has been made a witness is a proof that, in the opinion of the public accuser, he could not do without them. If the prosecutor's statement be true, these two accomplices were the property of the gibbet. Why, then, has justice been robbed of their lives? Because the Lord Advocate tells you that their being made witnesses was 'a *necessary* sacrifice'. . . .

Really, gentlemen, we give the prosecutor a most *un*necessary and unjust advantage when we talk of the credibility of these his *necessary* witnesses, and allow them to work up every circumstance according to their own pleasure. I cannot form the idea of any jury's being satisfied with less evidence than what the accuser thinks indispensable. Our learned friend who prosecutes here has demonstrated by his conduct that he is satisfied that you ought not to convict without the evidence of the associates; and thus we are absolutely driven to consider what credit is due to those witnesses. If you shall agree with me in thinking that it is an absolute sporting with men's lives, and converting evidence into a mockery, to give the slightest faith to anything that these persons may say, then we have the authority of the public accuser himself for holding that you must acquit. . . .

The prosecutor seemed to think that they gave their evidence in a credible manner, and that there was nothing in their appearance beyond what may be expected in that of any great criminal, to impair the probability of their story. I entirely differ from this; and I am perfectly satisfied that so do you. A couple of such witnesses, in point of mere external manner and appearance, never did my eyes behold. Hare was a squalid wretch – on whom the habits of his disgusting trade, want, and profligacy seem to have been long operating, in order to produce a monster whose will, as well as his poverty, will consent to the perpetration of the direst crimes. The Lord Advocate's back was to the woman, else he would not have professed to have seen nothing revolting in her appearance. I never saw a face in which the lines of profligacy were more distinctly marked. . . .

It is said that they are corroborated. Corroborated! These witnesses corroborated!! In the first place, I do not understand how such witnesses admit of being corroborated. If the prosecutor has a case without them, let him say so. But if he has not – if something material must depend upon these witnesses – it is in vain to talk of corroboration; because, in truth, the thing to be corroborated does not exist. You may corroborate a *doubtful* testimony – but the idea of confirming the lies of these miscreants is absurd. The only way to deal with them is to deduct their testimony altogether. It is like corroborating a dream. The fiction and the reality may possibly be both alike – but this accidental concurrence does not make the one stronger than the other.

It was close to quarter to eight when Cockburn – his throat raw by then, making his normal way or rolling the letter R more guttural – paused for a moment and then launched into the peroration of his great speech: a plea to the jury that they should be 'completely deaf to the cry of the public for a victim' –

The time will come when these prejudices will die away. In that hour, you will have to recollect whether you this day yielded to them or not – a question which you cannot answer to the satisfaction of your own minds unless you can then recall, or at least are certain that you now feel, legal grounds for convicting this woman, after deducting all the evidence of the Hares and all your extrajudicial impressions.

If you have such evidence, convict her.

If you have *not*, your safest course is to find that the libel is not proven.

The Lord Justice Clerk summed up, taking three-quarters of an hour about it, and the jury retired to consider their verdicts at half-past eight, as daylight greyed the court.

Reports say that the stubbled masses of spectators in the public enclosure stayed glued to the seats that they had occupied, most of them, for more than twenty-four hours; the substances of the gluing are nowhere intimated at.

Some of the same reports say that Burke was so confident that Helen M'Dougal would be found guilty too that he gave her directions as to how she should behave when the chancellor of the jury spoke of her, and 'desired her to look at and observe him' when the Lord Justice Clerk was passing sentence.

Other reports say that the crowd outside Parliament House was almost as dense as, and more unruly than, the crowd that had littered the forecourt till late on Christmas Eve.

Fifty minutes went by.

Then, at 9.20, the jury returned.

The chancellor, John M'Fie, announced the verdicts –

Burke: *Guilty*.

M'Dougal: *Not Proven*.

Applause broke out – noisy enough to be heard in the forecourt, where the crowd, though not knowing what was being applauded, joined in.

Helen burst into tears. One can be sure of that. But if the applause was as instantaneous, as thunderous, as all the courtroom reports say it was, one can only accept what the reporters claimed that Burke murmured to her by assuming that a reporter who could lip-read did so and was generous enough to communicate the reading to his rivals: '*Nelly, you are out of the scrape.*'

The dozen participating advocates – three quartets – were too tired to show much interest in the scene. Moncrieff shook hands with Cockburn. Rae concentrated on making his papers tidy. If he still believed that he was right to have employed the Hares, the subsequent information that the verdict against Burke was not unanimous – that two jurors had held out for Not Proven in his case – must have dented that belief. The two jurors' uncertainty could only have been raised on moral grounds.

As was the custom – ludicrous if a sentence was mandatory – the highest judge had to call upon another to propose the sentence. Lord Meadowbank having, at considerable length, proposed that Burke should be hanged and his body given for dissection, the Lord Justice Clerk, black-capped meanwhile, told Burke that the proposal was accepted and, departing from the mandatory on behalf of poetic justice, added: 'I trust that if it is ever customary to preserve skeletons, yours will be preserved in order that posterity may keep in remembrance your atrocious crimes.' Yes: *crimes*. Though Burke had been found guilty of only one, Lord Boyle had no doubt that he had committed others as atrocious.

The black cap removed, his Lordship told Helen M'Dougal.

The jury have found the libel against you Not Proven – they have not pronounced you Not Guilty of the crime of murder charged against you in this indictment. You know whether you have been in the commission of this atrocious crime. I leave it to your own conscience to draw the proper conclusion. I hope and trust that you will betake yourself to a new line of life, diametrically opposite from that which you have led for a number of years.

Less as a kindness to her than because the authorities were anxious to avoid breaches of the peace such as lynchings, she was taken with Burke to the gaol. For the same precautionary reason, the Hares had been returned to the gaol as soon as the Lord Advocate had begun his closing speech. It may have crossed some civil servant's mind that Robert Knox also was at risk; but the only precaution arranged in that regard was the stationing of two constables, one within sight of Knox's house, the other on the doorstep of 10 Surgeons' Square.

*　　　*　　　*

The hanging of Burke was scheduled for 28 January. Till then, the daily papers were always able to report incidents relating to the case; for some of the stories, particularly those given a 'MOB DISTURBANCE' sort of headline, the reporters were indebted to editorialists for having fomented them.

No later, apparently, than the early evening of the day after the trial, Burke handed a warder his pocket-watch and the remains of his share of the half-payment for the body of Mary Docherty, requesting that they be passed on to Helen M'Dougal. 'Poor thing,' he is reputed to have said, 'it is all I have to give her. It will be of some use to her, and I will not need it.' That evening, either Helen was forced to leave the gaol or she insisted upon her right to leave. Brazen or because she could not think of anywhere else to go, she walked to her home, slept there till late the next day, and then, naturally thirsty, went to a pub. She was recognised by the landlord, who so loudly refused to serve her that a crowd gathered and, also recognising her, became menacing. A pair of patrolling policemen intervened, needing their truncheons to do so, and hurried her to a watch-house. The crowd had followed, growing in numbers *en route*; their baying at the watch-house attracted more passers-by, and before long Helen's rescuers felt distinctly uneasy – so much so that they decided to bundle her out of a back window. The stealthy evacuation proved unnecessary, however, for when one of the policemen shouted through a front window that the woman was being detained as a witness against the Hares, the crowd contentedly dispersed.

Over the next couple of days, recognitions of Helen created other crowds, from whom she was rescued by other policemen; escorted out of the city, she returned; again recognised, she was rescued and escorted, not merely out of the city, but almost to her home-town. Continuing there, she received no welcome from relatives – they being relatives also of the disappeared Ann M'Dougal – and soon moved on, probably travelling south and eventually across the English border. (Forty years later, a newspaper[1] noted that 'It would seem that Helen M'Dougal, the paramour of Burke the murderer – and who gave origin to the word "burking" – was living in New South Wales until the other

---

[1] *Neither the title of the paper nor the issue-date is known. The complete cutting is reproduced by Jacques Barzun, op. cit.*

day, when she was accidentally burnt to death at Singleton. Such was the information, at all events, conveyed by telegraph from Sydney to Melbourne on the 13th of last August. It is stated in the message that the miserable woman was sent out many years ago to the colony in which she has at length come to a tragic end.' The phrases 'It would seem', 'Such was the information' and 'It is stated' suggest that the writer of the note was unconfident of it. Helen may well have been transported, either because she had again fallen foul of the law or because a guardian of the law, tired of the frequent need to rescue her, felt that she, he and his colleagues would be better off if she were out of harm's way.)

On Sunday, 28 December, while Helen was being dashed from one crowd or another in the region of the Royal Mile, an incident occurred to the south, in Newington Place, that caused the policeman stationed there to run off for reinforcements. A band of irreligious citizens gathered outside Dr Knox's house, shouting variations on the question, 'Where are the doctors?', which had been posed by certain editorialists who believed, or claimed to believe, that the deletion from the trial witness-list of Knox and his medical associates indicated a cover-up. By the time the posse arrived, the band had scattered, having chucked stones through practically every window in the house. The incident was the first of many representing the public's distrust of Knox and distaste for what he was guessed to have done. Even without such incidents, he would have had ample cause for concern: ever since he and his school had first been referred to in reports of the case, many registered students had cried off, applications for tuition had dried up – and conventional, grave-robbing suppliers of corpses had deserted him. A few friends were faithful, but efforts by some of them to restore his good name only provoked more-publicised opposition; on 14 January, Sir Walter Scott wrote in his journal, 'I called on Mr Robinson and instructed him to call a meeting of the Council of the Royal Society, as Mr Knox proposed to read an essay on some dissections. A bold proposal truly from one who had so lately the boldness of trading so deep in human flesh. I will oppose the reading in the present circumstances if I should stand alone.' Punsters were having a fine time, mixing the name Knox with the word 'noxious'; and printers of broadsheets and chapbooks were pocketing profits from their hacks' attacks on the doctor – one

example being a song, meant to be sung to the tune of 'Macpherson's Farewell', which had this rousing opening verse:

> In Scotland, the Slaughter-house-keeper may pay
> His Journeymen Butchers, and thrive on his prey;
> The victims are quickly cut up in his shop,
> And he pockets the profits, secure from the drop.

Burke too, languishing in a condemned cell, nursed a griev-
ance against Robert Knox. He felt that the doctor was morally
obliged to pay the five pounds owed on the body of Mary
Docherty, never mind that it had been confiscated, and that he
was entitled to receive the full sum, Hare having broken their
agreement in a most unbusinesslike fashion.

Speaking only of the mundane, Margaret Hare had come off
worse than the other three. Hare had had little to lose when, with
Log out of the way, he reprised his romantic overtures to her;
Burke and Helen M'Dougal had had nothing to lose when they
moved into Tanner's Close. She, on the other hand, had been a
woman of substance, nicely provided for by her inheritance of
the lodging-house. Now the substance was gone: her premises
were irreparable following their sacking by vandals and souvenir-
seekers. And, adding acid to the lemon, Hare had made her a
mother (not for the first time, according to a rumour that sprang
from the sighting of small bones, most likely animal, in the yard
at the back of Log's). All things considered, it is understandable
that she was so vexed with Hare that she vowed never to speak to
him again.

If nearly all of the circumstances had been different, there
would be a touch of *East Lynne* about the scene on the evening of
Monday, 19 January, when Margaret, carrying her child (recovered from whooping cough? – no one seems to know), was coaxed
through the small door set into the main door of Calton Gaol,
and, her feet crunching in the cold, cold snow, stumbled away
towards the Bridges. Recognised, hooted at, and followed
ominously by passers-by on one or other of the Bridges, she
broke into a trot, was pelted with snowballs, and was rescued by
constables, who took her into the nearest watch-house. (That
was the last that Edinburgh civilians saw of her. After a week or

so, she was smuggled out of the city. On 10 February, the *Glasgow Chronicle* reported that she was in one of that city's police offices, safe from 'the hands of an infuriated populace' –

> She had left Edinburgh a fortnight ago with her infant child, and has since been wandering the country *incog*. She states that she has lodged in this neighbourhood four nights with her infant and 'her bit duds'. . . . She occasionally burst into tears while deploring her unhappy situation, which she ascribed to Hare's utter profligacy, and said all she wished was to get across the channel, and end her days in some remote spot in her own country in retirement and penitence.

On the 12th, she sailed from nearby Greenock on the *Fingail*, bound for Belfast. Though there appears to be no report of her homecoming, there is no reason to suppose that she did not complete the voyage. And there is no reason for believing a story, put about more than thirty years later, that she and her daughter were then living, or had till recently lived, in Paris. I am intrigued by the thought that if her daughter survived long enough to have a child or children, someone reading this story may, certainly without knowing it, be descended from two of the protagonists.)

Had Burke made all of the long confessions published under his byline,[1] he would not have had the time for all of the intent bible-studying, loud lamenting and quieter praying that the prison priest said that he did – nor would he have had the energy, considering the indisputable fact that he was given only bread and water to keep him alive till the day of his hanging. The custom of offering condemned persons the opportunity of eating a last, hearty breakfast was a thing of the future: when Burke

---

[1] *Referring to one of them, James Hogg, the 'Ettrick Shepherd' (himself the author of* Confessions of a Justified Sinner*), complained that it was 'First ae drunk auld wife, and then anither drunk auld wife – and then a drunk auld or sick man or twa. The confession got unco monotonous – the Lights and Shadows o' Scottish Death want relief – though, to be sure, poor [Mary] Paterson, that Unfortunate, broke in a little on the uniformity; and sae did Daft Jamie. . . .'*

awoke, for the last time, on the Wednesday morning, he may have been given an extra-large chunk of bread, but that would have been the only culinary kindness.

The day before, he had surreptitiously been taken from Calton Gaol to the lock-up house in Libberton's Wynd, which was convenient to the High Street, the place of execution. It was a shame for the High Street traders that their upstairs windows had been booked long in advance: if they had delayed the opening of their respective box-offices till the Tuesday, when the city was perpetually drenched with rain, they could have been very exorbitant: as it was, none of them got more than thirty shillings per window. The rain eased off near two o'clock on the important morning. At about the same time, the carpenters finished making the scaffold. In common with present-day royal occasions, tourists and unemployed natives, some encumbered with babies, had been camping by the cordoning ropes for hours. They were dried out by a biting wind. They sang pop songs; it would be nice to know whether one of the numbers was to the tune of 'Macpherson's Farewell', but the reports give no details of the repertoire. By seven, they were forced to their feet; if they had continued to sit or lie, thereby taking up undue space, comparative late-comers – the latest only able, by standing on tip-toe, to glimpse the top of the scaffold – would have turned uglier.

While the crowd grew and was compressed, preparations went on within the lock-up house, where there was another crowd. Either through a wish for ecumenicalism, rare in Scotland, or from a desire to share the Catholic glory, some Presbyterian ministers had joined the priests; Burke accepted the diverse prayers, and joined in with some of them. As he was being led to a makeshift robing-room, he almost bumped into the executioner, a man named Williams. 'I am not just ready for you yet,' he remarked. He obeyed an order to put on the 'dead clothes', black with the exception of a thin scarf of white linen. The jacket and trousers, cut to accommodate men of all shapes and sizes, billowed around him. Glasses of wine were distributed. Burke spoke a toast which none of the others acknowledged: 'Farewell to all present and the rest of my friends.' Williams appeared. He knotted a rope round Burke's wrists. Everything was ready; and everyone – including bailies (magistrates), sheriffs, the clergy,

policemen. On the dot of eight o'clock, the procession emerged
into the daylight –

and proceeded up Libberton's Wynd, the windows of which were
also filled with spectators. When Bailies Crichton and Small, who
were foremost in the procession, reached the top of the wynd, and
were observed by that part of the crowd who were in a situation to
see them, a loud shout was raised, which was speedily joined in by
the whole mass of spectators. When the culprit himself appeared,
ascending the stair towards the platform, the yells of execration
were redoubled, and at the moment that he came full in view, they
rose to a tremendous pitch, intermixed with maledictions, such as
'the murderer! *Burke* him! choke him! hangie!' and other expres-
sions of that sort. The miserable wretch, who looked thinner and
more ghastly than at his trial, walked with a steady step to the
apparatus of death, supported between his confessors, and
accompanied by the [Presbyterian] Reverend Messrs. Marshall
and Porteous, and seemed to be perfectly cool and self-possessed.

When he arrived on the platform of the scaffold, his composure
seemed entirely to forsake him, when he heard the appalling
shouts and yells of execration with which he was assailed: he cast a
look of fierce and even desperate defiance as the reiterated cries
were intermingled with maledictions, such as we have already
described. His face suddenly assumed a deadly paleness, and his
faculties appeared to fail him. Deafening cries of 'hang Hare too',
'where is Hare?' 'hang Knox', were mingled with the denun-
ciations against Burke.

His appearance betrayed considerable feebleness, whether
from disease or emotion we cannot say. His head was uncovered,
and his hair, which was of a light sandy colour approaching nearly
to white, along with his dress, gave somewhat of a reverend aspect
to him.

Having taken his station in front of the drop, he kneeled with
his back towards the spectators, his confessor on his right hand,
and the other Catholic clergymen on his left, and appeared to be
repeating a form of prayer, dictated to him by one of these
reverend persons; the position called forth new shouts and clam-
ours of 'stand out of the way', 'turn him round'.

When he arose from his kneeling posture, he was observed to
lift a silk handkerchief on which he had knelt, and carefully put

it into his pocket. He then cast his eyes upwards towards the gallows; and took his place on the drop, the priest supporting him, though he did not seem to require it from any bodily weakness. There was some hesitation displayed in his manner, as if loath to mount; one of the persons who assisted him to ascend, having rather roughly pushed him to a side, in order to place him exactly on the drop, he looked round at the man with a withering scowl which defies all description. While the executioner, who was behind him, was proceeding with his arrangements, some little delay took place, from the circumstance of his attempting to unloose the handkerchief at Burke's breast. Burke, perceiving the mistake, said 'the knot's behind', which were the only words not devotional uttered by him on the scaffold, and the only time he spoke to anyone excepting the priests.

When the hangman succeeded in removing the neckcloth, he proceeded to fasten the rope round his neck, which he pulled tightly, and after adjusting it, and affixing it to the gibbet, put a white cotton nightcap upon him, but without pulling it over his face.

While this was going on, the yells, which had been almost uninterrupted, became tremendous, accompanied by cries of 'You ——, you will see Daft Jamie in a minute', 'give him no rope'. He seemed somewhat unsteady; whether from terror or debility, we cannot say.

When the Reverend Mr Reid retired, the executioner advanced, and offered to draw the cap over his face. He manifested some repugnance to its being done; but, with some little difficulty, this part of the fatal preparations was also completed.

The assistants withdrawn, he uttered an ejaculation to his Maker, beseeching mercy, and immediately gave the signal, throwing the handkerchief from him with an impatient jerk, as violently as his pinioned arms would permit, and was instantly launched into eternity.

The whole proceedings on the scaffold occupied only ten minutes, and precisely at a quarter past eight o'clock the drop fell. The fall was very slight. It was nearly so imperceptible that at one instant he seemed standing, and engaged in an active operation; on the next, with almost no change visible, he was hanging helplessly suspended only by the cord that was suffocating him.

Though no sympathy could be felt for such a despicable and

cold-blooded monster, it is still a fearful sight to witness death snatching his victim with such circumstance. If any feeling of pity could be aroused by this, it must have been heightened by the terrific huzza raised at the moment he was thrown off, and the populace saw their enemy in the death struggle. In all the vast multitude there was not manifested one solitary expression of sympathy. No one said, 'God bless him'; but each vied with another in showing their exultation by shouting, clapping of hands, and waving of hats. This universal cry of satiated vengeance for blood ascended to heaven, rang through the city, and we are assured was distinctly heard by the astonished citizens in its most remote streets. Never perhaps was such a noise of triumph and execration heard, and we may safely say never on a similar occasion.

The magistrates, clergymen, and executioners, immediately upon the drop falling, retreated from the scaffold, and left it under the charge only of about half a dozen city-officers, who walked about to keep them from the cold, and looked as if they would willingly have followed the example of their superiors.

There was nothing which could be called struggling observable on the now apparently lifeless body. It seemed as if, slight as was the jerk given by the fall, instantaneous death had been produced, although the neck could not have been dislocated, yet the body swung motionless except from the impetus given by the fall, until about five minutes after the suspension, when a slight convulsive motion of the feet and heaving of the body indicated that vitality was not entirely extinguished. Upon observing this, another cheer was raised by the crowd who were anxiously watching the body. It was repeated at intervals as the motions were renewed. This happened we think perhaps twice after the first, each time diminishing in force until the last seemed merely a slightly tremulous motion of the feet, imperceptible except to those who were gazing intently upon the body. A very gradual swinging round appeared to be produced by the action of the wind. The head also, as usual, leaned a little to one side, which added a more miserable character to the scene.

At a particular part of the crowd, a cry of 'to Surgeons' Square' was now raised by some individuals, and a large body detached themselves from the mass and proceeded in that direction. We are informed that the detachment which thus broke off, though large when it left the Lawnmarket, was gradually diminished by stragglers who dropped off in its progress, until upon reaching its destination it was not able to cope with the party of policemen who were stationed there in anticipation of such an attack. At this time a baker had the hardihood to attempt a passage down the High Street with a board on his head and a few rolls on it, and, contrary to expectation, succeeded in accomplishing it. At one time his board was nearly capsized, but an escort of fellow tradesmen quickly rallied round him, and guarded him safely past the danger. A chimney-sweeper with his ladder was not so fortunate as the baker, as his brethren probably did not muster so strong, and he had to retreat without accomplishing his purpose. With such incidents the mob was amused, while the melancholy spectacle was exhibited before them, and their laughter and glee continued unabated up to their dispersion.

After hanging a considerable time, some individual from below the scaffold, the under part of which was boxed in for the reception of the body when it should be cut down, gave the body a whirl round, but no motion except what was thus given was observable. From the same place was handed up to the town-officers on the platform shavings and chips taken out of the rude coffin underneath. These were held up to the populace, and some chips thrown over among them – conduct which did not appear very decorous from the official attendants upon such a solemnity. At ten minutes to nine o'clock, Bailies Crichton and Small again came up Libberton's Wynd, still habited in their robes and with their staffs, but did not ascend the scaffold. The executioner mounted it and immediately commenced lowering the body, which was done by degrees and rather leisurely. Again the people made the welkin ring with three hearty cheers when they saw their vengeance completed.

The body was lowered precisely at five minutes before nine o'clock, having hung exactly for forty minutes. Upon its falling into the space under the scaffold, a scramble took place among the operatives for relics, consisting of pieces of the rope, shavings from the coffin, &c. &c. The body was placed in the shell and almost immediately carried on men's shoulders to the lock-up house.

The populace, upon seeing this winding up of the business, quietly dispersed. All Wednesday, however, large groups visited the scene.

During the night, the body was removed from the lock-up house.

But for a chance encounter on South Bridge, exactly fourteen months before, Burke and Hare would have offered the body of Donald the pensioner to the university's anatomist, Alexander Monro III; they would probably have sold to him, or to his representatives, the bodies that they subsequently made. He, not Robert Knox, would have suffered as a result of the partnership's liquidation.

Burke's body was presented to Alexander Monro. He had the glorious task of dissecting it.

Before doing so, he hosted a private reception at which the body was centrepiece. Among those who accepted the invitation were the surgeon Robert Liston (who was famed for a brute force that allowed him to amputate limbs as if they were wishbones: some of his patients recovered); the phrenologist George Combe (who, along with other deducers from cranial bumps, would draw all sorts of conclusions, none controversial, from Burke's); the sculptor George Joseph (who sketched Burke's head and, vying with Combe, took measurements of it, with the intention of making a bust).

Reflecting upon Munro's drawing-power, his lecture-room within the precincts of the university was only 'quite crowded' when, at one o'clock on the Thursday afternoon, he began dissecting, 'having previously done everything in his power to satisfy the curiosity of those who wished to have a view of the features, by exposing them in the most favourable position'. By three o'clock, when he downed tools, the room was less crowded, probably because squeamish spectators had withdrawn, distressed by the fact that 'the class-room had the appearance of a butcher's slaughter-house, from blood flowing down and being trodden upon'.

The anxiety to obtain a sight of the vile carcass of the murderer was exceedingly great, particularly after the dismissal of Dr Monro's class; and the Doctor, in the most obliging manner, accommodated everyone to the utmost extent the apartment would admit of. About half-past two o'clock, however, a body of young men, consisting chiefly of students, assembled in the area, and becoming clamorous for admission *en masse*, which of course was quite impractical, it was found necessary to send for a body of

Police to preserve order. But this proceeding had quite an opposite effect from that intended. Indignant at the opposition they
met with, conceiving themselves to have a preferable title to
admission, and exasperated at the display of force in the interior
of the University, where they imagined no such interference was
justifiable, the young men made several attempts, in which they
nearly succeeded, to overpower the Police, and broke a good deal
of glass in the windows on either side of the entrance to the
Anatomical Theatre. It was attempted to clear the yard with but
indifferent success; indeed, the Police were overmatched, and
could only stand their ground by avoiding the open area.

The disturbance lasted from half-past two till nearly four
o'clock when an end was at once put to it by the good sense of
Professor [Robert] Christison, who announced to the young men
that he had arranged for their admission in parties of about fifty at
a time, giving his own personal guarantee for their good conduct.
This was received with loud cheers, and immediately the riotous
disposition they had previously manifested disappeared. We
cannot think why this expedient was not thought of earlier; for if
it had, there would have been no disturbances of any kind. The
whole fracas, indeed, was a mere ebullition of boyish impatience,
rendered more unruly by their extreme curiosity to obtain a sight
of the body of the murderer. Several of the policemen were
severely hurt; but, *en revanche*, we believe not a few of the young
men have still reason to remember the weight of their batons, and
some severe contusions were received. South Bridge Street, in
front of the College, was kept in a continued uproar, and almost
blocked up by the populace who were denied access to the interior, and had the approaches not been guarded, fresh accessions of
rioters might have given it a more serious aspect.

On Friday, however, matters were better arranged. An order
was given to admit the public generally to view the body of Burke,
and of course many thousands availed themselves of the opportunity thus afforded them. Indeed, so long as daylight lasted, an
unceasing stream of persons continued to flow through the
College Square, who, as they arrived, were admitted by one stair
to the Anatomical Theatre, passed the black marble table on
which lay the body of the murderer, and made their exit by
another stair.

To give a better idea of what the countenance had been, the

skull cap which had been sawn off the preceding day was replaced, and the outer skin brought over it, so as to retain it in the proper situation.

The immense concourse of people whose curiosity induced them to visit this sad and humiliating spectacle of fallen and degraded man may be judged of when it is mentioned that, by actual enumeration, it was found that upwards of sixty per minute passed the corpse. This continued from ten o'clock until darkening, and when we left at nearly four o'clock the crowd was increasing; we cannot compute the number at less than twenty-five thousand persons, and counting the other days on which many saw him, though the admissions were not so indiscriminate, the amount cannot be reckoned under thirty thousand souls. A greater number of males probably than was present at the execution, and a far greater concourse perhaps than ever paid homage to the remains of any great man lying in state.

We understand, though we did not witness it, that some women whose curiosity presented a stronger impulsive motive than could in them be counteracted by the characteristic grace of a female – modesty – found their way with the mob into the room where the naked body was exposed. It is not likely, however, that their curiosity will, in such a case, again get the better of their discretion, as the males, who reserve to themselves the exclusive right of witnessing such spectacles, bestowed such tokens of their indignation upon them as will probably deter them from again visiting an exhibition of the sort; seven in all is said to be the number of females in Edinburgh so void of decency; but in justice even to them we may presume that they did not anticipate such an exposure.

Next day, Saturday, all ingress was denied, and again the front of the College presented a scene of confusion sufficiently annoying to those in the neighbourhood, and to passers-by. Long after they had ascertained that no admission was allowed, the people continued gazing at the outer walls, and when their curiosity was abundantly gratified by this, or their patience exhausted, fresh arrivals of unwearied spectators arrived.

As a discreet fulfilment of the hope expressed by Lord Boyle: after the last member of the public had seen Burke's body, the fleshy parts of it were evacuated, what remained was put aside long enough to become no more than a skeleton, and that became – and is still – an exhibit in the university's unpublic medical museum. Appropriately, some of the discarded skin was treated by a tanner; when leathery enough for the purpose of binding, it was made into the cover of a pocket-book – thus making Burke, in Professor Richard D. Altick's words,[1] 'one of the select company of murderers who were hanged, drawn, and quartooed'. The pocket-book has, so to speak, joined the skeleton.

The people of Edinburgh were niggardly in one respect, generous in another. A subscription 'set on foot for the purpose of conferring on James Gray and his wife a lasting mark of gratitude' failed to raise more than about ten pounds. But a subscription to enable Jamie Wilson's mother and sister to bring a private prosecution (still known in Scotland as a Bill of Criminal Letters) against Hare raised so much money that the organisers could afford, not just one leading advocate, but two, as well as supernumeraries, and were left with cash in their hands. The action, opposed by the Lord Advocate, went through several hearings till, on 2 February, there was stalemate; three days later, the Wilsons' lawyers announced that their clients had given in.

In the evening of that day, a Thursday, Hare was slipped out of gaol by a turnkey, who accompanied him in a carriage to the place in Newington, just past Knox's house, which was the final boarding-point in the city for the mail-coach to Portpatrick, whence vessels sailed to Ireland. Hare would have been muffled up, leaving only his eyes and nose visible, even if the temperature had been above zero. A second-class, outside coach-seat had been reserved for him. The turnkey shouted, 'Goodbye, Mr Black,' as the driver whipped the horses.

---

[1] *In* Victorian Studies in Scarlet: Murders and Manners in the Age of Victoria, *Robert D. Altick, Dent, 1973. Altick, an American who has written several fine books, some dealing with aspects of life in Britain in the nineteenth century, only glances in this one at Burke and Hare; he takes more notice of William Corder, the murderer of Maria Marten in the Red Barn at Polstead, Suffolk, who was hanged in August 1828, not quite three months before the Edinburgh case was revealed. The Moyse's Hall Museum in Bury St Edmunds, the town which hosted that execution, has many associated items, including a copy of the record of the trial bound in Corder's skin.*

Hare's alias lasted about sixty miles, half the distance to Portpatrick. It was broken by a sort of coincidence that superstitious or religious readers may think was arranged. One of the other passengers was a lawyer; he had helped in the Wilsons' action; his position on rather than in the coach suggests that his bill was outstanding. Recognising Hare, he said nothing – till an incident indicated that Hare was financially better off than he was. According to a report that appeared in the following Monday's *Edinburgh Courant*, under the heading **'Riot at Dumfries!'**,

after travelling a stage or two, the guard, without knowing *Black*, consented to allow him to get inside the coach, as the night was damp and cold, but he had only got up one or two of the steps at the coach door when a highly respectable legal gentleman . . . called out, 'Would you put a murderer inside?' This led to the discovery, and the coach had not long arrived at Dumfries when the news of his infamous arrival became generally known. A crowd instantly assembled, evincing the most determinedly hostile intentions. For protection, the wretch was locked up in the tap-room of the Kings Arms Inn until the Portpatrick mail should start, which is usually about nine o'clock [on Friday morning]. Until that hour the mob, though it continued to increase, many coming no doubt to get a glimpse of such a notorious character, was tolerably quiet, under an expectation that he would take his departure by the Portpatrick mail. By nine o'clock, for half a mile on the road, the crowd became immense.

The coach drew up to the inn door, but for Hare to have ventured out would have been certain destruction, and, consequently, the coach drove off without him. It had not proceeded far when it was stopped by the populace, and a most strict search was made in case he was concealed; even the boot was examined. Being disappointed, the people became more enraged, and, in consequence, the magistrates were seriously alarmed for the peace of the town. As a *russe*, they caused a post-chaise to draw up at the front of the inn, into which, it was stated, Hare would proceed on his journey. They, at the same time, however, got another chaise to the bottom of the yard of the inn, from whence he contrived to escape unobserved from a back window and to walk along to the vehicle, which was driven rapidly to the gaol, followed by the mob, who soon found out the trick. The gaol was then assailed with stones, most of the windows of the Court Room were broken, and one of the doors forced. The police and constables, however, succeeded, with some difficulty, in restoring order, but the crowd remained in the street till after dark. During the night, the wretch was taken out of gaol and privately conveyed on foot out of town, on the Carlisle road, under an escort of police officers.

The last sure sighting of Hare was on the Sunday morning, when he was into England, a mile or so past Carlisle. There are legends, of course: most seem to have borrowed from earlier ones, at least so far as blindness is concerned: those of the 1830s have him tripping or being thrown into a pit, stirring a flurry of quick-lime, some into his eyes – and by the turn of the century, long after whenever he died, he was recollected as a blind beggar on the *north* side (a nice convincing touch, that) of Oxford Street in the West End of London. I shouldn't be surprised if he, in fact, returned to Ireland and lived there happily ever after.[1]

There was no need to make up satisfying tales about Robert Knox. The truth was good enough.

A week after Hare's release, it was announced that a committee had been formed, under the chairmanship of the Marquess of Queensberry, to evaluate the rumours against Knox; Sir Walter Scott had been invited to serve on the committee, but, not wanting the rumours to be disturbed, had refused 'to lend a hand to whitewash this much to be suspected individual'. Hundreds more who suspected a whitewash gathered in different parts of the city to scream and shout as much. Most of the gatherings centred upon effigies of Knox, and one of those became an

---

[1] *Thomas De Quincey (op. cit.), while speaking of 'Quintius Burkius and Publicus Harius', has the enquiry made of members of The Society of Connoisseurs in Murder, 'By the way, gentlemen, has anybody heard lately of Hare?' – and has the enquirer adding: 'I understand he is comfortably settled in Ireland, considerably to the west, and does a little business now and then; but, as he observes with a sigh, only as a retailer – nothing like the fine thriving wholesale concern so carelessly blown up at Edinburgh. "You see what comes of neglecting business" – is the chief moral . . . which Hare draws from his past experience.'*

unruly procession to Newington Place, where the effigy was hanged from a tree in the doctor's garden and set on fire. A subsequent effigy-following procession was more dense (advance notification of it having been published in the *Weekly Chronicle*: ' . . . the cavalcade will move in the direction of Portobello where, it is supposed, the Doctor burrows at night') and better prepared – in that a collection was taken beforehand to cover fines imposed on those arrested *en route* or at the destination, a long-disused gibbet near the Portobello sea-front. Very shortly afterwards, the Marquess of Queensberry, whose family motto was not 'Modesty is the Better Part of Valour', loudly resigned as chairman of the committee while being the soul of reticence as to the reason for his resignation.

The committee reported its findings in the middle of March. There were many, too many, of them, the main ones being that Knox had had no idea that he was using murdered subjects – but that if he had been at all inquisitive of the provenance of the bodies, of the men who had offered them for sale, he would have soon found out. Which meant, to those who were determined to find this meaning, that Knox was guilty, at the very least, of having turned a blind eye to clear indications of mass-murder. John Wilson, professor of moral philosophy at the university, hid behind the pseudonym 'Christopher North' when writing, in the next issue of *Blackwood's Magazine*:

> Dr Knox stands arraigned at the bar of the public, his accuser being – human nature. . . . He is not now the victim of some wild and foolish calumny; the whole world shudders at the transactions; and none but a base, blind, brutal beast can at this moment dare to declare, 'Dr Knox stands free from all suspicion of being accessory to murder.'

Knox was, to use a modern expression, on a hiding to nothing: any admission of laxity would cue a chorus of demands for a confession that he had been wittingly lax – silence was golden for his enemies. He kept silent; tried to persuade his supporters to keep their support discreet. Learning that his students intended to give him 'a lasting proof of their attachment', he wrote them a long letter, which ended:

In this situation I am unwilling to receive any token of your
friendship which must be associated in my own mind with the
heaviest calamity of my life, and which, moreover, I am perfectly
aware, cannot at present be accompanied by the sympathy of the
public.

Allow me therefore to say I shall consider your abandoning
your design as a stronger proof of your attachment than your ever
having formed it.

With the warmest wishes for your happiness, believe me very
gratefully,

Yours, etc.,
R. KNOX

But the students, feeling unable to forego 'the gratification of
carrying their design into effect', presented him with a gold vase;
the note with it, altogether protesting too much, reached an apex
of silliness at the end: 'The public voice has at length exonerated
you from charges of which we know you from the first moment
felt the injustice.' *The Scotsman* rightly described the gift as
'injudicious'.

The strength of Knox's self-control is indicated by the fact that
there is only one anecdote of its being broached. On a summer's
day, he went with another doctor to an Edinburgh park:

> They talked to a little girl who was playing there and at length
> Dr Knox gave her a penny and said, 'Now, my dear, you and I
> will be friends. Would you come and live with me if you got a
> whole penny every day?' 'No,' said the child, 'you would, maybe,
> sell me to Dr Knox.' The anatomist started back with a painfully
> stunned expression, his features began to twitch convulsively,
> and tears appeared in his eyes.[1]

There is no surer dating of that incident than that it happened
during a summer before the autumn of 1842. In most of the
seasons till then, Knox's troubles outweighed his joys. Continuing reduction of his student-roll caused him to leave Surgeons'

---

[1]*Quoted in Isobel Rae's good biography* Knox the Anatomist, *Oliver & Boyd,
Edinburgh, 1964.*

Square; he worked for a few months at another medical school in the city, for as short a time at a school in Glasgow, and then became a freelance lecturer, accepting whatever engagements were offered. In 1837, the professor of pathology at Edinburgh University gave notice of his retirement, and Knox applied for the Chair, making what appeared to be a one-horse race; but four members of the medical faculty, one of them Robert Christison, tried to have the race called off by proposing the abolition of the Chair, saying that they were willing to take turns at giving free lectures on general pathology; the city council, keen to keep the Chair but worried by the opposition to Knox's occupancy of it, got the professor of pathology to withdraw his notice. Knox then applied for the post of lecturer in anatomy to the art students of the Scottish Academy; he didn't get a single vote. Four years later, he applied for the Chair of Physiology; he was not surprised that it went to the son of the unretired professor of pathology. In that year, 1841, his wife died from puerperal fever; early in the next, one of his sons died from scarlet fever. In the autumn he moved from Edinburgh to London. None of the victory celebrations was reported in the Edinburgh papers.

He was poor. Unable to obtain a position in a London school of medicine, he gave talks on racial differences, and later turned his notes into a book, *Races of Men* (which contains prophesies on black and brown militancy that have come true). He wrote other books, some on anatomy, and may have made a decent amount from *Fish and Fishing in the Lone Glens of Scotland*, which was published in New York as well as in London, where its price was a shilling; he also contributed scores of articles, some on anatomy, to medical and veterinary journals.

In May 1847, one of the medical journals, *The Lancet*, published a letter from a lay person, expressing surprise at the fact that a young man of Nottinghamshire who had studied medicine for only nine months had won the College of Surgeons' diploma. The letter sparked off others, *The Lancet*'s leader-writer joined in, and before long there was proof-positive that the young man had forged several student-attendance certificates – one certifying that he had studied under Dr Knox in the winter of 1839. The forger was permitted to keep his diploma – and, of course, to continue practising in more ways than one. With a single exception, none of those whom he had claimed to be his

teachers was penalised for having 'evaded the faithful enforce-
ment' of regulations. The exception was Knox. The Royal
College of Surgeons of Edinburgh cancelled his licence to
lecture, and notified the twenty-two other licensing boards of the
decision, demanding that they follow suit. (Isobel Rae [see the
last footnote] remarks that 'one of the more extraordinary things
about this extraordinary case is that today not one of those
[boards] still in existence can produce the correspondence. So
Knox's letters in his own defence are for ever lost.')

In 1854, his sixty-first year, Knox applied to be sent to the
Crimea as a physician or staff-surgeon, and asked William Fergusson to support his application. Fergusson wrote to him: 'You
seem to me as full of energy as ever, and I need hardly say that
your intellectual powers seem equal to any of those former efforts
which in early days made you dux of the High School of
Edinburgh, and the first teacher of anatomy in Europe.' Knox
was turned down by the Army Medical Department.

Two years later, he at last got a job – as pathological anatomist
to the Cancer Hospital (Free) in London. He worked there till a
fortnight before his death, from heart disease, in December
1862. The corpse of the only survived victim of the West Port
murderers was buried in the nonconformist part of a graveyard,
eventually beneath a flat stone which, bearing no inscription,
might have borne this one, which is the final stanza of Southey's
'The Surgeon's Warning':

> So they carried the sack pick-a-back,
>   And he carved him bone from bone,
> But what became of the surgeon's soul
>   Was never to mortal known.

A Postscript on an Italian
(or Lincolnshire) Subject

The fact that the murders in Edinburgh, at least sixteen of them, had no parliamentary consequence, whereas a single similarly-motivated murder in London two years after the last of them *did*, may be seen by Scottish Nationalists as a further reason for patriotic paranoia.

The rarity of old books is governed, in the main, by whether they were published between boards or as paperbacks. Though titles published only in the latter format were almost always comparatively mass-produced, they were less likely to be kept, let alone treasured, by the owners of them new – less likely to be handed on or down – and still less likely to get to dealers in second-hand books who could be bothered to sort them into their subjects rather than shove them, any old how, in trays outside their shops, never minding showers and indiscriminate kleptomaniacs. I have one of the few remaining copies of a paperback that must have sold in thousands around the Christmas of 1831, and was probably sold out before the New Year came in. It is, so parts of the crowded title-page say,

THE TRIAL
of
BISHOP, WILLIAMS, AND MAY,
at the
OLD BAILEY, DEC. 2, 1831,
for the
MURDER OF THE ITALIAN BOY,
CARLO FERRIER

Corrected and Revised by W. Harding,
Short-Hand Writer.

LONDON:
PUBLISHED BY W. HARDING,
3, PATERNOSTER–ROW

Led along by three of the lawyers representing the Crown, of whom a Mr Adolphus[1] was most in evidence, the prosecution witnesses told the following story:

Just before noon on Saturday, 5 November (Guy Fawkes Day), the bell of the dissecting room at King's College,[2] London, was rung. The porter, William Hill, admitted John Bishop and James May, who were about the same age, in the early thirties.

He had known both of them before. May asked him if he wanted anything, and he said, 'Not particularly', but asked him what he had got. May said a male subject. Hill asked him what size? He said a boy about fourteen, and he demanded twelve guineas. Hill said that they could not give that price, for they did not particularly want it; but if he would wait, he would acquaint

[1] *I believe that this was the German-parented* John *Adolphus, who, astonishingly to mere mortals, wrote tomes on the history of Britain and its Empire while pursuing an extremely busy career at the Bar. In 1820, when he was fifty-two, he unsuccessfully defended Arthur Thistlewood and other Cato Street Conspirators who had intended to murder members of the Cabinet; during the next twenty years, he appeared in several celebrated murder trials (e.g. of James Greenacre, whom he successfully prosecuted). In 1840 he led the successful prosecution of the Swiss valet, François Courvoisier, for the murder of his master, Lord William Russell; though, during the trial, Courvoisier admitted to his counsel, Charles Phillips, that he was guilty, Phillips, in his closing speech, not only pledged his word to the jury that Courvoisier was innocent, but tried to fasten the crime on another. Adolphus stood aside from the furore when those deceits were found out, saying that he was absent for most of Phillips's speech, attending to business in another court.*

[2] *In 1840, Dr Knox's best student, William Fergusson, was appointed professor of surgery there; the surgeoncy to King's College Hospital went with the job. He resigned the professorship of surgery in 1870, but until his death seven years later, was clinical professor of surgery and senior surgeon to the hospital.*

Mr [Richard] Partridge, the demonstrator of anatomy, with the matter. He accordingly went to Mr Partridge, who said he would see them. Hill then went back to them, and told them to go round to the place appropriated for them.

There, Mr Partridge joined them. They could not agree as to the price. Mr Partridge said that he would not give twelve guineas for the subject. May then told him that he should have it for ten guineas. Mr Partridge left them, and went into the dissecting room. Hill followed Mr Partridge, and in consequence of what Mr Partridge said to him, he returned to Bishop and May, and told them that Mr Partridge would only give nine guineas for the subject. May said that he would be d——d if it should come in for less than ten guineas. May was tipsy at the time. On his going out to the door, Bishop, taking Hill aside, said to him, 'Never mind May, he is drunk; it shall come in for the nine guineas in the course of half an hour.' They then went away.

About a quarter past two o'clock on the same afternoon, they returned in company with Thomas Williams[1] and a man named Shields. They had a hamper with them: Shields seemed to be employed as the porter for carrying it. May and Bishop carried the hamper into another room, while Williams and Shields remained where they were. On opening the hamper, a sack containing a body was found in it. May and Bishop remarked that it was 'a good one', to which observation Hill assented. May being tipsy, they turned the body very carelessly out of the sack. Hill perceived that the body was particularly fresh, and that there was no sawdust about the hair of it. He asked the men what the subject had died of. They said that they did not know, and that that was no business either of his or of theirs. Hill replied that it certainly was not. In consequence of the opinion which he formed from the appearance of the body, he went to Mr Partridge, and detailed to him what he had seen, and what he thought about the matter.

Mr Partridge accordingly returned to the room where the body was lying, to see it. The prisoners May and Bishop had been removed from that room to the room into which they were originally introduced, and where the other two men were also. Mr

---

[1] As he was known. His real name, John Head, was tattooed on his left forearm, surrounded with 'rudely done flower-pots, etc.' It appears that he was about the same age as Bishop and May.

Partridge, without seeing them, after seeing the body, went to the secretary's office. In the meantime, several of the gentlemen connected with the College saw the body, and their suspicions were also excited.

Mr Partridge having returned to the place where the men were, showed them a £50 note, and told them that he must get that changed, and that then he would pay them. Mr Partridge having pulled out his purse while speaking to them, and there being some gold in it, Bishop said, 'Give me what money you have, and I shall call on Monday for the remainder.' May proposed that Mr Partridge should give him the £50 note, and he would go out and get it changed. Mr Partridge, smiling, said, 'Oh, no,' and then left them.

In about a quarter of an hour Mr Mayo, the professor of anatomy at the College, came down with Mr Rogers, a police inspector, and a body of police, and the men were all taken into custody. Before that took place, Bishop said to Hill, 'Pay me only eight guineas in the presence of May; give me the other guinea, and I will give you half-a-crown.'

The body was delivered to the police station in Covent Garden, together with the hamper and sack.

Joseph Sadler Thomas, superintendent of F Division of the Metropolitan Police (which, as it had been in existence for only two years, was usually referred to as the New Police):

The body was placed in the back room in the station-house, with the hamper. Bishop, May, Williams and Shields were put in the outer room. I asked May what he had to say, for he was charged with having come into the possession of the subject in an improper manner. He replied, 'I have nothing at all to do with it; the subject is that gentleman's' (pointing to Bishop). 'I merely accompanied him to get the money for it.' I then asked Bishop whose it was, and he said that it was his, and that he was merely removing it from Guy's Hospital to King's College. I then asked Williams what he knew about it. He replied that he knew nothing about it, and that he had gone with them to King's College to see the building. I asked Bishop in the first instance what he was, and his answer was, 'I am a b——y body-snatcher.' I think that all the prisoners at the time, Bishop and May especially, were labouring under the effects of liquor. May was carried into the station-house on all fours, and with his smock-frock over his head.

That night, a post-mortem examination was carried out by Richard Partridge, with the assistance of four other medical men. It is understandable why one of the assistants, Mr Mayo, the professor of anatomy at King's College, was not called to give evidence – for, according to another of the assistants, talking out of court, Mr Mayo, as well as being quaint of both stance and speech, was apt to jump from one conclusion to another, no matter how far apart conclusions were: 'The boy's teeth had been removed . . . but beyond this there was no trace of injury or poison. Mr Mayo, who had a peculiar way of standing very upright with his hands in his breeches' pockets, said with a kind of lisp he had, "By Jove! the boy died a nathral death." It was then found that one or more of the upper cervical vertebrae were fractured. "By Jove!" said Mr Mayo, "thith boy wath murthered."'

Over the next few days, several people identified the body as that of an Italian boy, Carlo Ferrier, who had been brought to England two years before by an Italian who seems to have been a sort of one-man band, playing the pandean-pipes as accompaniment to a street-organ, but who had been deserted by him after six weeks; from then until All-Hallows Day, when the boy was last seen alive, he had begged a living with the aid of what one of the witnesses described as 'a cage – like a squirrel-cage – with two white mice in it, which was suspended by a string round his neck', the usual site of his begging being in Oxford Street, near where it crossed Regent Street. (There is nothing to stop anyone who believes that William Hare became a blind beggar on the north side of Oxford Street from believing that he arrived there soon enough to be a competitor of Carlo Ferrier and his mice.)

A dozen witnesses spoke of happenings on Friday, 4 November. The first of the dozen was Thomas Mills:

I live at 39 Bridgehouse Place, Newington Causeway, Elephant & Castle, and am a dentist. Between nine and ten o'clock that morning, James May called and offered a set of teeth for sale; they were twelve human teeth, six for each jaw. He offered the set for a guinea. It was then that I observed that one of them was chipped; that lessened their value. I said that I would give twelve shillings for them, and I remarked that they did not belong to one set. He said, 'Upon my soul to God, they all belonged to one head not long since, and the body has never been buried.' I gave him the twelve shillings.

The evidence of some others of the dozen fitted together to make a pub-crawl. Henry Lock:

> I was in November a waiter at the Fortune of War, Giltspur Street, in the City. I saw Bishop, Williams and May there at eleven o'clock in the morning. They had some drink, and went away about twelve o'clock. There was a strange man with them. About three o'clock in the afternoon they came in again, and remained until about five. About eight o'clock the same evening they all returned with another man, who appeared to be a coachman. About nine o'clock May went to the bar, with something in a handkerchief, which proved to be teeth. I observed to him that they appeared to be young ones, and were worth two shillings. May said they were worth two pounds to him. He and his companions shortly afterwards left.

Thomas Wigley:

> I am a porter at coach-houses. On 4 November, early in the evening, I was in the Fortune of War, when Bishop came in, and was followed in a few minutes by May. In a few minutes Williams came in, and Bishop observed, 'Here he comes, I knew he was a game one.' Bishop said to May before they went away, 'You stick to me, and I will stick to you.'

James Seagrave:

> About six o'clock that evening I was with my cabriolet on the stand in Old Bailey [at the southern end of Giltspur Street]. Having put the nose-bag on my horse, I went into the King of Denmark watering-house to take my tea. I was called out, and saw May and Bishop. May asked me if I wanted a job, and said he had a 'long job'. He took me to one side and said he wanted me to fetch

a 'stiff'un', which I understood to mean a dead body. I told him I did not know, but asked him what he would stand; he said that he would stand a guinea. I said that I had not finished my tea and that my horse had not done his corn. I went into the public house, followed by May and Bishop. They took their seats, and called for tea for two. Some person in the room jogged me by the elbow and hinted that the men were 'snatchers', and I determined not to go with them. I afterwards saw them outside, making a bargain with another coachman.

Edward Chandler:

I was on 4 November porter of the King of Denmark. May and Bishop came in with Seagrave, a cabriolet-driver, and they had some tea and a pint of gin together. May put some gin into Bishop's tea, and Bishop asked him, 'Are you going to hocus me, or burke me?' I do not know what *hocus* means.[1]

George Gissing:

I am twelve years old. I go to school and church. My father keeps the Birdcage public house, Bethnal Green [just over a mile north-east of Old Bailey]. On the evening of 4 November, about half past six o'clock, I saw a yellow hackney-chariot draw up opposite my father's house, which is very near Nova Scotia Gardens. I know Bishop's cottage in Nova Scotia Gardens. Williams and his wife live with Bishop. I saw Williams standing on the fore-wheel of the chariot, talking to the driver. Then I saw a strange man carrying a sack in his arms, and Bishop holding up one end of it. They put it in the chariot. Williams helped it in. The sack appeared to be heavy, as if something heavy was in it. Bishop and the other man got into the chariot with Williams, and they drove up Crabtree Road and towards Shoreditch Church, on the road to the City. The strange man was not May. Bishop is Williams's brother-in-law, and they kept the wedding at my father's house.

[1]*According to Pierce Egan (Boxiana, London, 1821), 'To hocus a man is to put something into his drink, on the sly, of a sleepy, stupifying quality, that renders him unfit for action.'*

The present-day scarcity of porters – or rather, of porters who can be bribed to carry anything – makes one envious of the seeming ubiquity of them in London in 1831. Of course, the fact that such a lot of the evidence so far mentioned related to happenings in pubs helps to explain why a lot of porters have also been mentioned: porters' thirstiness for a kind of stout was so voracious that the drink itself had become known as porter. Two more porters helped the prosecution: their names were Thomas Davis and James Weeks, and they were both employed to carry things to, from, and within the dissecting room at Guy's Hospital, on the south side of London Bridge. They were on duty at seven o'clock in the evening of 4 November. Thomas Davis:

> Bishop and May came to the hospital, May carrying a sack. I knew them before. They asked me if I wanted to purchase a subject. I declined, and they asked if I would allow them to leave it in the hospital until the following morning. I acceded to their request, and locked the body up in a room. I only saw a foot out of the sack, and I believed that it was either that of a boy or a female; it was not large enough for that of a man.

Half an hour later, Bishop and May turned up at Grainger's Anatomical Theatre, in Webb Street, close to Guy's, and offered a subject to the curator, James Appleton:

> I knew them; Williams, too. They had not the body with them. Bishop said that it was a fresh subject, a boy of about fourteen years of age. I declined to purchase it, and they went away.

How they, and Williams (who, presumably, had loitered outside both Guy's and Grainger's), spent the rest of the night is not stated in the trial-transcript. May's tipsiness next morning would be excellent circumstantial evidence that he, at least, did not get to bed early were it not for the direct evidence of the aforementioned Henry Lock that, at eight o'clock that morning, May, Bishop and Williams were in the vicinity of the Fortune of War. They were accompanied by the porter named Shields. (As you know, later in the day he carried a hamper on their behalf. It seems likely that Shields was the 'strange man' observed by young George Gissing. Shields, who should have been a star witness at the trial, did not give evidence – which surely means that he had already given the police information, on the understanding that he would neither be charged as an accessory nor be called as a witness.) Henry Lock:

> Bishop, addressing Williams, asked, 'What shall we do for a hamper?' Williams made no answer. Bishop requested Shields to go over to St Bartholomew's Hospital [in West Smithfield, a short stroll from the Fortune of War] to get a hamper, but he refused to go. Bishop then went himself for it, and soon returned with a hamper. They then all left together.

Their destination was Guy's. They arrived in the dissecting room there shortly after eleven. Thomas Davis and James Weeks were still, or back, on duty. Weeks unlocked the anteroom, the sacked body that had been stored in it was put in the hamper, that was hoisted on to Shields's shoulders, and he and the three unburdened members of the party exeunted.

You will have noticed some time ago that, whereas in Edinburgh toutings and deliveries of bodies were restricted to hours of darkness, either no such restriction was put upon the three Londoners or they ignored such a restriction and were not told off about it. It seems safe to say that, whether they were unrestricted or undisciplined, they would hardly have undertaken their subsequent journey at such a busy hour of daylight if they had been quite sober. The party probably proceeded across London Bridge to the Monument, turned left into Cannon Street, passed St Paul's, and carried on down Ludgate Hill (where they, Shields especially, would have been tempted to pop into the King of Denmark in Old Bailey), along Fleet Street, and on to the Strand, which was then the sole location of the King's College that has since been distributed about London. Williams either departed from the others somewhere along the route or (as it appears he had done both at Guy's and at Grainger's) stayed close but out of sight, on this occasion with the hampered Shields as company, while Bishop and May opened negotiations with William Hill, the porter to the college's anatomists. You know what happened in and adjacent to the dissecting room.

Within the fortnight following Guy Fawkes Day, as the result of interviewing, rummaging and digging by many members of the New Police, the case against the three prisoners was clinched. It is unnecessary to mention, let alone to quote the evidence of, all of the trial witnesses who had helped during that fortnight. Two of the witnesses, both residing near Nova Scotia Gardens, swore that they had seen '*an* Italian boy' in their neighbourhood on Thursday, 3 November. More telling than their evidence was that of Edward Ward, who was aged six ('and a half,' he insisted):

> Previously to being sworn, he was examined as to the nature of an oath. The child, with infantile simplicity, said that he knew it to be a very bad thing to tell a lie; that it was a great sin; and that he who would swear falsely would go to h—l, to be burnt with brimstone and sulphur. He was then sworn.
> He stated that he lived with his father near to the Nova Scotia cottages; that a few days before Guy Fawkes Day, his mother having given him a half-holiday, he went to Bishop's cottage to play with Bishop's children, three in number, a boy older than himself, a little girl, and a boy about his own age. As a toy, Bishop's children produced a cage, which went round and round and which contained two white mice. He never before saw either a cage or mice with Bishop's children.

The evidence of Constable Joseph Higgins, more than being telling, made the case just about conclusive:

> He went to the cottage, 3 Nova Scotia Gardens, tenanted by Bishop, accompanied by another policeman. They minutely searched the premises and, with an iron-rod, probed the garden in several places. The rod met with resistance in one part of the garden, and on digging they discovered a cap, a jacket, a pair of trousers, and a small shirt. In another part they dug up a blue coat, a drab striped waistcoat (altered from man's size so as to fit a boy), and a pair of trousers with the braces attached to them. The waistcoat had stains of blood on the collar and shoulders. They were buried about 12 inches under the surface, and were covered with cinders and ashes. (The coat and one of the pairs of trousers were sworn to by those who had identified the body of Carlo Ferrier as having been his.)
> He – Constable Higgins – went to May's lodgings, near the New

Kent Road [the eastern end of which was only a few hundred yards from Webb Street, in which Grainger's Anatomical Theatre was situated], and found some awls. On one of the awls he discovered drops of blood apparently fresh. (Thomas Mills, the dentist, was here recalled for the purpose of stating that the awl was such as would serve to extract teeth in the coarse manner in which those sold to him had been extracted.)

Mr Adolphus having closed the case for the prosecution, the prisoners' written defences were read aloud by an officer of the court. *Bishop* stated that during the past five years he had 'occasionally obtained a livelihood by supplying surgeons with subjects' but that he had 'never disposed of any body that had not died a natural death – he had been in the habit of obtaining bodies from workhouses, with their clothes on'. He generously declared that neither Williams nor May knew how he had come by the body said to be that of the Italian boy. Unless the transcription of his written defence omits the most important part of it, he gave no indication as to where that body had come from. *Williams*, in his defence, stated that he had 'never engaged in the calling of resurrectionist' – it was 'by accident' that he had joined Bishop and May in the dissecting room at King's in the early afternoon of 5 November. *May*, though admitting that he had been a resurrectionist for six years, claimed that he had met Bishop quite by chance in the Fortune of War on 4 November, and had subsequently accompanied him for want of something better to do.

Bishop's counsel called one witness – a dealer in old clothes who remembered selling Bishop's wife a cloth cap in 1829 (as the cap dug up from the back yard of 3 Nova Scotia Gardens, and identified as that of the Italian boy, was 'of brown hair, with green-leather front', the dealer's evidence was peculiarly unhelpful to Bishop) – and May's counsel called three, all women 'who admitted themselves to be in the habit of seeing gentlemen': one said that May was with her, non-stop, from the early afternoon of 4 November till noon next day, and both of the others said that any blood on May's clothes 'was wholly owing to an accident which happened to a jackdaw' – an animal that deserves to have become as proverbial of moot serological evidence as has a trout in the milk of the undoubtable circumstantial kind.

The jury were sent out at 8 p.m. on the only day of the trial, and returned half an hour later.

Every eye was now fixed upon the prisoners.

Bishop advanced to the bar with a heavy step. There was something of heaviness in his aspect, but altogether his countenance was mild. His face had that pallid bluish appearance which so often betokens mental suffering.

Williams came forward with a short quick step. When he came in front and laid his hand on the bar, the rapid movements of his fingers on the board – the frequent shifting of the hand, sometimes letting it hang down for an instant by his side, then replacing it on the board, and then resting his side against the front of the dock, showed the perturbed state of his feelings. Williams had that kind of aspect with which men associate the idea of sharpness and cunning, and something of mischief, but nothing of the villain.

May came forward with a more firm step than either of his fellow-prisoners. He was the best-looking of the three; he had a countenance which most persons would consider open and manly. There was an air of firmness and determination about him, but neither in him nor in his companions was there the slightest physiognomical trait of a murderer, according to the common notions on the subject. They were that kind of vulgar men in appearance of which one sees hundreds every day, without being struck with any indication in them of good or evil disposition.

The jury returned the verdict of Guilty against all three defendants, and the judge, Lord Chief Justice Tindal, passed the sentence of death upon them.

They heard the sentence as they had heard the verdict, without any visible alteration in their manner. They stood at the bar as if they expected that something more would be added. When ordered to be removed, May raised his voice, and, in a firm tone, said, 'I am a murdered man, gentlemen, and that man' (pointing to Bishop) 'knows it.' Williams said, 'We are all murdered men.' He then addressed himself to one or two of the witnesses at the side bar, and said that before three months they would suffer for

the false evidence they had given against him. Bishop made no
observation, but retired from the bar even more absorbed by his
awful situation than he had appeared before. In a short time after,
the crowd outside the court dispersed –

perhaps before the crowd inside the court did, because the Duke
of Sussex, who had sat through the trial, stood up as soon as it
was over and made a lengthy speech praising everyone (well,
nearly everyone: he omitted reference to the tea-lady at Covent
Garden police station) who had 'helped towards redressing an
injury inflicted upon a pauper child, wandering friendless and
unknown in a foreign land'. Some of his unprepared audience
said 'Hear, hear' to his conclusion: 'I am indeed proud of being
an Englishman, and prouder still to be a prince in such a
country and of such a people.'

The Duke may still have been some way from that conclusion
when, next door, in Newgate Gaol, Bishop and Williams,
ignoring a chaplain's advice that they should compose their
minds after the 'agitation' of the trial, and partake of some
refreshment after standing almost snackless for eleven hours,
insisted upon confessing to the murder of 'the lad described in
the evidence' – who, they said (and it is hard to see why they
should have lied in this regard), was *not an Italian boy* but a
Lincolnshire one who had come up with cattle to Smithfield meat
market. They confessed also to the murder of a woman named
Fanny Pigburn, a boy perhaps named Cunningham, and a Negro
who was quite anonymous to them, adding that those victims, all
sold as subjects, had, like the 'Lincolnshire boy', been 'hocussed
by administering laudanum to render them insensible and then
suffocated by throwing them headforemost into the well in the
garden of 3 Nova Scotia Gardens'. And they 'entirely exculpated
May from all participation in the murders'.

The trial was on a Friday.

The hangings were scheduled for the following Monday.

On the morning of the Saturday between, May wrote poetry:

> James May is doomed to die,
> And is condemned most innocently.
> The God above, He knows the same,
> And will send a mitigation for his pain.

But on the Saturday afternoon, God learned, before May did, that *His* mitigation was not needed: the Sheriffs decided that May's sentence should be mitigated to transportation for life. When he was told that he was being sent to Australia,

> the poor wretch fell to the earth as if struck by lightning. His arms worked with the most frightful contortions, and four of the officers could with difficulty hold him; his countenance assumed a livid paleness – the blood forsook his lips – his eyes appeared set, and pulsation at the heart could not be distinguished. It was nearly a quarter of an hour before May was restored to the use of his faculties. Until then, all persons present thought that he could not possibly survive – it was believed, indeed, that the warrant of mercy had proved his death-blow.

(In a different way, it *was*. Soon afterwards, he was put on board a prison-hulk, the *Grampus*, bound for Botany Bay; but he did not complete the voyage. A careful report of his death at sea ascribes it to 'the annoyance he received from the other convicts'.)

On Monday, 5 December, as arranged, the brothers-in-law Bishop and Williams were hanged concurrently outside the Debtor's Door of Newgate, across the road from the King of Denmark watering-house.[1] There was a tremendous turn-out. By half-past six in the morning, the crowd was packed so tight in Old Bailey that a 200-strong contingent of policemen, ordered to form a cordon around the gallows, was unable to get through; an emergency arrangement was made for the policemen to file through the court-building, into the adjoining gaol, and out through the Debtor's Door. The crowd stretched west along Holborn as far as Hatton Garden, east along Newgate Street to St Martin's le Grand, and north along Giltspur Street, past the

---

[1]*No doubt actual brothers were executed in tandem before adequate records of capital punishment were kept, but what appears to be the first such event in fairly modern times took place on 23 May 1905, the brothers on that occasion being Alfred and Albert Stratton, the murderers of Thomas and Ann Farrow in the 'colour and oil store' in Deptford High Street, South-East London, that Thomas Farrow had managed for a quarter of a century; the Strattons were the first persons found guilty of murder chiefly on the basis of fingerprint evidence. Their execution was performed by the brothers John and William Billington.*

Fortune of War, to Smithfield. At eight o'clock, when Bishop
and Williams were led on to the scaffold, the crowd in Giltspur
Street, suddenly become a mob, pressed forward with such force
that a heavy barrier toppled –

> and a number of persons of both sexes fell with it. The screams of
> the females, and the confusion that ensued, was truly alarming.
> One female, of very respectable appearance, with her husband,
> was most dreadfully injured, the barrier having fallen upon their
> chests, and a number of others pressing upon them. A city
> constable was also under the barrier, and his cries were most
> deplorable. In this dreadful situation did the sufferers remain for
> some minutes. A cry of 'Stand back; for God's sake, stand back!'
> was raised, but all to no avail, and people in all directions were
> trampling upon one another. At length, a space of ground was
> obtained, and the individuals were rescued from their perilous
> situation, and carried to St Bartholomew's Hospital. Before nine
> o'clock every bed in Colston Ward was occupied by persons who
> had been injured, many of them seriously so, and a number of
> others who had been brought in much hurt had, after being bled,
> been enabled to proceed to their homes.

Bishop and Williams were dead by then, their bodies being cut
down. Past nightfall, Bishop's body was delivered to King's
College, and Williams's to the Tuson Theatre of Anatomy in
Little Windmill Street,[1] each to be dissected in compliance with
the law. The work on and in Bishop's body was done by the
lisping Mr Mayo, a running commentary being provided by the
college professor of forensic medicine, a Dr Watson. George
Guthrie, the surgeon at Tuson's, had been premature with an
announcement that he had been allotted the body of May. On
Sunday, 4 December, hearing a rumour that that body would not
be available, he had written to the secretary of the College of
Surgeons of England: 'If May is not executed, pray do me the
favour to beg Mr Clift [who appears to have been the clerk in

[1] *The southern bit of Windmill Street that, speaking of the present topography
of the area near Piccadilly Circus, makes a short-cut – east of the London
Pavilion and west of the Trocadero – from Shaftesbury Avenue to Coventry
Street, which leads towards Leicester Square.*

charge of the despatch department at the surgeons' headquarters in Lincoln's Inn Fields] to send to Little Windmill the best of the two remaining.' Supposing that Mr Clift was of an obliging nature, it would be interesting to know the criteria he applied in choosing Williams's body as the better.

The porter Shields. What of him? Soon after the trial, the news broke that he worked part-time as watchman and grave-digger at the cemetery of the Roman Catholic Chapel in Moor-fields. Sacked from there, without notice, the minute the report was published, he applied to be a porter in Covent Garden fruit market. He was recognised by some marketers, who, downing their baskets and shouting 'Burker!' and other less apt epithets, chased him off the premises and along Russell Street, the fleetest of them almost catching up with him before he reached the sanctuary of the police station where he was well-known. There is no further report of Shields's movements, whether fast or at his working pace.

On 15 December, Henry Warburton, a radical Member of Parliament (for Bridport, Devon), who had tried before to get changes made to the law governing the dissection of human bodies, tried again – and this time, with the invaluable post-humous aid of the Italian or Lincolnshire Boy, succeeded. The clauses that concern us in his 'Bill for Regulating Schools of Anatomy' gave permission for bodies to be given up, no fewer than forty-eight hours after death, by executors 'or other persons having lawful possession' (those including functionaries in charge of hospitals or workhouses), so long as (a), at least twenty-four hours before a giving-up, the person occupying the specially-created post of Inspector of Anatomy had been told, (b) a death certificate had been signed by someone with a suitable medical qualification; the bodies of executed criminals were not to be dissected but were either to be 'hung in Chains or buried within the Precincts of the Prison'. The Bill passed through both Houses, and received the Royal Assent on the first day of August, 1832.

Politicians have been, and are, indirectly responsible for many murders. But some of them, by being sufficient for the passing of the Anatomy Act, the 'Surgeons' Charter', made the multifarious motives for murder one fewer.

A Wolf in Tanned Clothing

Accepting that Sweeney Todd[1] didn't happen, the trade of barbering is less blemished by murderers in its midst than are nearly all others that are comparable in terms of number of traders. Generalising psychiatrists, which means nearly all of them, will deduce from that fact that the 9-to-5 plying of scissors and cut-throat razors works 'cathartically' upon barbers, turning them against using these instruments lethally from 5 to 9. Till 1987, the public relations officer of the Hairdressing Council could, if he or she had wanted to, have proclaimed that there was a sort of minus-quantity of illegal dangerousness attributable to barbers – a deduction arising from the perception that there had

---

[1] *Prior to Stephen Sondheim's musicalising of the tale, the man most associated with stagings of it was Tod Slaughter, author of* Sweeney Todd, The Demon-Barber of Fleet Street, *and, from about 1922 till the late '50s, the almost invariable player of the eponym. 'Slaughter' really was his name (his brother, Ernest Slaughter, was a Fleet Street reporter for almost as long as he himself was an actor-manager), but 'Tod' was a replacement for 'N. Carter'; his secrecy about what lay behind the initial suggests that it stood for a name as innocuous as Neville or Noel. The moment that audiences of his playing of Sweeney Todd most savoured came when, after dropping a caricatured-as-Jewish customer, chair and all, through the trap-door and then exiting to 'finish him off', he re-entered, his hands and forearms drenched with 'blood' (a mixture of olive-oil and cochineal), and ruminated: 'The old Jew – hmf – I thought he was anaemic.' His extensive repertoire of melodramas of the Grand Guignol genre included some that were loosely based upon the doings of real mass-murderers:* Landru; Jack the Ripper *(which he presented at, among many other theatres, the Granville, in the London suburb of Walham Green, while an uncle of mine was its manager), and* The Wolves of Tanner's Close *(he as William Hare). A friend of mine, Richard Carr, stage-directed the last of his 'farewell tours'. I had tea with him once – which is to say that I drank tea; he was abstemious of that beverage, fearing that it might mar his fine-tuned taste for Scotch, of which he drank the equivalent of a bottle a day, none during performances.*

been more deaths caused by barber-hangmen than by barber-murderers. (The most household-named of the former were James Billington, who executed during the last ten years or so of Queen Victoria's reign, meanwhile running a barber's shop in Farnworth, Lancashire; his sons William and John, who followed in both sets of his footsteps, William for the longer in the executional set; and John Ellis, who combined the same occupations – the barbering one in Rochdale, also in Lancashire – between 1907 and 1923, and who, eight years after retiring as a hangman, committed suicide with a razor that he had used professionally.) However, the outcome of proceedings at the Old Bailey in the summer of 1987 would have prompted the PR person to put any proposal for a You're Safe and Sound When Your Barber's Around press-release on what PR people refer to as the back-burner.

Michele de Marco Lupo was born to working-class parents, the father a bricklayer, in the northern Italian city of Bologna, which should be famous for things other than a spaghetti-sauce and a sort of sausage, in 1953 or thereabouts.

Lupo, a not uncommon Italian surname, is the Italian word for *wolf*.

As soon as Lupo was old enough to be a choirboy in the cathedral, he became one; and, as his voice took longer to break than is normal, he grew to be the leading juvenile chorister. When he left school, meaning to go to a college of art, his form-master gave him a reference: 'A boy of high quality whose morality is beyond question.' Since hardly any boys of school-leaving age have proved that they are more or less moral than other boys (or girls, for that matter) of the same age, the teacher's tribute may actually have been a retort to rumours or a groundlessly optimistic prophesy that Lupo's morality would become unquestionable. I must emphasise that that is only a guess. In 1971, he was conscripted. To anyone who remembers World War Two jokes about Italian servicemen but did not fight any of those servicemen, the idea of that country subsequently having commandoes will seem as preposterous as the idea of Switzerland having sailors; but Italy did, and perhaps still does: in 1971 there were at least twenty-two Italian commando units. Private Lupo was assigned to the 22nd.

One gathers that he served his time untroublesomely – that, while doing so, he was taught how to kill with efficiency and, if necessary, without the aid of blunt or sharp or explosive instruments – and that, also while serving his time, he either discovered or had a pre-conscription suspicion confirmed that he was unequivocally homosexual.

The latter knowledge, so it is said, worried him only in so far as his parents – rigid adherents to Catholic doctrines, including some regarding matters that a growing number of Catholics believed that God had no strong feelings about – would be shocked, shamed, even made to feel guilty, if they learned of his condition. With the intention – again, so it is said – of preventing that, he, demobilised from the army, decided to emigrate, at first with no particular other country in mind. He could speak, with varying degrees of fluency, four languages in addition to Italian, and so he believed that he had a wider choice of other countries than the average educated intending emigrant. English was one of the foreign languages he could speak.

In the end, it was a toss-up between the United States (or rather, some of them: he excluded Alaska, Hawaii, those in the rather unCatholic Bible-Belt, and those that also were predominantly rural) and England – or rather, London. His choice, which was London, may be blamed upon the time when he was choosing, which was in the early 1970s, closely following the decade when London was supposed, mostly by people not living there, to be an especially 'swinging' city. Small incidents sometimes have large effects: Lupo may have been lured to London because of an article about it in a once-glossy magazine that he picked up in a Bolognese dentist's waiting-room. London had swung in a number of directions, several towards destinations that were either downright sleazy or attractive to sleazy people. Not only in Soho, there had been an uncontrolled infestation of establishments offering pornography on the premises or to be taken away; the word 'kinky' had been coined as a replacement for 'perverted', and shops specialising in merchandise appealing to kinky people had opened, not unlike sores, on prime sites in high streets, juxtaposed with branches of Woolie's and Marks' and of the brand-new chains of stores selling 'natural Swedish pine' (unpainted Taiwanese chipboard) furniture and 'farmhouse' (heavy and lopsided) crockery; transvestites had transvested in public, for money, in certain pubs and membership-at-the-door clubs, and some of those pubs and clubs, and others that provided no advertised entertainment, had become '*in* places' for people who needed drugs or desired to meet male or female whores; etc.

By 1973, when Lupo arrived in London, it had swung in more directions, and farther in those directions, than most founder-members of its 'permissive society' had ever, in their wildest, wettest dreams of 1959, dreamed possible. It lived down to Lupo's expectations. He was enchanted. There is no accounting for taste.

Quite as enchanted as he was by what he saw were many natives (leaving out greengrocers, milkmen, people like that, but not excepting one or two heterosexual wealthy men) who caught sight of him. He was darkly handsome, he wore his white shirts, always white, open to the button above his Gucci belt, as if forgetful of buttoning, and his jeans looked painted on; those lucky spectators who got close noticed that he smelt only of anti-perspirant; and those luckier ones who struck up a conversation found it hard to continue, having been thrilled so by his funny accent, his charming smile, his lovely manners.

He soon had many male friends, and as each of them already had many gregarious male friends, he was almost as soon friendly with the friends of the first friends, and as each of them had other gregarious male friends, it wasn't long before he was friendly with them as well; and so on. I understand that there are marine protozoa that have a similar colonially multiplying facility, though I don't understand how, in their case, each of the ever-increasing multitude of organisms is able, as the fancy takes it, to adjoin any of the others. Lupo did not have sexual relations with all of the friends. Not quite all.

If he needed to rent a flat or bed-sitter when he arrived, I don't know where it was. He had no trouble in finding a job – doing something at a London branch of the French fashion and cosmetics firm, Yves Saint Laurent. (Most of the other male employees took to him – he, showing slight discrimination, only to most of them.) He did not stay there long because, meanwhile, having been advised – wrongly, as it turned out – that the easiest way for him to make lots of money was as a hairdresser in an elegant 'salon', he trained to be one. The training must have been

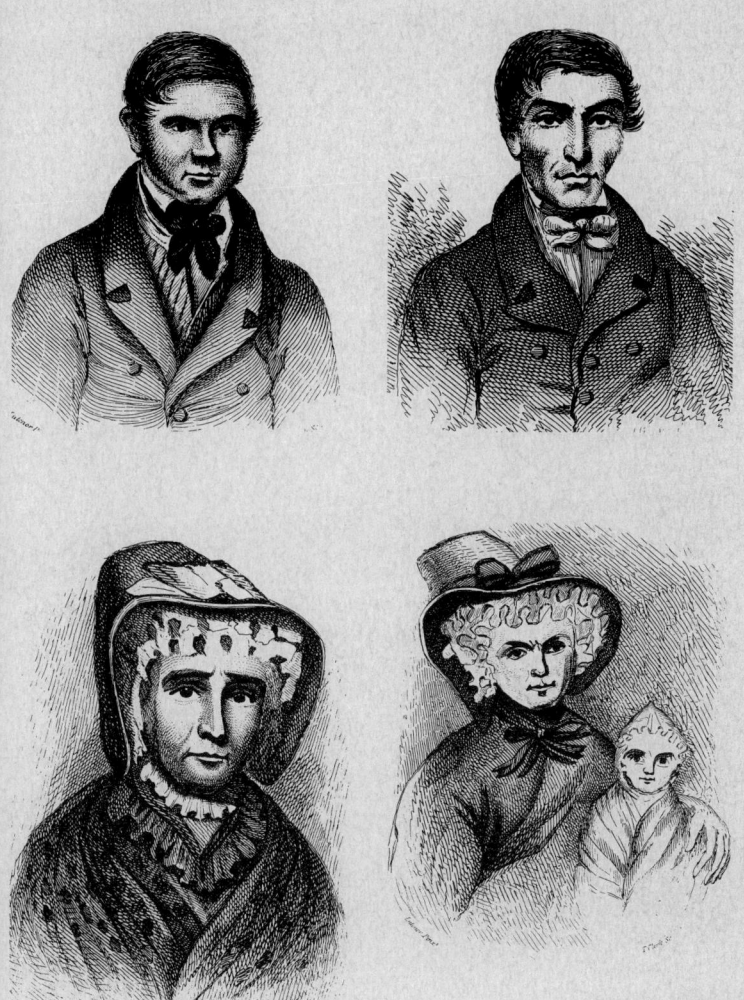

Drawings, made during the trial, of *(above)* William Burke and
William Hare, *(below)* Helen M'Dougal and Margaret Hare holding
her daughter.

Caricature of Dr Knox, the anatomist, drawn at the time of the trial.

The rear of Burke's residence, showing (A) his window and (B) the
door through which the body of Mary Docherty was brought out.

THE TRIAL, SENTENCE, FULL CONFESSION, AND EXECUTION OF
BISHOP & WILLIAMS,
THE BURKERS.

BURKING AND BURKERS.

The month of November, 1831, will be recorded in the annals of crimes and cruelties as particularly pre-eminent, for it will prove to posterity that other wretches could be found base enough to follow the horrid example of Burke and his accomplice Hare, to entice the unprotected and friendless to the den of death for sordid gain.

The horrible crime of "Burking," or murdering the unwary with the intention of selling their bodies at a high price to the anatomical schools, for the purpose of dissection, has unfortunately obtained a notoriety which will not be soon or easily forgotten. It took its horrify-ing appellation from the circumstances which were disclosed on the trial of the inhuman wretch Burke, who was executed at Edinburgh in 1829, for having wilfully and deliberately murdered several persons for the sole purpose of profiting by the sale of their dead bodies.

APPREHENSION OF THE BURKERS.

On Tuesday, November 8th, four persons, viz., John Bishop, Thomas Williams, James May, and Michael Shield, were examined at Bow Street Police Office on the charge of being concerned in the wilful murder of an unknown Italian boy. From the evidence adduced, it appeared that May, *alias* Jack Stirabout, a known resurrection-man, and Bishop, a body-snatcher, offered at King's College a subject for sale, Shield and Williams having charge of the body in a hamper, for which they demanded twelve guineas. Mr Partridge, demonstrator of anatomy, who, although not in absolute want of a subject, offered nine guineas, but being struck with its freshness sent a messenger to the police station, and the fellows were then taken into custody, examined before the magistrates, when Shield was discharged and the others ultimately committed for trial.

THE TRIAL.

Friday, December 2nd, having been fixed for the trial of the prisoners charged with the murder of the Italian boy, the Court was crowded to excess so early as eight o'clock in the morning.

At nine o'clock the Deputy Recorder, Mr Serjeant

Part of a contemporary broadsheet.

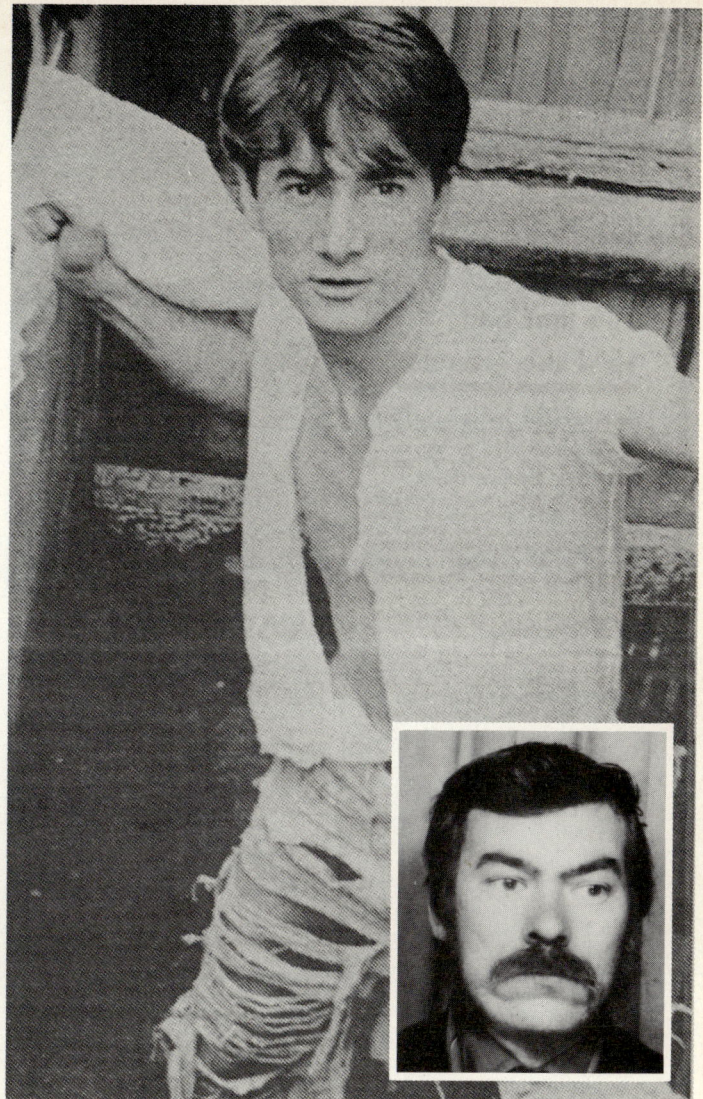

Michele de Marco Lupo.
Inset: his first victim, James Burns.

(above) Norman Thorne, and
(below) his 'living apartment'.

Henry Jacoby, in custody for the murder of Lady Alice White *(inset)*.

Ronald True, circa 1915.
Inset: Olive Young.

extremely unarduous, considering that he completed it in a month or so while he was working five or six days a week for Yves Saint Laurent and either enjoying the gay social whirl or recuperating from it at most other times. He then practised shampooing, snipping and setting in one small salon after another, and eventually was engaged to perform in a large yet chic 'unisex' salon in Belgravia. The total of his tips there, only a small percentage of which he declared to the Inland Revenue, dwarfed his properly-taxed salary.

After a couple of years, he bought – apparently without the need of a mortgage – a flat in Roland Gardens,[1] a select, dog-legged turning off Old Brompton Road, within easy walking distance of his daytime work-place. Though some of his friends who were interior decorators gave him ideas, his initial fur-bishing of the flat was fairly conventional. Over the years, however, as he sought more and more idiosyncratic sexual pleas-ures, and as he entertained more and more men who were as sexperimental as he was, he put in a number of fixtures and fittings that were so unconventional that he cannot, surely, have had them fixed or fitted by workmen who were at all narrow-minded or inquisitive of the items' intended purposes; suffice it to say that among the items were shackles, either suspended from a ceiling (more dependable than most) or attached to posts of Lupo's four-poster bed. Lying loose about the flat, much as in bourgeois living-rooms copies of *The Official Sloane Ranger Handbook* and pottery souvenirs of places on the Costa del Sol are deposited as if casually, were whips, riding-crops and une-questrian but just as hurtful implements, several of which had been bespoken by the occupant. By no means all of the visitors who, shackled or not, were given a taste of Lupo's leather or ironmongered bricabrac received the treatment on the house: as a moonlighting trade, drummed up by small ads in which he used the business-name of Rudi and which he inserted under the headings of 'Esoteric' or 'Bondage – No Holds Barred' in 'homosexual-contact' weeklies, he tortured for cash (paid in

---

[1] *Fewer than 200 yards west of the Onslow Court Hotel – the residence, till 18 February 1949, of Mrs Olivia Durand-Deacon, the only one of the heaven knows how many victims of John George Haigh, the 'acid-bath murderer', whom he was charged with having dissolved.*

advance by the torturees; Lupo's period of operation was one of high inflation, and so the best idea of his tariff is given by what he charged for the de-luxe treatment in 1985, towards the end of the period, which was £100; I cannot tell whether his satisfied customers, not knowing that he was also a hairdresser and therefore expectant of tips, gave him any – but even if none of his regulars did, some of them must, like some drug-addicts, have needed to thieve so as to afford their habits). Every so often, one or other of Lupo's neighbours complained about his loud playing of records (especially those made by his friend, the rock-singer known as Freddie Mercury), but none of the neighbours seems to have complained about, or even commented upon, the thwacking sounds, the screams of pleasure and/or pain, the cries for mercy or greater punishment, which frequently disturbed the peace of that part of the Royal Borough of Kensington & Chelsea.

Lupo was insatiable. Not content with his sexual busyness at home and in the London homes of friends, he travelled far and wide in the pursuit of being sadistic to masochists – for instance, a ballet dancer in Amsterdam, an unemployed aristocrat in West Berlin, a dress designer in Paris, a commercial artist, a shop-assistant, a stockbroker, and a fashion photographer in Manhattan. And he exhibited himself, gossiping with old acquaintances while keeping his mascaraed eyes open for prospective friends or clients, in London clubs popular with homosexuals, such as a place called Heaven (owned by a company called, oddly enough, Virgin), underneath the Arches that Flanagan & Allen had made famous many years before. On one occasion, in one of the clubs, he caused an especial stir by popping up, dressed to some extent as a nun, out of a coffin, and then made everybody laugh by lifting the skirt, to reveal that he was wearing fishnet tights, and doing a bump-and-grind dance. It would be interesting to know whether that act was witnessed by an acquaintance of his, a radio disc-jockey who had turned to slapstick comedy, for the act was of a kind that has been performed by the versatile entertainer in his own series of television shows.

Lupo had a penchant for dressing up, and black leather was the material he most favoured for his costumes. He seems to have had only one *all*-black-leather costume, and that costume he wore only at home, tête-à-tête, and then only in the company of one or other of the friends or clients who were prepared to go to almost any lengths in aid of getting goose-pimples all over. The outfit consisted of a hood, slitted so that he had no difficulty in seeing, breathing and speaking (but, as it was not slitted at the sides, requiring whoever else was present to speak clearly), and with thongs, a little like spring-onions, planted in and drooping from it; a leotard that had large holes in it, so that Lupo must have resembled a negative of a Henry Moore statue; a wristband, just one, that was embellished with and clasped by iron studs and bits of chain; boots of the type associated with wine-treaders and soccer-hooligans. There were no smalls. One of the clients for whom Lupo often donned that costume often brought along a costume of his own, which was that of a pre-war preparatory-schoolboy – cap, blazer, Aertex shirt, striped tie, short trousers, socks that were kept up by rubber bands, plimsolls, and an accessory satchel – and I hope that most readers will find it hard to imagine the scene of the elderly schoolboy and the leathered Lupo doing whatever it was they did.

Until fairly recent times in England, any white woman who wore a thin gold-looking anklet was advertising that she was a prostitute, any white man or woman whose hair was of fairground colours was to be pitied, and kept well away from, because that could only mean that he or she was being treated for fleas or lice with something like gentian violet, any white woman wearing an ear-ring through her nose almost certainly had one brown parent, and any man of any colour who wore an ear-ring on an ear was undoubtedly a merchant seaman. But such decorations are no longer sure signs. It won't be long before diminutive men – and certain women too, perhaps – take to wearing the necktie of the Brigade of Guards, simply because the combination of blue and red goes nicely with a shirt or blouse. I must warn any heterosexual and occasionally slovenly man who possesses leather clothes or jeans that have come apart anywhere, that he should either have them mended or throw them away – the reason being that, in some homosexual circles (which are sometimes unwittingly trespassed into), the wearing of such torn garments is interpreted as an indication that the wearer is 'into violent sex'.

It is at this point that the story of Michele Lupo becomes appropriate to a book about murder in low places.

For months, maybe years, before the spring of 1986, he had sometimes worn leather clothes that he had torn to signify that he was into violent sex – to act as a tacit invitation to like-minded men. During a short period before that spring, he was able to buy leather clothes at a discount-price, for he had left the unisex salon in Belgravia and become manager of a clothes shop, Tan Guidicelli, in Beauchamp Place, about halfway between Harrods and the Brompton Oratory. He had flaunted himself, and the tears in his leather clothes, in clubs and pubs in various parts of London, some of the parts very seedy indeed, and the violent sex that he had enjoyed with some of the men whom he had met on those premises had whetted a desire to extend violence to mutilation and murder.

On Saturday, 15 March 1986, he visited the Coleherne pub in Old Brompton Road, and picked up, or was picked up by, James Burns, a railwayman in his mid-thirties. They did not go to Lupo's home, only a stroll to the east, but about the same distance north, to the derelict basement of a house in Warwick Road, near the Earls Court Exhibition Building. Shortly afterwards, two tramps entered the basement, meaning to make themselves unconscious with methylated spirit, and found the body of James Burns, who had been strangled with his Burberry-check scarf and, either before or after death, savagely bitten, as if by a rabid wolf. The tramps reported their discovery at the Kensington police station, in the parallel Earls Court Road. An investigation was begun. No one who had noticed Lupo and Burns conversing in the Coleherne, and leaving the pub together, imparted that information to the police.

On Thursday, 3 April, Lupo visited the Prince of Wales pub in Brixton Road – south of Elephant & Castle, and still farther south of Blackfriars Bridge, over the Thames. There he met Anthony Connolly, a 26-year-old native of Newcastle-upon-Tyne who had had brief spells of employment as a waiter but who was presently on the dole, and who considered himself fortunate to have been given accommodation in a nearby council flat, the registered tenant of which was a carrier of AIDS. Lupo left the pub ahead of Connolly – who, as he left, remarked to friends at the bar, 'I have just met the most beautiful man.' Two days later, his body was found in a disused railway-shed even closer to the Prince of Wales than the council flat which he had shared. He had been strangled and, either before or after death, savagely bitten, as if by a rabid wolf; the most noticeable difference between his murder and that of James Burns, less than three weeks before, was that, in his case, the strangling ligature had been taken away by the criminal. An investigation was begun by detectives working from the police station in Kennington Road, to the north of Brixton Road. Strangely, and worryingly, The Kennington detectives were unaware that the Kensington detectives were investigating a similar crime – and vice versa. The Kennington ones were hindered by a forensic-medical delay: when Connolly's erstwhile flat-mate went to Southwark Mortuary to identify the body, he happened to mention that he was a carrier of AIDS, and the mortuary staff, frightened that Connolly might have contracted that disease from him, refused to let a post-mortem examination be conducted, and were supported by colleagues in other mortuaries, who refused to cross the picket-line as stand-ins; and so a fortnight passed before a pathologist was able to venture within the vicinity of the body.

By then, Lupo had strangled (and, before or after, bitten) Damien McClusky, an Irish hospital-porter, just past his majority, whom he had lured to the derelict basement of a house in Cromwell Road, South Kensington, between the Victoria and Albert Museum and Baden-Powell House, the headquarters of the Scout Association. There was no serendipity in this case – no one stumbled upon the body. Officers of Special Branch who, knowing that McClusky belonged to the IRA, had been keeping tabs on him, took his sudden disappearance concernedly, suspecting that he was lying low alive, making ready to use his membership of the IRA as the excuse for doing something psychopathic.

On Friday, 18 April, Lupo left Heaven late at night and started walking across Hungerford Bridge, which is meant as much for trains as for wayfarers. His intended destination can only be guessed at; the bridge leads, from Heaven's side, towards, among other districts of South London, Brixton – nowhere near Roland Gardens. Halfway across the bridge, he was accosted by a male vagrant, ostensibly 'bumming for a fag' (but hoping for greater generosity – much as, when an October comes, children pleading for 'a penny for the Guy' are actually so contemptuous of that coin that they are liable to mug any literal-minded donor). Lupo – who was not only a non-smoker but also an ardent supporter of the ASH anti-smoking organisation, because he considered smoking to be a filthy habit – enticed the vagrant across the bridge and, on waste-ground in the region of the Royal Festival Hall, strangled him with a black stocking which he, Lupo, happened to be carrying. There appears to be no information as to whether it was the stocking he had used on Anthony Connolly and Damien McClusky, or one of them, or fresh hose; a matter relating to a subsequent incident suggests that he did not use one stocking murderously more than once. The body was soon found, but the identity of the vagrant is still unknown. It is understandable that the detective or detectives who dealt with this case did not connect it with either of the cases that the respective detectives of Kensington and Kennington had not yet connected, for Lupo had not bitten the vagrant. He would say that, try as he might, he could not explain what possessed him to commit this particular murder: 'I just decided to do it,' he would remark with a shrug – adding, so that none of the audience ran away with the idea that his libido was grateful for even the grubbiest of small mercies, 'I certainly did not get any sexual feelings – certainly not,' and then uttering an afterthought that sounds suspiciously like a misquotation from William Burroughs, Jean Genet or Barbara Cartland, or all three of them: 'Something inside me was screaming to the world.'

Presumably, something inside him was still screaming twenty-four hours after the murder of the vagrant, when, having coaxed or been coaxed by a young cook named Mark Leyland to one of the increasing number of public conveniences in Central London from which water has been cut off, he attacked him with a length of iron adrift from the redundant plumbing. Leyland, unpartial to sex as violent as that, fled – eventually to a police station, where he told a no doubt dubious detective that he had gone to the loo simply and solely to relieve himself and had suffered attempted *robbery* with violence.

Less than three weeks later, between one and two o'clock in the morning of 8 May, a Thursday, Lupo was in or loitering near the Market Tavern, Nine Elms, which is about a mile and a half north-west of the Prince of Wales, Brixton. The Market Tavern is so named because of its proximity to the New Covent Garden wholesale fruit market; and because of that proximity – the law being sympathetic of the fact that much marketing is done in unsocial hours and that some marketing is thirsty work – the tavern is entitled to be open when most others have to be shut. The law ignores the fact that comparatively few of the people who take advantage of the Market Tavern's entitlement are marketers of fruit. David Cole, one of the early-morning regulars there, was – as James Burns had been – employed by British Rail; he was in his late twenties; he is homosexual.

According to his recollection of events in the small hours of 8 May, he got talking to Lupo, whom he knew only by sight, and, at Lupo's suggestion, walked with him from in or near the Market Tavern to the market's main lorry-park. Lupo or Cole produced and broke an ampoule of amyl-nitrate, a drug whose primary proper use is to relieve angina but which is used improperly, and dangerously, as an aphrodisiac. Squatting in a space shadowed by banana lorries, they sniffed the drug. Neither was quite recovered from its physical effects when Lupo pulled what he thought was a black stocking from one of the pockets of his black-leather trousers. It appears that he had come out in rather a hurry: he had pocketed, not a black stocking, but a black sock. In the darkness, he realised his error only when he tried to circle the sock round Cole's neck and found that it was nowhere near long enough. By then, his efforts to make a little go a long way were starting to make Cole suspicious of his intent. Cole's suspicion was confirmed when Lupo gave up with the sock and made a noose of his beautifully manicured hands. Cole's heart, still thumping as an effect of the drug, thumped even harder, faster, from fear. He chiselled his hands through the noose made by Lupo's, scrabbled it apart, shoved Lupo back, staggered to his feet, and ran: all the way home – though, even before he was out of the lorry-park, his heart felt as if it might burst.

He rested. He wondered what he ought to do. And having decided what he ought to do, he wondered if that was wise. He telephoned an organisation that offers guidance to homosexuals, gave a counsellor an account of his experience, and was told that he should not inform the police. (A spokesman for the organisation has denied that Cole was given such negative counsel.) He had read of the murder of James Burns, and the more he now thought about it, the more firmly he believed that the murderer and the man who had tried to strangle him were one and the same. He telephoned Scotland Yard, and was told to telephone Kensington police station. A Kensington detective took a statement from him, and decided that the man who had tried to strangle him was not the man who had succeeded in strangling James Burns; however, the detective had heard of the strangling of Anthony Connolly, and so he sent Cole's statement to Kennington police station. By the time it arrived there, the 'Connolly-murder squad' was working from a police station in Stockwell, closer to the scene of the crime. The statement was sent to that station – and eventually read by Detective Superintendent John Shoemake, the officer in charge of the Connolly-murder investigation. Shoemake interviewed David Cole. Fortunately, Cole's memory of the events in the early morning of 8 May had not been dimmed by time.

In the early evening of 15 May, four male members of the Connolly-murder squad paraded in black leather clothes that they had begged, borrowed or hired, and, after being inspected by Shoemake and Cole, set off with the latter on a tour of places frequented by homosexuals; Cole had had to be cajoled into acting as look-out for his assailant, and was so apprehensive of success that he often trembled and then had to be 'jollied along' by the largest of the disguised detectives. The posse cannot have looked as strange as it sounds as if it did; the detectives must have marched separately, pretending that they were not in one another's company, otherwise the progress of a 'heavy mob' of men dressed as they were would surely have caused beat-policemen along the route who had not been let into their secret to band together and trail them precautionarily. The tour began north of the Thames, taking in such places as Heaven and the Copacabana Club (which, despite its name, is in the Australian part of London), and continued on the south side: the Royal Vauxhall Tavern, adjacent to the plain Vauxhall Station of British Rail . . . the Market Tavern – and the Prince of Wales, Brixton. It was in that hostelry that David Cole spotted the man who had tried to strangle him, first with a black sock, then with his bare hands. Cole began trembling so violently that his escort knew at once that they were at journey's end – that the one man in the bar whom he was now determined not to look at was the man they were after.

Lupo came quietly. If any of the other customers guessed that the men leading him out were, in the argot of most of them, 'pigs', none was intrepid or tipsy enough to utter the word 'harassment' above a whisper. One surmises from Superintendent Shoemake's subsequent comment that his officers had 'acted exemplarily in the face of harrowing and difficult experiences' that they would have reacted roughly to rudeness or ridicule of the slightest kind.

During his accompanied walk to Stockwell police station, and for some time following his reception there, Lupo insisted that he didn't know David Cole from Adam. But then, as if orgasmically, he spilt out such a diverse confession that Shoemake and anyone else who was present must have been somewhat taken aback. Yes, he *had* tried to strangle David Cole – and yes, he *had* murdered Anthony Connolly – and oh, by the way, he had also murdered James Burns and the unidentified vagrant and Damien McClusky. He needed to give directions as to where McClusky's body was decomposing. A few days later, Mark Leyland, having read of Lupo's arrest, suggested to the detective who had taken his statement regarding the attempt to 'rob' him that Lupo might be the culprit – and when that suggestion was eventually mentioned to Lupo, he agreed that it was so.

By then, Shoemake had visited, and some of his subordinates had taken stock of, Lupo's flat in Roland Gardens; Shoemake had also visited a flat in Chelsea which Lupo had cited as a 'temporary residence', explaining that he had stayed there for some weeks, looking after the occupant, an elderly Italian widow whose daughter was married to an 'art director' who was best known for his work on many of the James Bond movies. The daughter said that Lupo was 'a lovely man who was very kind to a lonely old lady'.

Among other possessions of Lupo's that Shoemake took from the guest-bedroom in the Chelsea flat were some leather-bound volumes: albums of snapshots, not all of which Lupo would have dared show the old lady; appointment registers (in which the handwritten word *Surgery* recurred), and address books. Leaving no stone unturned, Shoemake got a subordinate to count the entries in the address books: there were over seven hundred (a total considered insufficient by all of our comic daily papers, the least untrustworthy of which reported it as a thousand). Several of the entries were incomprehensible; perhaps they were in code, or perhaps they had been scrawled, ouija-fashion, by Lupo while he was under the influence of an hallucinogenic drug. A number of the decipherable names were of much-publicised persons, one or two of whom so relished publicity that they employed press agents to buy them more. Included in that entire number were the names of smart photographers (it would be interesting to know whether any of them had taken any of the snaps in Lupo's albums), transvestites and transexuals whose birth-certificates described them either as male or as female, dress designers (one of them peculiar in that he had become famous without having designed anything for either of our newest princesses by marriage), far-distant relatives of royal rulers of places like Monaco, and Society ladies (one of them best-known by her nickname of Bubbles, which seems more likely to have been derived from a Shirley Temple perm that Lupo gave her than from her being associated with the song about bubbles which begins, 'I'm for ever blowing'). Speaking only of male names in Lupo's address books, he had entered an unrepresentatively large number of social workers.

I cannot tell you why the law's usual delays were added to in Lupo's case. More than thirteen months passed between his arrest and his trial, which was held in Court No. 7 of the Old Bailey, before the Recorder of London, Sir James Miskin, and a jury, on Friday, 10 July 1987. Part of the unusual delay may have been due to if-at-first-we-don't-succeed efforts by psychiatrists, none successful, to find that Lupo was suffering from 'a recognised mental illness or personality disorder'. His claim, made to most of the psychiatrists, that he had had four thousand sexual partners since his arrival from Italy (which works out, on the basis of six-day weeks, and without allowing for holidays, as an average of one conquest per diem) is unlikely – as it would be impossible to verify – to get into the *Guinness Book of Records*; if it did, the editor might add a footnote to the effect that the slang-word *baloney* is a corruption of the place-name *Bologna*.

Lupo's trial-counsel, Lord Gifford – not for the first time defending a defendant who had no defence – said little more during the proceedings than did his client, who, apart from saying 'Guilty' to all of the counts of the indictment, said nothing. The Recorder, illustrating the illogic of post-capital-punishment legal arithmetic, sentenced Lupo to life imprisonment on each of the four murder charges, and to consecutive terms of seven years for the two attempts, and told him: 'I am confident that you will never be released until it is totally safe for the public at large.'

But Lupo is unlikely to live that long. He has contracted AIDS. It is reasonable to guess that his greatest punishment is that the prison authorities do their utmost to keep him away from other convicts, even those who are affected by the same disease. That is a punishment that comes close to being fitting to his crimes.

NB.   In December 1987, following the seizure by the police of two quantities of amyl-nitrate that were estimated to have a 'street-value' of £40,000, one from a house at Strood, Kent, the other from the Royal Vauxhall Tavern, six men appeared at Horseferry Road Magistrates' Court, London, charged with 'conspiring to cause people to take a noxious substance with intent to injure, aggrieve or annoy'. One of the defendants, the licensee of the Tavern, was discharged; the others were committed for trial at the Old Bailey. A medical witness for the prosecution at the committal proceedings was Professor G. Newell, an American, who treated the first patient diagnosed as having AIDS, at Houston, Texas, in 1972, and who, it was stated, was 'one of the world's leading researchers into the virus'. During his examination-in-chief by Miss Anne Goddard, QC, Professor Newell said: 'It is my belief that susceptibility to the AIDS virus is increased by the inhalation of [amyl-] nitrate . . . or that it increases the susceptibility for AIDS to be expressed as a clinical disease . . . That is my firm opinion.'

Two Slight Uncertainties

The Hollinwood Horror

The word 'mugger' has become common only over the past twenty years or so. I don't know if one can conclude from this that attacks on pedestrians, with robbery the usual but not invariable aim, have meanwhile become so common that a single word seemed needed to describe the species of attacker. Perhaps so. But it would certainly be wrong to gather, as some people have, that the rather sudden ubiquity of that word means that 'mugging' is a new sort of crime so far as England is concerned, let alone that it is an import from Caribbean places.

In one of the anthologies of true-crime stories that I have edited,[1] I include the text of a broadsheet reporting a fatal mugging in Fig Lane, near St Pancras Church, London, in 1685. Nearly two centuries later, in the Sessions Papers of November 1862, a police witness is quoted as saying: 'When I apprehended Roberts, he exclaimed, "You want me for putting the mug on, do you? I will put the b——y mug on you!"'

And recently I came across some yellowing cuttings from a newspaper published in 1831. The headlines on one proclaimed:

THE HOLLINWOOD HORROR
A Fiendish Atrocity

The next word that caught my eye was 'mugging'. I read on.

At eight o'clock on the evening of Wednesday, 22 December 1830, Mrs Bridget Cheetham, an Irish resident of the Lancashire cotton-town of Oldham, had two reasons for feeling worried.

[1]The Pleasures of Murder, *Jonathan Goodman, Allison & Busby, 1983.*

The first was that her small daughter, Bride, had become ill earlier in the day. Now the sound of the cuckoo clock, perched high above the kitchen range, woke the sick child, who started crying.

Bridget, who had been chatting quietly to a visiting neighbour, Norah Mahony, muttered, 'Saints protect us. The doctor said let her sleep as much as she can. I wish I had throttled the old cuckoo. I must go up and give Bride a sup of cold tea.'

Bridget's other reason for worry was the non-arrival of her mother, Sarah McCrinn, who had written to say that she would be setting out from her home in Bolton that morning, to spend Christmas with the Cheethams. Though Sarah McCrinn was at least sixty-four (it appears that she herself was unsure of her exact age), and 'had had bad times of late and been well clemmed' (that last word meaning starved), she had told her daughter that she intended to 'pad the hoof' from Bolton to Oldham – a distance, roughly west to east, of a dozen miles.

Sarah McCrinn had, in fact, started walking from Bolton in the early hours of the morning. She was wearing, among other garments, a cloak that she had borrowed from a friend.

At about the time her daughter was wishing that she had 'throttled the old cuckoo', Sarah was six miles from Oldham. She was seen by Thomas Jones, a watchman at Newton Heath, who enquired after her health and was told that she was 'feeling rather light in the head'. As they were speaking, a man named Robert Lees approached. Upon hearing the old woman's destination, he said that he would accompany her part of the way. This he did.

When they had walked about a mile and a half, Sarah became faint and murmured that she could not keep up with Lees. The last he saw of her, she was leaning against a bridge over the Rochdale Canal.

Soon after that, Sarah knocked at the door of a cottage on the Oldham Road and was given a drink of water by the person who lived there, a Mrs Agnes Moon.

Round about ten o'clock, a conscientious and apparently owlish-eyed land surveyor named Schofield, who had been measuring some fields off 'The Street', the disused remains of a Roman road in the district known as Hollinwood, decided to call it a night. He walked across the fields towards the Oldham Road. As he made to hop across a ditch, he saw, lying in the ditch, the body of an old woman, 'her skirts drawn up so that her person was exposed from the waist downwards'.

Schofield noticed smidgens of blood around the woman's mouth and a scratch above one knee; but it never occurred to him that the woman, subsequently identified as Sarah McCrinn, had been murdered.

Nor was murder considered as the cause of death by Alfred Newton, the surgeon who performed a post-mortem examination the next day. The presence of some extravasated blood on the brain led him to believe that Sarah McCrinn's death was due to apoplexy. In his report to the coroner, he gave his view that the proper inquest verdict would be 'accidental death'.

That might well have been the end of the matter so far as the law was concerned. But a day or two after Christmas, a young man named Ashton Hutton, a native of Hollinwood, was quizzed by the police about his possession of a woman's cloak. It was the cloak that Sarah McCrinn had borrowed before starting the journey from Bolton.

Hutton explained that, at half-past nine on the evening of 22 December he left his local pub and started across the fields beside 'The Street', on his way home. A short way ahead of him were two brothers, Ashton[1] and William Worrall, who had left the pub a few moments before his own departure from it. He lost sight of them when they passed through a hedge.

Then, Hutton claimed, he heard a woman's voice from the far side of the hedge: 'Oh, dear me, this will never do!' Soon afterwards, there was a shrill cry of 'Murder'.

The sound of 'deeper tones' was followed by the woman's voice again: 'Surely you will not abuse an old woman so? For heaven's sake, think of your own mothers.' Those words were followed by further cries of 'Murder'.

By now, Hutton had reached the hedge. Looking over, he saw three men holding an old woman down. He was sure that two of the men were the Worral brothers. He thought that the third (who presumably was attacking Sarah McCrinn before the Worralls turned up) was another local man, Robert Chadderton. Hutton watched as the three attackers tipped the body into a ditch.

---

[1] *A popular male forename in the area.*

Hutton joined the Worralls and the man he thought was Robert Chadderton, and they all walked as far as Ashton Coast (a place that, despite its name, was land-locked – lying a mile or so from the nearest appreciable expanse of water, which was and is called Crime Lake, but not because of its being the scene of a crime), where Ashton Worrall stopped a passer-by and handed him something, saying: 'Here, take this and say nowt.'

It would be interesting to know how Hutton explained his possession of the cloak, but the accounts of the case that I have seen are silent on this point.

Anyway, the police considered Hutton's story strong enough to justify the arrest of the Worrall brothers and Robert Chadderton.

Before the trial at the Lancaster Spring Assizes, the police received peculiar evidence from a man who had guarded the body after its discovery by the surveyor, Mr Schofield. He said that Ashton Worrall had come into the field and, after asking if it was true that a dead woman had been found in a ditch, complained, 'Damn it. I wish I had never had anything to do with her.'

That seems to have been the whole of the prosecution case. The trial lasted from nine in the morning till ten at night on Saturday, 12 March 1831. Robert Chadderton was acquitted, since he had a cast-iron alibi for the time of Sarah McCrinn's death. But the jury, without even bothering to retire, returned a verdict of Guilty against the Worrall brothers.

Sentenced to be executed on the following Monday, they were taken to a communal condemned cell, where they were presently joined by two men who were to be hanged for forgery. Saying that he had 'no intention of stretching a rope', one of the forgers produced a home-made saw and proceeded to cut away the iron bars on the window.

The forgers scrambled through the opening, and the Worralls followed. They made their way across roofs, through corridors, and into a room at the side of the gaol. There they prised a bar from the window.

The forgers clambered out and made good their escape, but the burly William Worrall, the first of the brothers to try to follow them, got stuck in the opening. He was still there, with Ashton staring dolefully at his waggling legs, when guards entered the room.

The brothers were hanged at the appointed hour on the Monday.

It strikes me that justice would have been better served if they had managed to escape from Lancaster Gaol. I believe that Sarah McCrinn, malnourished and exhausted, was probably the victim of a stroke rather than a mugging. It may be that the Worralls, or just one of the brothers, stole some of the old woman's paltry belongings when she was dying or dead. Even that possibility seems unsupported by any real evidence.

Hutton's tale is so riddled with implausibilities, and raises so many unanswered questions, that one suspects that he concocted all or most of it as a means of evading the dire penalty at that time for stealing the borrowed cloak. If the brothers had managed to escape and had then wreaked vengeance on Ashton Hutton, I am inclined to think that they would have had excellent reason for not pulling any punches.

There are several touches of sadness in the story of 'The Hollinwood Horror'. But to end on a happy note, let me mention that there was no vacant chair at the Cheethams' Christmas dinner-table: little Bride Cheetham had recovered from her illness and sat at the place intended for her grandmother.

The Ending Of Elsie

1924.

If you are old enough to have memories of that year, what do you recall? What happenings, other than purely personal ones, were sufficiently *special* – not necessarily important – as to have lodged in your mind meanwhile? Perhaps you remember, not a happening, but a song that was made ubiquitous by dance-bands hired by the fledgling British Broadcasting Company: the song was by Cole Porter, and the bit of its lyric that everyone seemed to know by hear commented that

> I'm in love again,
> And the hymn I'm hummin'
> Is the 'Huddle Up, Cuddle Up Blues'.

Or maybe you remember that, on St George's Day, you were one of the six million or so people, hardly any of whom had heard a monarch's voice before, who listened in to the BBC's relay of King George V's speech at the opening of the British Empire Exhibition at Wembley.

I am willing to wager that if you were living in Sussex – or, to be more exact, in or near Crowborough, which was then not much larger than a village (the population of the entire parish was fewer than 6000) – your strongest memory of the year is a mystery that arose during the last few weeks of it. The mystery concerned a 26-year-old woman called Elsie Cameron who, on Friday, 5 December, had travelled by train from London to Crowborough, intending to visit her fiancé, Norman Thorne – and had vanished from the face of the earth.

Elsie and Norman had known each other for four years, and had been engaged to be married for about half that time, since Christmas 1922. It was religion that had brought them together; living with their respective parents in the Kensal Rise area of North London, they had attended services at, and joined in social activities of, the local Wesleyan chapel, and eventually – to use Norman's words – 'started walking out as sweethearts'.

There was always an imbalance of love, of passion, in their relationship. From the start, Elsie was far keener on Norman (who, incidentally, was her junior by two years) than he was on her; and her devotion, her dependence, increased – to such an extent that, according to one of her women-acquaintances, 'Norman Thorne filled her thoughts.'

Someone else said of her that she was imbued with 'the iron tenacity of the feeble'. Tenacious she certainly was – but *feeble*? That word needs to be explained. One doesn't need to rely on her doctor's diagnosis of neurasthenia to say that she was an extremely nervous person. She exemplified what is nowadays known as a 'self-fulfilling prophecy' in the sense that her anxiety that she would not be able to cope often resulted in an *actual* inability to cope. When, at about the time she first met Norman Thorne, she lost the job she had had since leaving school, as a typist for the Triplex safety-glass company, her attempts to find employment were half-hearted, and the few jobs she did find never lasted long. In one instance, she was dismissed after a few days' trial, and in another, her nerves were so tattered by the end of the first week that she declared herself too ill to work and was escorted home by kindly fellow-employees (one of whom subsequently recalled: 'When we were on the platform at Aldgate railway station, she walked towards the edge. We walked her back. In the train she said she felt she was going mad. She was very strange – not like an ordinary girl at all. She said her head had felt very curious ever since she had had a nervous breakdown').

A plain-featured girl – and, more to the point, a girl who was very much aware of her plainness – Elsie Cameron had probably resigned herself to spinsterdom, to a life bereft of 'huddling up, cuddling up', before Norman Thorne began courting her. Once she had got over her surprise, though not her delight, at having such a charming and good-looking beau, she was determined to hold on to him, to become his wife.

One must give Norman Thorne the benefit of the doubt and assume that when he became engaged to Elsie, he intended to marry her. But whereas Elsie straightway started filling her bottom drawer, he was in no hurry, none at all, to take the plunge. Though his tardiness may not have been due to his parlous financial state, that was certainly a quite reasonable excuse for it. In the early summer of 1921, he was made redundant by the motor-engineering firm that had employed him as a mechanic since his demobilisation from the Royal Naval Air Service at the end of the Great War; unlike Elsie, he tried hard to find employment – but to no avail. After being on the dole for over a year, he prevailed upon his father, an inspector of Admiralty shipyards, to lend him £100 so that he could purchase a field at Crowborough, and there breed poultry. The field was at the junction of Luxford Road and Luxford Lane, on the edge of Crowborough that was known as Blackness. Indicating that he remained a staunch Methodist, he christened the smallholding Wesley Farm. Despite his frugality – the most visible sign of which was his use of the largest of the sheds he had erected as a 'living apartment' – and though he laboured seven days a week, he was unable to make the farm pay; by the start of 1924, he was deeply in debt.

Elsie was a frequent visitor; usually, she stayed in cheap digs close to the farm, but on one or two occasions she slept in Norman's shed. Desperate to see him more often, she took a job as a nursemaid in Crowborough – but had to leave within a fortnight because of 'ill health'.

On Whit Saturday of 1924, Norman Thorne went to a dance, and afterwards accompanied a girl called Elizabeth Coldicott to her home in South View Road, Crowborough. Before saying good-night, they fixed up a 'date'. Over the next few months, they got to know each other very well. Norman did not hide the fact that he was betrothed to Elsie Cameron.

Nor did he keep his friendship with Elizabeth Coldicott a secret from Elsie; he even arranged for the two girls to meet during one of Elsie's visits. In October, he took a day off and escorted Elsie to the British Empire Exhibition. Among the stands they entered was that of the Alliance of Honour, an organisation dedicated to 'preventing young people from indulging in sexual intercourse with one another before marriage'; Norman, already a member, paid a year's subscription of a shilling, and Elsie joined too.

That they were not whole-hearted supporters of the Alliance is shown by, among other things, a letter that Elsie wrote to Norman in November. She informed him that he had made her pregnant, and asked what he intended to do about it. His reply was not merely disappointing to Elsie but shocking: he was, he said, 'between two fires' because he had just learnt that he had put a local girl in the family way. Neither Elsie nor Norman was telling the truth. If Elsie had still been alive on Saturday, 6 December, she would have menstruated. No Crowborough maiden was pregnant by Norman.

On the morning of Friday, 5 December, Elsie, wanting to look her best, went to a hairdresser in Kensal Rise for a marcel. At about midday, she packed a suitcase with articles of clothing – including a baby's frock – and set off for Crowborough. After buying her ticket – a single, for she intended to stay with Norman for good – she had only three-ha'pence in her purse.

At the start of the following week, Norman addressed letters to Elsie at her parents' home. Towards the end of the week, her father sent him a telegram: ELSIE LEFT FRIDAY. HAVE HEARD NO NEWS. REPLY. Norman wired back at once: NOT HERE. OPEN LETTERS. CANNOT UNDER-STAND. He followed this up with a letter saying that, though he had expected Elsie on the Friday and had gone to the railway station to meet her, she had not arrived; he urged the Camerons to report Elsie's disappearance to the police. As soon as he had posted the letter, he asked the Crowborough police to make inquiries.

By the weekend, a full-scale investigation was under way; and the hotels of Crowborough were filling up with reporters and photographers from Fleet Street. Norman Thorne struck the police as being extremely helpful (for instance, without having been asked if he had any snapshots of Elsie, he provided some), and the newspapermen found him most co-operative, always ready to give interviews and to pose for photographs while standing ankle-deep in pullets outside his 'living apartment'.

But the publicity was his undoing. No one in Crowborough was unaware of the disappearance of Elsie Cameron; just about everybody was talking about it. Two nurserymen told the police that in the late afternoon of the 5th, while they were standing together in Luxford Road, Elsie Cameron – or her spitting image – had passed them, walking towards Wesley Farm. Acting on that information, a superintendent and an inspector examined the sheds on the farm; they found no evidence to support the nurserymen's story. A couple of weeks passed; then the police received a call from a Mrs Annie Price, who lived in a cottage close to Wesley Farm. Her memory had been jogged by something she had read in a newspaper. She remembered seeing the nurserymen in Luxford Road – and, at the same time, a young woman with a suitcase 'turning into the gate of Mr Thorne's farm'.

And so Norman Thorne was taken to the police station to make a further statement. And as soon as he was there, a squad of policemen, some with spades, began a thorough search of the farm. Many hours later, a constable digging near the gate unearthed a suitcase; inside it were a woman's jumper, some high-heeled shoes, and a broken pair of spectacles.

Thorne was told of the find; was asked if he wished to amend his statement. Eventually, he decided to do so. Yes, he said, Elsie Cameron *had* come to the farm that Friday afternoon. He had not expected her. When she had informed him that she intended to stay, and demanded that he marry her, he had become angry. They had argued, on and off, for hours – until about half-past nine, when he had walked out, telling Elsie that he was keeping a date with Elizabeth Coldicott. He had returned two hours later:

'When I opened the hut door I saw Miss Cameron hanging from a beam by a piece of cord as used for the washing line. I cut the cord and laid her on the bed. She was dead. . . . I lay across the table for about an hour. I was about to knock up someone to go for the police [but] *I realised the position I was in*, and decided not to do so.' He stripped the body and burned the clothes in the fireplace. After covering the floor with sacks, he used a hacksaw to decapitate and dismember the body. Apart from the head, which he put in an Oxo tin, the remains went into the sacks. 'Next morning, just as it got light, I buried the sacks and tin in a chicken run. It is the Leghorn chicken run, the first pen from the gate.'

Long before all the remains had been unearthed, Norman Thorne was charged with murder.

His trial, at Lewes Assizes in March 1925, resulted in a verdict of Guilty. It was Sir Bernard Spilsbury, the Home Office pathologist who had been vested with a reputation far in excess of his talents, who made that verdict almost a foregone conclusion. The all-important question – *Had Elsie Cameron died from hanging?* – was answered affirmatively by three eminent pathologists called by the defence; but negatively by Spilsbury, appearing for the Crown. The jury needed less than half an hour to agree with the judge, who in his summing-up had said that Sir Bernard's opinion 'is the very best that can be obtained'.

Despite efforts to save Norman Thorne from being hanged, the sentence was carried out on 22 April 1925, which would have been Elsie Cameron's twenty-seventh birthday.

Sir Arthur Conan Doyle, who at that time was living just outside Crowborough, commented: 'In any case where there is the faintest doubt, I do not think the death sentence should be carried out. In the Thorne case there does seem to me to be that faint doubt existing.'

Faint doubt . . . ? An understatement, surely. One wonders whether Conan Doyle would have liked to speak out more strongly, but was constrained from doing so by the fact that he, in common with all but a few people, had been taken in by the hyping of Spilsbury as 'Saint Bernard', whose deducing was as infallible as that of Sherlock Holmes. Even now, more than forty years after Spilsbury used household gas to bring his own life to an unnatural end, I feel a little bit heretical in stating my belief that though Norman Thorne was guilty of several crimes, murder was not among them.

Murder in Deansgate

As Olive Balchin traded as a prostitute, one may suppose that she was considered physically attractive by at least some men during the latter part of her forty years of life.

But her dead body was very ugly indeed.

Battered and contorted, it seemed appropriate to the surrounding debris on the bomb-site in the main thoroughfare called Deansgate, close to the corner of Cumberland Street, in the centre of Manchester.

Eleven o'clock on the morning of Sunday, 20 October 1946 – just over a year after the Second World War but still a time of ration cards and 'utility' goods, and with as many men wearing demob suits, stiffly obvious as such, as were clothed in garments bought from the Fifty Shilling Tailors.

Deansgate was relatively quiet. Two schoolboys, with nothing better to do, wandered through the jagged tear in the shop-facade and kicked at the bits of brick that littered the bomb-site.

Their attention was caught by some buttons, as shiny and as large as half-crowns. They saw that the buttons, reflecting the weak autumn sun, were sewn to a rusty-red coat. And then, after tentatively approaching, they realised that the coat was inhabited by a body.

A woman's body.

Was she a dosser, oversleeping because she had drunk too much meths the night before?

One of the boys called out, but the woman did not stir.

The boys moved slightly closer – sufficiently to see over the weeds and stones and garbage. The blotches on the woman's face matched the colour of her coat.

The boys scampered off the bomb-site. They raced to the

corner, turned into Cumberland Street, rushed into a newsagent's shop, and told the owner what they had seen. Leaving his daughter behind the counter, James Acarnley went to the bomb-site, and then ran to the nearby police headquarters in Bootle Street.

A full-scale investigation was set in motion. Detectives who had expected a quiet Sunday at home were telephoned and told to report for duty. By the time the first of them arrived at police headquarters, uniformed constables in Deansgate were ensuring that passers-by passed by, canvas screens had been erected around the bomb-site, and within them a doctor was making a preliminary examination of the body, a photographer was taking pictures of it from different distances and angles, and detectives were scouring the ground.

There was not much in the dead woman's pockets. Enough, though, to make it virtually certain that her name was Olive Balchin. On a scrap of paper, handwritten, was a man's name and an address in the Hertfordshire town of Cheshunt, not far from London. After the man had been interviewed by the Hertfordshire police, to whom he said that he had known Olive Balchin for nine years and had last seen her three years before in Cheshunt, he was driven to Manchester, where he formally identified the body at the mortuary in Platt Lane.

By then, the Manchester police had taken a statement from Sarah Bayley, the manageress of the city's women's hostel in Corporation Street, who had checked her records and established that Olive Balchin had stayed at the hostel from 25 August until the morning of the Saturday before she was murdered.

There was no doubt about the method of murder and the weapon that had been used. On the ground near the body was a rather unusual hammer. The police also found a ragged, crumpled sheet of brown paper which, going by certain deep creases in it, looked as if it had been wrapped round the hammer. That tool – of a sort intended primarily for leather-dressing – had been used to inflict the many wounds on the right side of Olive Balchin's head, breaking the bone around the eye, causing brain tissue to protrude, and splashing blood on her dyed hair, tincturing it a darker shade of red.

Domestic murders apart, Sunday is the worst day of the week on which to start an investigation of a murder committed in the centre of a large city: that was even more true back in 1946, when, in the absence of an evening paper, there was no television service to report what had happened and to elicit help from the public. And, of course, with only a few small shops open and almost all offices closed, there was no point in starting door-to-door inquiries or seeking information from people who worked in or near Deansgate.

And so the investigation did not get into top gear until first thing on the Monday.

One of the places visited by the police was the Queen's Café, which was in a basement in Queen Street, leading off Deansgate towards the town hall. A waitress, Elizabeth Copley, remembered that between half-past ten and eleven on the Saturday night, Olive Balchin had been in the cafe with an elderly woman – *and a youngish man*. She didn't know the man's name, but she was sure that she would recognise him if she saw him again. Oh yes, there was one other thing: she had noticed that the man was carrying a thin, brown-paper parcel.

Had that parcel contained the leather-dresser's hammer? The police thought it extremely likely.

But, before long, they had far more definite evidence concerning the murder weapon.

As a result of one of the several accounts of the case that appeared in Monday's editions of the *Manchester Evening News* (the offices of which were within a stone's throw of the bombsite), detectives traced a shopkeeper in a southern district of the city who, late on Saturday afternoon, had sold just such a hammer for 3/6d to a customer who said that he wanted it for 'general purposes'. The shopkeeper, Edward MacDonald, had wrapped the tool in brown paper of exactly the sort that was found at the scene of the murder. MacDonald, so he said, had a clear recollection of the young man who, 'strange in any case', had added to his strangeness by insisting on buying a leather-dresser's hammer for purposes other than leather-dressing.

Within two or three days of the murder, the police had a decent collection of evidence and 'leads'. They were thankful that there was no need to rely on the always doubtful opinion of doctors as to the time of death: the prostitute had been seen by at least three people on the Saturday night, and the juxtaposition of those witnesses' statements with the fact that most of the wounds on Olive Balchin's head were dried or drying when she was found showed that the murder must have been committed during the very small hours of the Sunday.

Edward MacDonald's description of his customer tallied in several respects with that given by Elizabeth Copley – not all that helpfully, however. The descriptions, though quite detailed, could have been applied to thousands of men. MacDonald's, for instance, included the following components:

> About 5 feet 8 inches, medium build, pale face, thin features, clean-shaven, quiet-spoken; dark suit and tie, fawn cotton raincoat.

It is true to say that, nine times out of ten, the success of a police investigation depends upon hard, grinding, boring routine-work – plus a liberal sprinkling of luck. Those two ingredients certainly led to an arrest in the Olive Balchin case – but the 'luck' was the outcome of both dogged perseverance by the whole investigating team and a touch of what has become known as lateral thinking on the part of one detective.

As well as conducting inquiries house-to-house, office-to-office and shop-to-shop in central Manchester, the police visited lodging-houses and men's hostels within a far wider radius of Deansgate. And a resident of one of the hostels took the opportunity of making a complaint that – on the face of it – seemed irrelevant to the reason why the police had come calling. He had lent a fawn cotton raincoat to someone, and the borrower – a man whom he knew only as 'Roland' – had not returned it.

Considering how much the police had on their hands, it would not be surprising if the opportunistic complainant had been told 'we'll look into that, sir,' and been left with the choice of acquiring a replacement raincoat or catching a cold when the weather turned sour. But no: Detective-Sergeant Emrys Jones Trippier (you are right – he was a Welshman) recalled Edward Mac-Donald's reference to the hammer-buyer's fawn cotton raincoat, and went in search of Roland.

In a short time, Trippier had added a 'w' to the name, had learned the Christian names, and was looking for *Walter Graham*

Rowland – a man from New Mills, Derbyshire, who had spent a good many of his thirty-eight years in prison. Among the first of the many and diverse entries on Rowland's police record was one for June 1927, when he was sentenced to three years in Borstal for attempting to strangle a woman. After being released on licence, he worked as a labourer. He got married in 1930, but his wife died ten months later in childbirth.

The following year he married again, and in 1932, while he was unemployed, his wife (almost certainly the person he had tried to strangle five years before) gave birth to a girl, who was given the names of Mavis Agnes. In 1934 Rowland was convicted of murdering his child by strangulation. He was reprieved from the death sentence, and spent ten years in prison. As soon as he was released, he joined the army.

Rowland had been a civilian for about three months when Detective-Sergeant Trippier took an interest in him.

After noting that Rowland matched the descriptions given by Edward MacDonald and Elizabeth Copley, and learning that Rowland was staying at the Services Transit Dormitory in the part of Manchester called Long Millgate, Trippier reported his suspicions to a superior officer, who sent Detective-Sergeant Joseph Blakemore and Detective-Constable Douglas Nimmo (subsequently a Deputy Chief Constable of Manchester) to the dormitory. Nimmo knew Rowland, having been involved in a recent investigation of a case of warehouse-breaking for which Rowland was convicted but put on probation at Manchester Quarter Sessions.

When the two detectives arrived, at eleven o'clock on the night of Saturday, 26 October, they found Rowland asleep. They woke him up, and Rowland, recognising Nimmo, asked: 'Is it about that coat?' According to both detectives, neither of whom responded to Rowland's question, he then enquired: 'You don't want me for murdering that fucking woman, do you?' (At his trial, Rowland insisted that he had said no such thing.) As soon as he had dressed – whether or not inclusively of the fawn raincoat, I don't know – he was taken to police headquarters.

There is some uncertainty as to what Rowland actually said when he was questioned by Detective-Inspector Frank Stainton, the officer in charge of the investigation; but he never denied stating that he had known Olive Balchin for a couple of months immediately prior to her death and that during that time he had had intercourse with her at least twice – once on a bomb-site (though not, he hastened to add, the one in Deansgate). Then – certainly to the astonishment, and probably to the gratification, of the listening detectives – he said that he believed that he had caught a venereal disease from the prostitute; had he been sure of that diagnosis, he added blithely, he would have had no hesitation in strangling her.

But he had *not* murdered Olive Balchin, he insisted. The last time he had met her was on the Friday before the murder: catching sight of her in the café in Littlewood's department store, in Manchester's Piccadilly, he had treated her to a cup of tea and a cake.

Identification parades were arranged, and Rowland was picked out not only by Edward MacDonald and Elizabeth Copley, but also by Norman Mercer, the landlord of the Dog & Partridge pub in Deansgate, who said that when he was taking his dog for a walk at about midnight on Saturday, 19 October, eleven hours before Olive Balchin's body was found, he had seen her quarrelling with Rowland just a few yards from the bomb-site.

The police decided that they had enough evidence – more than enough – to justify charging Walter Graham Rowland with the murder in Deansgate.

Less than a fortnight before Christmas 1946: for most people in Manchester, no different from most people in most other parts of the country, a time for sending cards, shopping for presents, and looking forward to the bank-holidays.

But Rowland had something more important on his mind.

He sat in the dock at Manchester Assizes, knowing that there was a strong probability that he would be found guilty of bludgeoning Olive Balchin to death.

The old Manchester Assize Courts, adjoining Strangeways Gaol in Great Ducie Street, had been destroyed by enemy action at the end of the first year of the war, and so Rowland was tried in the far less splendid surroundings of a magistrate's court in Minshull Street.

Rowland's leading counsel was Kenneth Burke, a well-known barrister on the Northern Circuit. He achieved some success in his cross-examintion of one of the first prosecution witnesses, Charles Jenkins, the doctor who had performed the autopsy, by persuading him to agree that the absence of blood on Rowland's clothes was unexpected considering the likelihood that a good deal of blood became 'airborne' during the attack.

Mr Burke tried to capitalise on that success when he examined the following witness, Edward MacDonald. However, the shopkeeper refused to be flustered by the volleys of quick-fire questions. He was sure, he said, taking his time about it, that the leather-dresser's hammer produced as an exhibit was the self-same tool that he had sold in the late afternoon of Saturday, 19 October. And he was no less certain that the customer was the accused.

At the end of his re-examination by Crown counsel, Basil Nield, KC, MacDonald turned his head towards the dock, looked closely, but only for a moment or so, at its central occupant, and said; 'That is the man I sold the hammer to.' The resultant 'stir in court' must have been slight compared to the one that, overlapping it, was caused by a shindy in the dock, as Rowland, screaming 'You're a liar!' at MacDonald, tried to stand up but was kept in his place by the flanking warders.

Though Mr Burke did his best to discredit the evidence of both the waitress, Elizabeth Copley, and the publican, Norman Mercer, neither witness fell into the trap of reacting to defence counsel's sarcasm about their powers of observation and the excellence of their memories. Each of them, one after the other, stepped from the witness-box without having succumbed to any of the tricks of advocacy – and presumably returned straightway to their respective places of business, one to serve tea and coffee, the other, mild and bitter.

Mild was the response of the police witnesses to Mr Burke's bitter attack on their notes and claimed recollection of what Rowland had said when he was arrested at the Services Transit Dormitory and during the long interrogation at police headquarters. The detectives had good reason for feeling calm and confident: after all, since Rowland's imprudent remarks concerning VD were admitted by the defence, it would hardly matter if Mr Burke managed to make any or all of the detectives appear sheepish in regard to discrepancies between Rowland's claimed recollection

of some other things that he had said and their own claimed
recollection of his words.

The so-called 'VD statement' was the subject of many questions put to Rowland when he gave evidence on his own behalf,
starting in the afternoon of Friday the thirteenth. During his
cross-examination, he was asked: 'This much is plain, isn't it?
You felt that you had contracted the disease from that woman,
and she deserved to be strangled?'

'I didn't say she deserved to be strangled,' Rowland protested.

The judge, Mr Justice Sellers, interposed: 'What *did* you
say?'

And Rowland showed – impressively – that he understood the
difference between a likely motive and a hypothetical justification by replying: 'I said, my Lord, that if I had known she
had given me VD, I would have strangled her.'

During his interrogation at police headquarters, Rowland had
told Inspector Stainton that he had spent the night of the murder
at a lodging-house in Hyde Road, on the south-eastern outskirts
of Manchester – but after the inspector had mentioned that
inquiries would be made at that address, Rowland had retracted
the statement, saying that he had stayed at another place in the
same road. Inquiries at that address, however, showed that
Rowland had stayed there, not on the night of the murder, but on
the following one.

At the trial, after Rowland had returned to the dock, the
defence called a man named Beaumont, who swore that Rowland
had stayed at his lodging-house in Brunswick Street, Chorlton-
on-Medlock (the district, in which Edward MacDonald's shop
was situated), on the night of the murder. But Beaumont's evidence was easily negated by the prosecution, for his visitors'
book, produced as an exhibit, showed that Rowland had arrived
on Saturday, 19 October – and *departed* later the same day. Even
if one or two members of the jury believed Beaumont's assertion
that the departure-date should have read '20/10/46', they must
have disregarded his evidence when he admitted that Rowland
could have left the premises at any time – and returned – without
anyone else in the lodging-house being aware of the fact.

At twenty minutes to five on the fourth day of the trial, after the
closing speeches and the judge's summing-up, the jury retired to

consider their verdict. The returned just under two hours later, and the foreman pronounced the single word: 'Guilty.'

'May God forgive you,' Rowland shouted from the dock. 'You have condemned an innocent man.'

Pretending that he hadn't heard the outburst, the Clerk of Assize intoned the ritual question: 'Have you anything to say why sentence of death should not be passed according to law?'

Customarily, persons asked that question remained mute, either because they felt unable to speak or because they didn't feel like talking, or insisted upon their innocence in a single breath. Rowland was exceptional. 'Yes, I have, my Lord,' he said – and went on, so fluently, never hesitating or stumbling, that people in the public gallery craned forward and sideways to see if he was reading the speech, which he wasn't:

> I have never been a religious man, but as I have sat in this Court during these last few hours, the teachings of my boyhood have come back to me, and I say in all sincerity and before you and this Court that when I stand in the Court of Courts before the Judge of Judges I shall be acquitted of this crime. Somewhere there is a person who knows that I stand here today an innocent man. The killing of this woman was a terrible crime, but there is a worse crime being committed now, my Lord, because someone with the knowledge of this crime is seeing me sentenced today for a crime which I did not commit. I have a firm belief that one day it will be proved in God's own time that I am totally innocent of this charge, and the day will come when this case will be quoted in the Courts of this country to show what can happen to a man in a case of mistaken identity. I am going to face what lies before me with the fortitude and calm that only a clear conscience can give. That is all I have got to say, my Lord.

No doubt there was a moment of silence; then a rustle of whispers – growing in volume till the Judge's Clerk read aloud from a card: 'My Lords the King's Justices do strictly charge and command all persons to stand up and keep silence whilst sentence of death is passed upon the prisoner at the bar upon pain of imprisonment.'

The black cap was placed on Mr Justice Sellers' wig. He, also reading from a card, told Rowland that he was to be hanged by the neck until he was dead.

No one considered that there would be any hitch in the arrangements towards the carrying out of that sentence. No one, that is, with the possible exception of a man named Ware.

I, David John Ware, wish to confess that I killed Olive Balshaw with a hammer on a bombed-site in the Deansgate, Manchester, on Saturday, October 19th, about 10 p.m. We had been to a Picture House near the Belle-Vue Stadium earlier in the evening. I did not know her before that night. I wish this to be used in evidence and accepted as the truth.

That written statement, made by a prisoner who was serving a sentence for the theft of cash from the Salvation Army hostel at Stoke-on-Trent, was handed to the Governor of Walton Gaol, Liverpool, on 22 January 1947.

Ware had got the name of the victim wrong (in early press reports of the murder in Deansgate, Olive Balchin was referred to as 'Olive Balshaw'), but there was no doubt that he was confessing to the crime for which Walter Graham Rowland had been sentenced to death.

The Governor informed the Liverpool police, who telephoned the Chief Constable of Manchester, who instructed Detective-Inspector Stainton and Detective-Constable Nimmo to drive to Walton and interview David Ware.

He told them that, on Friday, 18 October, having committed the theft in Stoke, he travelled first to Uttoxeter, a distance of about fifteen miles south-east, and then to Manchester, forty miles north, where, on the following afternoon, he bought a hammer in a shop 'on the road from Piccadilly leading to Manchester Hippodrome', with the intention of using it to commit robbery with violence.

He said that he met Olive Balchin, a stranger to him, at about six o'clock outside the Hippodrome, and took her to a cinema near Belle Vue: 'my idea was to kill time till it got dark.' He said that when they came out of the cinema three hours later, they had coffee, then boarded a bus into the centre of Manchester.

I did not know whether to leave her or not but after finding a dark place not far from Piccadilly I decided to spend a while with her. The spot where we stopped was a place or building that I took to be bombed in the war. We went inside the ruins & stood for a short while near the entrance. We were quite close to each other & being so near she took the opportunity of going through my pockets. I was aware of this but did not show her. I was ate up with hatred & felt immediately that I'd like to kill her. I realised I had the hammer so suggested that I'd like to make water & went further in the building. In there I took the brown paper off the hammer & threw it in the corner.

I went back to her & suggested moving further inside where we could not be seen. She agreed to this & we moved further inside. She was on my left & with my right hand I got the Hammer out of my pocket. While she was still in front & had only a few paces to go before reaching the wall I struck her a violent blow on the head. (I should say the right side.) She screamed & before her scream lasted any length of time I struck her again this time she only mumbled. Her hands were on her head protecting it the second time she fell to the floor up against the wall & I repeated the blows. Blood shot up in a thin spray. I felt it on my face & then I pannicked threw the hammer & left everything as it was. I made no attempt to get my money. I ran & ran zig-zag up & down streets I didn't know eventually getting to Salford Station. I was frightened of going on the station so decided to go to Stockport. I caught bus to the Hippodrome then another to Stockport, sleeping at a lodging House there. On Sunday I tramped to Buxton & on to Chapel en le frith where I stayed the night at the institution. On Monday I Hitch Hiked to Sheffield & surrendered to the Police for the stealing of the money at the Stoke on trent salvation Army Hostel.

I have been in custody since.

One doesn't know what the two detectives thought of Ware or of his confession. It seems clear that the confession was all Ware's own work: that neither of the detectives prompted him, suggested that he should amplify certain points, or (and their apparent silence in this regard is hard to understand) asked him a question the answer to which was known only to themselves, a few other investigators of the murder in Deansgate, lawyers for the Crown and for the defence in the proceedings against Rowland – and the murderer of Olive Balchin. Of several such questions, probably the most obvious was: How much money, and of what coins or notes, or both, did the woman steal from you?

The detectives travelled back to Manchester, and Inspector Stainton at once informed Rowland's solicitor of the development.

Rowland's appeal against his conviction was due to be heard in the Royal Courts of Justice, London, in three days' time; but because of Ware's confession, the proceedings were postponed until 10 February. Meanwhile, Rowland's legal advisers interviewed Ware and took a statement from him. One of the sentences in the statement read: 'After I had felt this woman feeling in my pockets, I felt in my trousers cash pocket and found that a 10s. note, which I was certain I had put in that pocket, had gone.' Supposing that none of the lawyers, while interviewing Ware, had inadvertently let slip any informtion about the murder that was not known to the public, then Ware's reference to a ten-shilling note may have given a slight, a very slight, fillip to the lawyers' hopes. For a ten-shilling note *had* been found on Olive Balchin's body. That good news, so far as Rowland's lawyers were concerned, was greatly diminished in value – indeed, almost wiped out – by details of the state and precise location of the note. In the words of Mr John Jolly, KC (whose role in this story will soon be explained), '. . . when Olive Balchin's body was found, there was discovered a ten-shilling note in the left-hand bottom pocket of her overcoat. This note was carefully folded into a small capacity and placed at the bottom of a Midland Bank paper cash packet. On the top of the ten-shilling note there were 8 half-crowns, 1 two-shilling piece, 1 shilling, 1 sixpence, 1 penny and 2 half-pennies, making a total of £1.13.8d. The cash bag was then filled up with letters and bed tickets. It was placed at the bottom of the pocket and the pocket was then filled up with papers and other property.' And so, unless Olive Balchin had been marvellously manipulative (a notion that, if Ware was to be believed, was contradicted by the unsubtlety of her rummagings in *his* pockets), it was unlikely that the ten-shilling note found deep-down in her pocket was her final acquisition.

Unlikely? Well, yes, Rowland's lawyers admitted. But not impossible. Rowland's appeal was heard by three judges, including the Lord Chief Justice, Lord Goddard. They allowed the defence to call a new witness, who swore that he had briefly encountered Rowland, or his spitting image, in a pub in

Stockport at about the time that Rowland was supposed to have been drinking tea with Olive Balchin in the Queen's Café, near Deansgate. Among several reasons why this witness failed to impress the judges, one was that he admitted that when he had approached Rowland's solicitor, he had been unable to recognise Rowland from a photograph that was shown to him. (The judges were not able to look at the photograph, to decide whether or not it was a good likeness, because it had been returned to its owner, none of the defence team having presumed that the judges would want to look at it.) Another reason was that the witness had an idiosyncratic way of remembering when things had happened: it was all very well that he connected his sighting of 'Rowland' with a visit to the Plaza cinema, Stockport, where he had paid 2/9d to see a thriller entitled *Cornered*, starring Dick Powell (his reference to the price of the ticket, together with his saying that he had given 'Rowland' 10½d for ten Woodbine cigarettes – that transaction making up the whole of their encounter – suggests that monetary matters loomed large in his mind) – but there was a concerted puckering of judicial brows at his remark that he could only work out when he had first been interviewed by Rowland's solicitor by reference to when Stockport County had played Bolton Wanderers in the competition for the Football Association Cup.

The judges refused to hear anything about Ware's confession, noting that, Catch-22ishly, 'if we had allowed Ware to give evidence before us, and he had persisted in his confession of guilt, the Court would have been compelled to form some conclusion as to his guilt or innocence and to express that opinion in open court. In effect, therefore, the Court would have been engaged in trying not only Rowland but also Ware, and thereby usurping the function of a jury.'

However, the judges suggested that the Home Secretary should look into the matter.

As soon as Rowland realised that the appeal had been dismissed, he shouted out that he had not been allowed justice because of his past. As he was led from the court, he was still protesting: 'It would have knocked the bottom out of English law to have acquitted me and proved my innocence. I say now I am an innocent man before God.'

* * *

Heeding the judges' suggestion, the Home Secretary appointed Mr John Jolly, KC, to conduct an inquiry into Ware's confession. During the inquiry, Ware admitted that his statements to the prison governor, the Manchester detectives, and Rowland's lawyers were false. 'I'd better turn it in,' he said. '. . . I have never seen the woman Balchin . . . in my life. I did not murder her and had nothing whatever to do with the murder. I made these statements out of swank more than anything, but I had a feeling all along that I wouldn't get very far with them. My health has not been too good since the outbreak of war and I really do feel I want some treatment. I also thought I was putting myself in the position of a hero. I wanted to see myself in the headlines. In the past I wanted to be hung. It was worthwhile being hung to be a hero, seeing that life was not really worth living . . . I would like to say that I am sorry I have given the trouble I have and I didn't realise the serious consequences it might entail had the confession been believed.'

Even so, Mr Jolly investigated particular passages in the statements and arranged for an identification parade: none of the three eye-witnesses against Rowland recognised Ware. On 25 February, Mr Jolly reported that he was satisfied that there were no grounds for thinking that there was any miscarriage of justice in the conviction of Walter Graham Rowland for the murder in Deansgate.

He was scheduled to die on the morning of the 27th – that being a Thursday, the conventional day for hangings. During the Wednesday evening, he wrote some letters, one to his parents:

Dear Mother & Dad,

I understand just how you must have been feeling today when you came to see me for the last time in this world. I ask you to forgive me for trying to cheer you up in the way I did. I just had to keep you up or I would have broken down myself. I am sure you will understand Mother and Dad. You know I have told you the truth all along, and you have promised never to doubt, or sease [*sic*] from seeking the truth of my total innocence. The truth will out in God's own time, so just go on with this firm believe [*sic*] in your hearts. Please dont mourn my passing Mother and Dad, I am going into God's hands and into his keeping. I shall walk beside you until we meet again in God's Kingdom. I am just going on before. Away from the unjustness and the strain of all the past long days. When you receive this letter I shall be at my rest so do not grieve my passing. Hold up your heads for I die and innocently, Christ said on the Cross, for others sin. I die for anothers crime. I tell you mother and dad that before my maker I swear that I am completely innocent of the death of that poor woman. You have each other and those around you to comfort you in your sorrow, hold on to your faith in God. He will make all clear in His own good time and way and hold on to your believe [*sic*] in my innocence. May God Bless you all and comfort you, until we meet again by His grace in His Kingdom where unjustness is no more and all shadows flie before His Light.

With deepest love to you both. Good bye in this World.

Your loving and Grateful Son,

WALTER

In the space between his signature and the foot of the sheet of prison-issue notepaper, he put three rows of kiss-crosses.

In July 1951, about four and a half years after Rowland's death, David Ware, who was then living in Bristol, sought to kill a young woman whom he had just met for the first time, in an area of common land, using a hammer that he had bought earlier in the day. Fortunately for the woman, the hammer was of shoddy workmanship, its head coming away after the first blow; Ware then 'laid into her with the shaft', causing ugly wounds but none that was lethal, and ran off. Soon afterwards, he walked into a police station and confessed to the crime, explaining that he had 'felt the urge' to kill a woman, any woman would do, and had bought the hammer for that indiscriminate purpose. At his trial, which took place in November, he was found 'guilty but insane',[1] and was ordered to be detained in the Broadmoor asylum 'until His Majesty's Pleasure was known'. On April Fool's Day, 1954, he committed suicide by hanging himself.

Ever since the Bristol jury had delivered their verdict, thereby making it legally safe to state publicly that Ware had tried to

[1]*A form of words that in 1965 was replaced by 'not guilty by reason of insanity'.*

hammer a woman to death, campaigners for the abolition of
capital punishment had, in pamphlets and on platforms, insisted
that that fact proved conclusively, no ifs or buts, that Ware had
hammered *Olive Balchin* to death – that, more to their point,
Walter Rowland had been executed for another man's crime.
You may need to be reminded that, till 1953 (when the abolitionist cause was boosted by public disquiet at, first, the hanging of
Derek Bentley for a murder that his youthful partner-in-crime,
Christopher Craig, had committed in his presence, and second,
the discovery that John Christie, who in 1950 had helped
towards the hanging of his erstwhile upstairs-neighbour,
Timothy Evans, was a mass-murderer), abolitionists were
stumped when asked to name anyone other than Edith Thompson
(hanged in 1923, chiefly because she had committed adultery
with the young man who, perhaps to her surprise, murdered her
husband) in firm support of their contention that some hangings
were miscarriages of justice. And so there was a paradox: many
abolitionists were so distressed by the thought that innocent
persons had been, might be, hanged that they were *delighted* to
believe that Rowland had been hanged in error. They were
determined not to allow facts to diminish their delight.

I have mentioned some of the inconvenient facts. Before
mentioning some others, I shall say a little about Ware.

He was born in 1908 – as was Rowland – in the small Welsh
town of Skewen, which lies between Swansea and Neath. His
police record began in 1931, when he was sentenced to twelve
months' imprisonment with hard labour for a clumsy attempt at
blackmail. Six years later, he deserted his wife and two children,
and five years after that, in 1942, he was conscripted into the
army. He had served less than a year when he was discharged
because of a doctor's belief that he was suffering from manic-
depressive psychosis. In 1943, and again in 1945, he was
imprisoned for theft. And, as you know, he was a convict in
Walton Gaol, Liverpool, when he confessed to the murder of
Olive Balchin.

In the days when a convicted murderer might be hanged, it
was not unusual for a much-publicised murder case to produce a
rash of bogus confessions – some from people whose lives were so
dreary that they were keen to 'swank' responsibility for just about
any unclaimed shock-horror act (one is reminded of the tale of

the Catholic spinster who, having confessed innumerably to immoral sexual conduct, was asked by the priest if she had really sinned in that way, and replied, 'No, father, but I do love talking about it'); some from people who, wanting to opt out of life but not having the courage to commit suicide, looked upon the hangman as someone who might do the job for them (there is evidence, decisive as well as ample, of that phenomenon). Other false confessors had other motives; often, those liars did not understand what prompted the lies – or, understanding, were either not articulate enough to explain or too bashful to try.

When Ware retracted his confession to the murder in Deansgate, he referred to both of the motives that I have outlined. It appears that he was a practised confessor: soon after saying that he had killed Olive Balchin, he told a prison doctor that, at some time prior to his present imprisonment, he had falsely confessed to a murder in Edinburgh. Whether what he told the doctor was true or false, it proves that he was a liar of some strange sort.

Of course, that fact, by itself, does not mean that he lied when he said that he killed Olive Balchin. The fact simply makes one a trifle suspicious.

But suspicion grows into certainty when one takes other matters into account. Ware explained to John Jolly that he had first thought of confessing after reading an early account of the crime in the *Daily Herald*. Following his remand on the charge of the theft from the Salvation Army hostel at Stoke-on-Trent, 'I set myself to get all the details of the murder in my mind and continuously repeated the story to myself until I knew it right off. After I knew Rowland was arrested for the murder, it magnified the thing and made it bigger altogether. I wanted him to be sentenced to death and to make my confession just before he was hung so as to make it spectacular in the way I snatched him from the gallows.'

Asked by Mr Jolly to recall his actions and whereabouts directly before and at the time of the murder, Ware gave a minutely detailed account of places that he had visited, people whom he had met, buses and trams that he had travelled on, and things that he had done. This made it clear that he couldn't possibly have killed Olive Balchin.

*　　*　　*

But so far as propagandists against capital punishment were concerned – never mind. They used – or rather, *mis*used – the Rowland case in aid of their objective (which was achieved, to all intents and purposes, shortly before Christmas 1964, when the Murder [Abolition of Death Penalty] Bill, framed by Sydney Silverman, MP, was given a second reading in the Commons).

In the early 1970s, the crime-writer Rupert Furneaux provided me with transcripts of some post-war murder trials, including that of Rowland. As general editor of the *Celebrated Trials*, I persuaded Judge Leon (more widely known by his forenames, Henry Cecil, which he used pseudonymously as a novelist – most successfully, of the 'Brothers-in-Law' series – and author of works on legal matters) to edit and introduce a Rowland volume.[1] Both of us came to the case with little knowledge of it; with no preconceived notions. And we soon discovered that Sydney Silverman was – in Henry's carefully chosen words – 'a literary psychopath': in an essay that Silverman had contributed to a book purporting to show that three persons, one of them Rowland, had been wrongfully executed,[2] he had completely misrepresented salient passages in Ware's retraction of his confession.[3]

No doubt Silverman believed that deceitful means were justified by what he considered a worthy end. He was not the only abolitionist who told lies, or left out hindering truths, on behalf of the cause. (And I must say that some of those who spoke for

---

[1] Trial of Walter Graham Rowland, *Henry Cecil, David & Charles, 1976.*

[2] Hanged – and Innocent? *by R. T. Paget, QC, MP, and S.S. Silverman, MP, with an epilogue by Christopher Hollis, MP; published in London (by Victor Gollancz, an influential abolitionist), 1953.*

[3] *In 1967, while I was writing a book on the Wallace murder case, I had dinner at the House of Commons with Scholefield Allen, who had been one of William Herbert Wallace's defence counsel and was now Labour MP for Crewe. As we were preparing to leave, Sydney Silverman entered the dining room, and Scholefield Allen (who, incidentally, had campaigned against capital punishment ever since, in 1931, Wallace had come close to being hanged for another man's crime) suggested that I should meet him. I cannot remember a single thing that Silverman said to me, or I to him – perhaps because my mind was engrossed by what Scholefield Allen had added to his suggestion: 'But I should warn you that Sydney is as likeable as most expert confidence tricksters.'*

the silent majority of unparliamentarian retentionists used similar tricks, only less skilfully.) The Silverman version of the Rowland case helped towards persuading sufficient members of both Houses of Parliament that capital punishment should be done away with. Not only did the abolitionists win the day, but they celebrated a double victory: the end of hanging – and no insistence by anyone in either chamber that the till-then alternative 'life sentence' should be redefined so that, in some circumstances, it would mean what it said.

Walter Rowland was already a murderer when he killed Olive Balchin. Though I vacillate on the subject of capital punishment – one day being against it; the next, following news of some heinous crime, being for it – I am unwaveringly glad that Rowland was hanged. For the simple reason that, if he had not been, he might by now have murdered several times more.

Two Sketches of Monsters

Of Mice and Murder

'The mice are still eating the mattresses,' Elizabeth Pearson informed her mother-in-law as they sat in the kitchen of the small house in the village of Gainford, to the west of Darlington.

The mother-in-law tut-tutted sympathetically and asked if the powder she had bought on Elizabeth's behalf a few days before had had any diminishing effect on the problem. Well, a little, Elizabeth allowed – but it was like 'scooping a pail of water out of the Tees to stop flooding'. Better than nothing, the mother-in-law commented – and was rather surprised when Elizabeth at once agreed and asked her to pop round to the appropriately-named Mr Corner's grocery shop for another threepennyworth of the powder. Elizabeth explained that she couldn't go herself because, sure as death, the minute she left the house the old man lying abed upstairs would need her attention.

And so the mother-in-law – her name was Jane Pearson – went on the errand. John Corner, the grocer, recalled her earlier purchase of a packet of Battle's Vermin Powder; he remembered, too, that on that occasion he had neglected to make a note of the sale of the poison. He had better do that this time. Apologising for the slight delay, he scribbled the details of the transaction in the poison-entry book, complete with the date: 2 March 1875. As he did so, he made what he thought was a joke, words to the effect that he hoped the stuff wasn't being used to kill anybody.

Mr Corner's joke would – and in a very short while – be seen as an awfully unfunny one by the people of Gainford. So that you may understand why, I must tell you something about an old man named James Watson.

Only a year younger than the century, he had lived in Gainford all his life, toiling as a herdsman, lastly for wages of fifteen shillings a week. He had outlived two wives, the first of whom had borne him a son, named Robert. After the death of his second wife, in the spring of 1874, he had decided to retire; he didn't have much in the way of savings, but he reckoned that if he took in a lodger at his small house, on which he paid rent of £7 a year, he could just about make both ends meet.

No sooner had he retired than his house became overcrowded. His first wife's niece, Elizabeth Pearson, locked up her own house at the far end of the village and, with her husband and baby girl, moved in with him. It appears that neither the old man nor his recently-ensconced lodger, a labourer called George Smith, had much, if any, say in the matter: once the thin-faced, 28-year-old Elizabeth had embarked on a course of action, she was devilish hard to resist.

Of course, James Watson's female neighbours, tittle-tattling among themselves, surmised that Elizabeth hoped to profit from the move in some way. However, when one of them, Annie Hall, came straight out with it and asked Elizabeth for an explanation, the reply she got was itself a question: 'What are kith and kin for, if not to help in times of sickness?'

Sickness? Well, yes, it was true that, these days, the old man was poorly. He had developed some sort of chest complaint, and there were times when he needed to fight for breath.

Despite the doctor's potions and Elizabeth's ministrations, James's condition worsened. By the end of February 1875 – which, you will remember, was when Elizabeth suddenly became concerned about the mice in the house – he was virtually confined to his bed.

Hearing of this, Robert Watson came over from his home in the village called Barnard Castle. Perhaps trying to make up for the fact that he had hardly seen his father during the past twenty years, he made an offer: 'If you sell your furniture and come and live with me, I'll allow you a few shillings a week.' James asked for a little time in which to make up his mind.

The thought that he might accept must have worried Elizabeth no end.

Two days later, at about five o'clock in the afternoon of Monday, 15 March, George Smith, the labourer-lodger, called Annie Hall into the house. He told her that James seemed 'none too well'. Mrs Hall ran upstairs to James's bedroom. Elizabeth was standing beside him, holding his wrists. 'He appeared to be cringing himself up in the bed, and his head was thrown quite back, so that his form was arched. He said, "Annie, I don't think I shall be able to tremble this one out." I told his niece to fill a bottle with hot water, then I sent my little girl for Dr Homfrey.'

By the time the doctor arrived, James Watson was dead. Mrs Hall sent a telegram to Robert. Reaching Gainford at nine that night, he found that the house, as well as being empty of people, had been stripped of all furniture except the bed on which the body lay, uncovered, resting on the bare steel trellis.

Shocked and angry, he rushed to the Pearsons' house. Elizabeth's husband was anxious to 'come to an arrangment' about the dead man's belongings. But not she. 'I'd sooner make firewood of everything than let you have any of it,' she shouted. 'What's mine's mine, and what's thine's thine, and what I have I'll keep.'

Robert wasted no words on her. He went in search of a constable. The policeman sought out Dr Homfrey, who at once admitted having a suspicion that James Watson's 'cringing' might have been due to strychnine poisoning. That suspicion was confirmed next day, when an autopsy revealed traces of strychnine, Prussian-blue ferrocyanic acid, and starch – the constituents of Battle's Vermin Powder.

Elizabeth Pearson was charged with murder. At her trial at Durham Assizes in July, the defence made the half-hearted suggestion that George Smith – who, having been deprived of his lodgings, had disappeared from Gainford – was the true culprit. Unimpressed, the jury found her guilty of having killed in the furtherance of acquiring a few sticks of furniture, and the sentence of death was passed.

Elizabeth claimed that she was *enceinte*, but the prison doctor could find no sign of pregnancy. On the morning of Monday, 2 August, she was hanged together with two men who had killed during street brawls, one in Darlington, the other in Barnard Castle, on a specially-constructed gallows with three beams. Maybe coincidentally, at the very time that her body was buried within the precincts of the prison, miles away, in Gainford, John Corner was tending a bonfire on which he had tipped his entire stock of the powder that was a destroyer of mice and of men.

The Other Moors Murderer

There is some truth in the saying, 'Murder will out.' Only *some* truth. Like most statistics, those relating to crime rates, percentages of convictions, and so forth, need to be taken with a pinch of salt, if for no other reason than because a good many crimes are not reported to the police or simply go unnoticed. Criminologists have a term for the number of crimes that, for one reason or another, are not recognised as illegal acts by the authorities: the 'dark figure', they call it.

Occasionally, the stygian gloom of one year's dark figure is alleviated, a long while after the fact, by the recognition that someone has been 'getting away with murder'. Perhaps a hidden body comes to light – as was so to the detriment of Eugene Aram, whose victim remained out of sight and out of mind for fourteen years, till 1758. Or perhaps an unapprehended murderer, lulled into a false sense of security, kills again, is caught this time, and is revealed as a practised hand at homicide. That, you will remember, happened in 1965, when the 'shopping' of Ian Brady and Myra Hindley for a murder in a council house at Hyde, in Cheshire, led to the discovery that they were indiscriminate killers who had buried all of their victims save the most recent on nearby Saddleworth Moor.

Brady and Hindley were not the first 'moors murderers'. Some forty years earlier, a man named Albert Burrows had turned a place on the moors to the south of Saddleworth into an illicit graveyard. Burrows was a resident of the grey-stone town of Glossop, which lies a mile or so east of Hyde, and which was later to be a favourite haunt of Brady and Hindley. Like that foul couple, he remained unsuspected till he committed one murder too many.

It is rarely easy to assign a precise starting-date to a murder case; a killer's motive, often hazy anyway, may have been sown many years before the crime. Thursday, 10 October 1918, towards the end of the Great War, is a convenient date, no more than that, on which to start the history of the events that culminated in Albert Burrows' appointment with an executioner five years later.

On that day in 1918, Hannah Calladine, a short and naturally stout woman of twenty-eight, gave birth to a child whom she

named Albert Edward Burrows, an exact replica of the name of
the father, a 57-year-old itinerant labourer whose travels had
taken him from his home-town of Glossop to Hannah's, which
was Nantwich, a distance of about forty miles south-west. The
nativity was marred by two related facts, one being that the
senior Albert was not married to Hannah, the other being that he
was legally debarred from marrying her because he had a wife
back in Glossop. But still, considering that Hannah already had
one illegitimate child, a two-year-old girl called Elsie, she may
have been concerned only in regard to finance. Whether it was
Hannah's idea or the still-labouring Albert's, we don't know, but
a few weeks after the birth of the son, she went through a form of
marriage with Burrows at the Nantwich registrar's office.

The 'marriage' was only a couple of months old when the
Nantwich police were informed of the real Mrs Burrows in
Glossop. Burrows was sentenced to six months' imprisonment
for bigamy in February 1919. He visited Hannah as soon as he
was released in July – but she, rather than welcoming him back
with open arms, applied for a bastardy order against him. This
was granted, the order being for the payment of seven shillings a
week (which would today, what with inflation, be about ten
pounds).

Either because he wouldn't or because he couldn't keep up the
payments, Burrows went back to prison, for twenty-one days, in
November.

That sentence served, he returned to his wife in Glossop
rather than to the troublesome Hannah in Nantwich.

In the absence of an explanation from Hannah, what happened next seems inexplicable. When Burrows had been back in
Glossop for only a day or so, Hannah turned up on the doorstep;
with her were her two children – Albert in a push-cart which also
contained a large brown-paper parcel of clothing. Not surprisingly, as soon as Hannah and her offspring entered the
house, Mrs Burrows flounced out. She didn't go far, though: just
to the nearby house of a friend, Mrs Streets, who was willing to
put her up. Soon after Christmas, she issued a maintenance
order against her husband, which was made returnable for 2.30
in the afternoon of 12 January 1920.

Burrows, who was hard pressed for cash, seriously in arrears
with the rent, was presented with a choice of evils: if he sent

Hannah packing, he would have to make the payments on the bastardy order – if he let her stay, he would be faced with the maintenance order on behalf of his wife. There seemed no way that he could stay out of prison.

No way, that is, short of committing murder.

The last time that Hannah was seen alive was as the bell of the parish church was tolling for the evening service on Sunday, 11 January: Eliza Hammond, who lived across the road from Burrows, observed Hannah standing at the door of the house, 'dressed in dark clothes, as if to go out'.

Next morning, some time before seven o'clock, Mrs Streets happened to glance through her window as she was preparing her husband's breakfast. She saw Burrows walking towards the moors in the company of a small girl.

A couple of hours later, Burrows knocked at Mrs Streets' door. He was alone. He asked to see his wife, but was told that she had gone to work. Soon afterwards, he visited a newsagent named Dale, brother of the man who employed Mrs Burrows as a char. He wanted the newsagent to pass on a message to Mrs Burrows, telling her that Hannah Calladine had 'gone housekeeping for a widower' who was prepared to give board and lodging to the two children, and imploring her to withdraw the maintenance summons.

Mrs Burrows ignored the message, and that afternoon, at the town hall, an order was made for her to receive £1 a week. But by the following Friday, Burrows had persuaded her to return home.

Subsequently, Burrows gave a variety of answers to questions concerning the whereabouts of Hannah and the children: 'a secret between us,' he told Eliza Hammond – but on another occasion informed her that Hannah was 'in a bacon shop with a relation of mine at Stretford' (a district of Manchester). He was speaking the truth when he added: 'She will never come to Glossop again.'

Over the next few weeks, he sold several of Hannah's belongings to local people, none of whom seems to have thought it at all odd that she had left the things behind.

Months went by; *years*. And meanwhile Burrows showed neighbours letters that he said he had received from Hannah. And meanwhile he wrote to relatives and friends of Hannah, saying that she sent her love – and enclosing with one of the letters to Hannah's mother a fuzzy snapshot of a small boy: 'I send you this photograph of your grandson, hoping you will like it . . . We are all happy.' And meanwhile a friend of Hannah's, living in Nantwich, received letters that seemed to have been written by Hannah: 'The children, Albert and Elsie, are got big now . . . I have the best husband in the world and everything I want.' And meanwhile Burrows applied for and was granted extra dole money in respect of Hannah and the two children, 'who are now living' and 'maintained wholly at my cost'.

On Sunday, 4 March 1923, Burrows murdered again. His victim was Thomas Wood, a boy of four, whom he abused before killing. During the police investigation into the boy's disappearance, Burrows blithely volunteered the information that he had been with Thomas on Symmondly Moor shortly after the boy was last seen by his mother. He pointed out the place, which was close to the Dinting shaft, one of the many airshafts over the disused mines in the area. A search of the shaft revealed the body. A further search revealed three other bodies lying in stagnant water more than a hundred feet below ground.

The rest of the story can be quickly told. The bodies found at the foot of the shaft were examined by a pathologist and an anatomist at Manchester University; though it was not possible to establish the cause, or causes, of death, there was no doubt that the bodies were those of Hannah and her children.

Yet, even then, Burrows thought he could get away with murder. While in Strangeways Prison, he tried to persuade a fellow-prisoner to write him a letter: 'I and the children are all right, Hoping to see you soon, HANNAH, x x x.' The prisoner was one of the witnesses for the Crown at Burrows' trial, which turned out to be a little more than a formality; the jury needed but eleven minutes to find him guilty of murdering Hannah and Elsie, the only charges on which he was tried.

I think it is safe to say that when Albert Burrows was hanged for his awful crime, no one, least of all his widow, felt any emotion far removed from gladness.

The Pantry-Boy and the Toff

As I was going up the stair,
I met a man who wasn't there;
He wasn't there again today,
I wish, I wish he'd go away.
'The Psychoed' by Hughes Mearns

Times have changed. No more so than in regard to London's residential hotels. Nowadays, most of the proprietors of such hotels profit profiteeringly at the expense of rate-payers, many in boroughs distant from those in which the hotels they are unwillingly supporting stand, by taking in parolees, illegal immigrants, single parents and their offspring, displaced patients of mental institutions that the government has thought it sensible to close, and others who for other reasons are homeless. Many of those many hotels have been made to spin even more money for their proprietors, not all of whom pay tribute to persons in town halls, by the dividing of rooms – with, for instance, bits of hackneyed hardboard or with lengths of curtain material from a local Oxfam shop – into cubby-holes called rooms; speaking of the sparcity of tended amenities, not of the extravagance of ill-gotten gains, such hotels are the London-in-the-1980s equivalent of Log's lodging-house in Edinburgh in the 1820s; even allowing for the fact that some of them will have burnt down by 1990, there will be more of them by then.

They are a far, a very far, cry from what most residential hotels used to be like; their denizens are extraordinarily different from the clients of most residential hotels in days not long gone by. Those clients, generally known as paying guests, were either wealthy enough to foot the bills or fortunate enough to have relatives wealthy enough and willing to foot them. The hotels' respective clienteles were not entirely composed of genteel spinsters, legacied widows, retired officers of good regiments who grunted 'Qui-hi' for service, second or subsequent-to-second sons of aristocrats, and recent products of finishing schools that had not taught common abilities such as egg-boiling, bed-making, shoe-polishing or furniture-dusting – but a quite large percentage of the guests fell into those categories. In one way or another, all were privileged. And most of the people who looked after them were of that stratum of society now referred to as the Under-Privileged; it may be that the main difference between the majority of the British-born Under-Privileged of those days and the majority of the British-born Under-Privileged of these is not that the former were willing to accept servants' work at servants' wages – that being an optical illusion of those who have worked their way out of the Under-Privileged stratum and who perceive a dearth of persons ambitious to do likewise.

In the early spring of 1922, the Hotel Spencer was among the poshest of its residential kind. If the management (who were all, of course, male; who, whatever the hour, were immaculate in morning-dress) had been forced to *advertise* vacancies, they would have done so demurely and in an organ like *The Times of India* – not in the native *Times*, where the announcement would be seen by far too many people who were totally unqualified as applicants, or, perish the thought, *The Tatler* or *Dalton's Weekly*. But the management had no need of printed publicity: the attractions of the establishment were broadcast by the Right People to their peers by perfectly articulated word of mouth; there was a short list, winnowed from a far larger one, of persons who, when accommodation became available, could be invited to fill it in the sure knowledge that none of the already-chosen guests would, on that account, complain to neighbours, let alone to the management, that the Hotel Spencer wasn't what it used to be.

The hotel was on the west, considered best, side of Portman Street – convenient to Regent's Park, a stroll farther north from the northern end of the street, and (though Oxford Street intervened) to Bond Street and other thoroughfares of nice shops, all to the south, in or adjacent to Mayfair, and with the streets of surgeries (Harley, etc.) hearteningly handy eastwards. Before the bricks and mortar had become the Hotel Spencer, they had made four identical four-storeyed and basemented houses of a terrace. Nothing had been done to the façades, which were already visually linked by a wrought-iron baluster of the balconies of the first-floor-front, french-windowed rooms, the most desirable in the hotel; four of the balconies were supported by the Corinthian porches of the front doors, each of which was four marble steps up from the street; the end-doors were permanently bolted, one of the central doors was usually bolted, and the other, the entrance to the hotel, was always locked, requiring guests either to use their keys or to ring a bell that sounded in the hall-porter's box which, jutting from the wall of the manager's office, faced the door. Archways had been cut in the common walls, thereby turning short, lateral passages into long corridors, and an elevator – operated manually, only by servants, by pulling on a rope – had been installed at the centre of the block. In those parts of the hotel that were meant to be noticed by guests, the ceilings were ornate, like wedding-cakes, the walls were covered with red or green flock paper, and red, figured Wilton was laid on the floors.

The basement was not like that. What the eyes of the guests didn't see, their hearts didn't grieve about. The basement was where meals and refreshments were made, the washing-up done, the mock-silverware polished, guests' footwear cleaned, fresh linen and towels stored, soiled linen and towels put by for the daily-visiting launderer, tools and cleaning things kept; it was where the coke-consuming boilers were – continually on the go, warming the upstairs rooms in the cold months and providing piping-hot water all the year round, and (it couldn't be helped) making the whole below-stairs area ever like an oven; it was where all but one of the living-in domestics lived – paying for that right through having their wages docked on account of bed as well as board.

In March 1922, there were five male living-in domestics. The lowliest of them, the pantry-boy, was also the youngest, being barely nineteen, and the newest, having been taken on at the start of the year. He was slightly-built, pale-faced, hook-nosed; he wore his fair, wavy hair longer than was fashionable, brushing it diagonally back from a parting on the left. His name was Henry Julius Jacoby.

He and most of the other servants who did not serve food and drink were superintended by Margaret Harvey, a widow, whose position as housekeeper entitled her to a room in the attic and who was directly responsible to the manager, Frederick Eden, whose living quarters were next to but larger than hers and who was also assisted by two under-managers and a maitre-d'hotel, each of whom had a room in the attic of the same size as Mrs Harvey's.

One of the longest-served guests was Lady Alice White, the 65-year-old daughter of an army officer, who, having stayed at the hotel, on and off, since 1914, following the death of her husband, Sir Edward White, whose second wife she was, had taken up permanent residence there in the summer of 1921. Her husband, who had begun his career as a working stonemason, had created a construction company that, while growing large, carried out several important projects in the West End. Helpfully to his business interests and associates, he became a local councillor, calling himself a Moderate & Municipal Reformer: he was for many years chairman of the Marylebone Vestry (which was supposed to work for the good of the rate-payers of that borough, the owners of the Hotel Spencer among them), later represented Marylebone on the London County Council, and in 1911 was elected chairman of the LCC. During his term in the latter office, the foundation-stone of the new County Hall was laid, and – presumably therefore – he was knighted. He left effects that were officially valued at about £35,000 (the present-day purchasing-power of which would be close to half a million), the beneficiaries of the estate being his seven children, some of whom were Lady Alice's as well; she received an annuity of £350. As cash, shares, and property (including, it seems, a house in Upper Berkeley Street, Mayfair) had been hived off to her long before his death, the annuity was her pin-money. Or rather, perhaps, her philanthropic money – for she contributed to many causes that she thought good, and was an extremely generous pedestrian, doling out silver coins to flag-sellers and beggars from a regularly replenished fund of them in a particular pocket of her purse.

Gossip at the Hotel Spencer – which was much the same, whether among guests and their visiting confidants or among the staff – had it that Lady White was uncordial with all of her children and most of her step-children, an assumption based on the fact that, though she received lots of visitors, the only relative who came to see her was her step-son Arthur, who practised as a dentist in one of the streets of surgeries. When he visited her early in March, she, savouring gossip as much as the next guest, gave him a whispered, don't-look-now account of incidents in the lives of other guests present in the drawing-room, which was on the first floor; an incident common to several was attendance at the recent wedding in Westminster Abbey of the King's only daughter, Princess Mary, to Henry Lascelles, the elder son of the fifth Earl of Harewood. Perhaps with a hint of sour grapes, for she had not been invited to the ceremony, she whispered comically of the attire and accoutrements of the women guests who *had* been invited – and, so much less confidentially that Arthur became a trifle embarrassed, complained that one of the women still hadn't returned her 'enormous amount of jewellery' to its safe-deposit, and was thus 'making a danger for the rest of the people in the hotel'.

During the evening of 13 March, a Monday, Lady White played auction-bridge in the drawing-room with three other widow-guests – one of whom, Adeline Grainger, Lady White's partner, would subsequently insist, and keep on insisting, that they did not play for cash. The last rubber was completed at ten minutes to eleven, and the partners vanquished by Lady White and Mrs Grainger instantly exeunted, blaming each other for the defeat. Though whichever of them opened the door did not do so abruptly enough to make a draught that caused the french-windows to burst open, that *had* happened at least once or twice in the past, much to the annoyance of Mrs Grainger; and as she followed Lady White over to the fire – which Alfred Platt, the night-porter, wearing a green monkey-jacket, had banked up a few minutes before – she complained retrospectively of those happenings, saying that it was a positive disgrace that the work-man who was supposed to see to window-catches hadn't seen to this one, and that the under-manager who was supposed to see to it that the workman saw to window-catches was neglectful of seeing to it. There is no information as to whether or not Lady White tut-tutted in agreement. Perhaps she tagged an addendum to the complaint, noting that there was such an insufficiency of upright chairs in the drawing-room that she had had to bring one from her own room to make four around the card-table. Admittedly, she had not had to bring it far: her room was next door to the drawing-room. She and Mrs Grainger sat by the fire for twenty minutes, till ten past eleven. Noticing that she looked 'rather pale and tired', Mrs Grainger insisted on carrying the chair back as far as the door of Lady White's room. There they said good-night. The last Mrs Grainger saw of her neighbour, she was switching on the light in her room and going inside, trailing the chair behind her. But for the superstition, the number of her room would have been, not 14, but 13.

Before the ormolu clock in the entrance hall had sounded the last of its muted chimes at midnight, Alfred Platt, confident that all of the guests were within, began the first of his rounds – this one to ensure that unnecessary lights were out, that the quarter-globe guard of wire-mesh was tight against the fireplace in the drawing-room, that the cloakrooms were tidy and unblemished. If he had had his way, he would have combined this round and the one that followed, the purpose of which was to collect grubby shoes from outside guests' doors and, with each pair carefully united and identified by a label showing the room-number, carry the loaded collecting-basket to the basement – where, taking his time before daylight, he brushed and buffed the shoes, and then, all finished, retraced the steps of his second round, meanwhile depositing the pairs of gleaming shoes appropriately. But Mr Eden, the manager, fearing that Alfred's mind was unversatile – that if he had to think concurrently of more than a few disparate duties, the risk might arise that, say, Lieutenant-General Bincks (Retd.), of room No. 27, would be offered the pompommed winkle-pickers of the Hon. Penelope ffolkes, of room No. 72, and she his burly veldschoens – was adamant that Alfred's first two rounds had to have different purposes. And so it was nearly half-past one when Alfred, having lugged the basket of shoes down to the entrance hall, rested there and, still puffing a bit, rolled a cigarette, meaning to have a quiet smoke before continuing, basket and all, to the basement.

As he was about to light up, he became aware that Henry Jacoby, the pantry-boy, was standing by the door to the basement. It gave him rather a start. He was on the point of reminding the boy that he, the most menial of the servants, was not permitted to ascend even a single step above the ground floor: that, dressed as he was, with a jacket and trousers that didn't match only partially covering striped pajamas, he was taking a liberty by coming anywhere near where guests might be – but decided that he had better not say anything, not yet awhile at any rate, because of the further observation that the boy, as well as being wide-eyed, as if from fright, was tapping his lips with a finger. Alfred watched, a match in one hand, its box and the ragged fag in the other, as the boy tiptoed to within muttering distance of him – and strained to catch the muttered words, which were to the effect that Jacoby, awoken by collywobbles, had got out of bed, meaning to go to the lavatory, the route to which was through the kitchen, but had stopped short of his intended destination upon hearing two or more men talking in 'grunted whispers', had flashed his torch around without seeing anyone, and, though he was by then (even more so now) hard-pressed to contain what was rumbling inside him, had thought that Mr Platt, the hotel's expert in observing anything at all suspicious, should be asked to investigate. The latter was in two minds: yes, it was perfectly true, he modestly agreed, that he was eagle-eyed – but it was equally true, thought not to be admitted, that he didn't fancy succeeding in finding two or more trespass-ing men who grunted when they whispered. He went to the porter's box and made himself empty-handed so as to pick up a torch and two old pokers, one of which he gave to Jacoby, at the same time telling him to lead the way down to and in the basement. They looked high – which, in the basement, was no more than a few inches above the head of Alfred Platt, who was the taller – and low; they found no sign of anyone other than sleeping servants, no sign that anyone had trespassed and gone. The porter, relief making him affable, grinned as he said that Jacoby must have heard men talking in the street; and Jacoby – who, strangely enough, no longer needed to relieve himself – smiled sheepishly before going back to his little room.

Alfred returned to the entrance hall and, after smoking his cigarette, carried the basket downstairs, cleaned its contents, and then did his final, shoes-returning round. At five o'clock, he returned to the basement to stoke the boiler; then, all of a sudden encumbered with chores, he hurriedly unlocked the doors to the basement areas, front and back, took in the crates of milk that had just been left outside one of those doors, awoke the servants (or, speaking of Jacoby, believed that he did), ran up the two flights of stairs to the drawing-room, there to rekindle the fire, and then, moist by this time, ran up to the attic to tap on the doors of the rooms occupied respectively by Mrs Harvey, the housekeeper, and the under-manager who was on the early turn. And that, so he imagined, was the last of his labours prior to half-past eight that night, when he was due to take over from the day-porter, a living-out employee who, like himself, did twelve-hour stints.

At five past eight, twenty-five minutes before Alfred, prematurely somnolent in the porter's box, was due to clock off, a squeak of alarm, emitted from the region of the first floor that was almost exactly above his head, caused him to sit up straight. There was a patter of feet on the stairs down to the entrance hall. That sound too was made by Sarah Pocock, the 20-year-old chambermaid for the first floor. She was carrying a cup of tea. Though she was trembling, almost hysterical, none of the tea had slopped in the saucer.

The reason for her untoward behaviour was this:

Having delivered early-morning tea from her trolley to those occupants of rooms 1 to 12 who took it, she poured a cup for Lady White, tapped on the door of room No. 14 and, without waiting for a reply, entered. The only sound was the bombastic ticking of a tiny clock on the bedside table. When Lady White had applied for permanent residence at the hotel, requesting a large room, she had been advised that the only large room available, No. 14, was presently twin-bedded, but that one of the beds could be removed or both could be replaced by a double bed; she had, for some reason, preferred to leave things as they were, and, perhaps after trying both beds, had settled on the one farther from the door.

Sarah Pocock found the room twilit, faintly buff-coloured, as she usually had when entering it at this time of the morning, for Lady White, who occasionally suffered from insomnia but who was frightened of side-effects of soporifics, always drew the canvas blind over the french-window and drew back the green-and-gold striped curtains before retiring. She also believed that she slept better when wearing a veil, and she had a small collection of them, each attachable around her forehead by means of a circle of elastic, each dyed a different colour. One of the veils was dyed a dark pink.

Sarah casually glanced at Lady White as, still balancing the cup and saucer, she moved towards the window to pull the cord that made the blind roll out of sight behind the valance; she saw

that Lady White was lying propped up against the pillows, as if
waiting for her tea, and that, whereas the flowered eiderdown
was usually pushed to the foot of the bed, it was at full stretch,
tidy and symmetrical – and she thought she saw that Lady White
was wearing her dark-pink veil.

Turning from the now-unblinded windows, she saw – and a
moment later realised that she was seeing – that Lady White was
not wearing a veil. The coloured stuff covering her face was not
gauze; was not dark pink but brownish red. The things that, in the
half-light, she had assumed were curlers in Lady White's dark but
greying hair were splinters of bone, bits of brain-tissue; the hair,
every tress of it, was an awful auburn. The top pillow was
drenched with blood. The headboard was no longer recognisable
as of mahogany; the wall behind it, above and on each side, was
splashed, and there was a puddle between the beds, most of it
shadowed by the table that separated them, and upon which the
tiny clock with the loud tick was hooded with blood as if by an
egg-cosy.

Sarah must have smelt the blood when she entered the room;
one's senses can be misled by contexts that the mind says are
inappropriate to what is sensed: Sarah, her mind confident that
room No. 14 could not smell like an abattoir, must have sub-
consciously ignored that smell, and smelt what her memory of
many early-morning visits had led her to expect: the smell of
4711 Eau-de-Cologne, cachous, prettily-fashioned soaps, naph-
thalene, lavender-tinctured furniture-polish, starch on the
sheets – ingredients, no longer individual, of the special, perhaps
unique aroma that Lady White and some servants of the Hotel
Spencer had unwittingly composed. It was when Sarah's mind
accepted the different smell, making her want to vomit, that she
fled from the room. Symptomatic of the discipline that kept her
off the dole, she closed the door behind her.

A squeak of alarm, hurried footsteps – in the Hotel Spencer,
they constituted a commotion. Before Sarah could blurt out the
reason for her untoward behaviour to Alfred Platt, made moon-
faced by perplexity, the early-turn under-manager emerged from
the office, and Mrs Harvey cruised into the entrance hall from
wherever she had been. Sarah gave them a rough idea of why she
was distraught. Mrs Harvey ordered Alfred to remove Sarah to
the basement. As Mrs Harvey and the under-manager started –

sedately – up the stairs, Alfred advised Sarah to take a sip of the still-steaming tea, but she declined, pointing out that it was more than her job was worth to be caught using the guests' Doulton crockery.

Mrs Harvey and the under-manager, having confirmed Sarah's account – and having ascertained, to their surprise, that Lady White was still alive – decided that the circumstances justified awakening Mr Eden. They ascended to his quarters and told him what they had seen in room No. 14. He asked the under-manager if he had telephoned for a doctor. The under-manager, who hadn't, said of course he had, and went back to the office to do so. And, on his own initiative, he telephoned Arthur White, whose number was in a ledger of guests' next-of-kin, to tell him that his step-mother had 'met with some sort of accident' and to suggest that he should come to the hotel.

While Mr Eden dressed, Mrs Harvey instructed the chamber-maid for the second floor, who had almost reached the end of the corridor with her tea-trolley, to make haste right to the end and at once take over Sarah Pocock's trolley, starting – she emphasised this – at room No. 15. She then went to the basement, where Sarah was the centre of attention, and warned that if anything Sarah or the now-ascended Alfred had said reached the ears of any guest or journalist, the informer would be unemployed before the day was out.

Now came a lull. Quite a long one. The under-manager paced the entrance hall; so did Mrs Harvey; and when Mr Eden arrived there, spruce as could be, he did too – but they paced separately, pretending that they were not pacing at all, and whenever a guest came in sight, they nodded and smiled with the degree of deferentiality that was apt to their respective positions in the hotel's hierarchy. Alfred Platt, told by one of his superiors that he was to stay on duty though the day-man had arrived, did his best, which wasn't very good, to look continuously on the point of clocking off. It would be fascinating to know how the early-morning rush below stairs was amended: in particular, whether or not Henry Jacoby contributed (indeed, as the most menial of the servants, was permitted to contribute) to what must have been a wild surmise; but, probably because Mrs Harvey's Warning rang in the servants' ears, giving them the shivers, even when some of them no longer needed to fear her, the scene has never been described first-hand.

Frederick Eden exhibited patience that was both remarkable and – considering that, when last seen, Lady White was still alive – remarkably stupid. At half-past nine, about an hour and a quarter after the under-manager had telephoned for a doctor, that doctor had still not arrived. Only then did Mr Eden tell the under-manager to telephone for a different doctor. That doctor arrived about half an hour later, and was ushered into the office; he was still there when the other doctor turned up. The doctors were dressed almost exactly as were the managers, whom they eventually followed upstairs, Mrs Harvey having meanwhile returned to whatever she had been interrupted in doing two hours before.

Either the doctors took three-quarters of an hour to agree that Lady White was still alive but beyond their joint ability to save from death, and to suggest to Mr Eden that the police should be informed, or they took a shorter time – and the rest of the three-quarters of an hour, till eleven o'clock, was taken up by Mr Eden's appraisal of the suggestion. He himself made the telephone call – not to the local station but to New Scotland Yard – to Frederick Wensley, the recently appointed Superintendent of the Criminal Investigation Department. Before explaining the reason for the call, he explained who he was, stressed that the Hotel Spencer was a most respectable place, and requested that only one, or at most two, detectives, of the most discreet sort, should be sent there. Wensley listened to all that, gave an assurance that the investigation would be as clandestine as was practical, and as soon as Mr Eden had rung off, passed on part of what he had heard to Detective-Superintendent Arthur Neil – who, in turn, passed on part of what he had heard to Detective-Inspector George Cornish, at the station in Marylebone Lane, just to the east of Portman Street.

Cornish – who was referred to by some policemen, speaking behind his back, as 'the pasty' – seems to have been born under a lucky star. Throughout his career as a plain-clothes officer of the Metropolitan Police (ending in 1933, by which time he had been promoted to the rank of superintendent and was stationed at Scotland Yard), he was assigned to many sensational murder cases: most of the murderers either were waiting to confess when he appeared or were profligate with evidence of their guilt, and the others who were convicted owed that misfortune to observations or deductions made by investigators who were junior to and cleverer than Cornish.[1] He had so many deficiencies that it is hard to say which was the worst: perhaps it was his tendency to go galloping off in all directions; perhaps it was his quaint idea of the arithmetic of logic, which, time after time, gave him the answer of three or five when he put two and two together.

But he may not have been altogether to blame for the initial cock-up at the Hotel Spencer: it may be that Neil's résumé to him of Wensley's résumé of what Eden had said made the case sound like *The Crime of the Century*, requiring the presence at the scene of every available policeman of the Marylebone Division, uniformed as well as plain-clothed, and that therefore, as he rushed out, determined to be first on the spot, he shouted an order to that effect – and another to the effect that every national newspaper was to be informed that something (he wasn't sure what, but whatever it was was certainly sensational) had happened at the Hotel Spencer, Portman Street, London, W.1.

The under-manager who had telephoned Arthur White had been over-successful in sounding unperturbed. Gathering that his step-mother was recovering from a fainting fit, something like that, Mr White spent the morning extracting, filling and cleaning other people's teeth, and then, at noon, the usual time at which he began his lunch-break, strolled from his surgery towards the hotel. But as soon as he came in sight of the building, he quickened his pace – the reason being that the stretch of pavement by the entrance was hidden underfoot; and so were the steps leading up to the door – which, most unusually, were wide open. Arrived among the outdoor crowd, he pushed his way through it – only to find that that crowd was the preliminary to a larger, indoor one, filling the hall. The unsheltered members of the entire assembly were persons swayed from being passers-by; the rest were motley – detectives, reporters, guests of the hotel, uniformed policemen, press-photographers, hall-porters (two of them, crammed together in a box made for one; they looked, in

[1] *Anyone wishing to learn about any of the cases in which he was involved should avoid his memoirs,* Cornish of the Yard, *published by The Bodley Head two years after his retirement; he, or the ghost-writer, omitted or perverted every one of the many facts that proved that he was a poor detective.*

their green monkey-jackets, rather like bottled gherkins); standing abreast on the main staircase, so as to prevent anyone who was not accompanied by Mr Eden ascending it, were the early-turn under-manager and Mrs Harvey, the more daunting of the pair. As no one was standing guard at the door to the basement, some reporters were down there – getting no truck from the servants but nosing around and taking notes, in case a description of the nether-region became important to the story or useful towards filling a column.

No one asked Arthur White why he was pushing his way to the office. Having reached the grey-glassed door of it, panting by then, he entered it. He may have knocked first. Mr Eden, who only appeared to be calm, introduced him to Inspector Cornish, who seemed oblivious of the shemozzle in the hall, and one of them told him that Lady White had been attacked and, if she was not yet dead, was dying. Mr Eden – and Inspector Cornish – accompanied him upstairs.

At about that time, a laundry van drew up by one of the outside entrances to the basement. The driver carried clean stuff inside, and lugged bundles of soiled stuff into the van. One of the bundles may have contained servants' personal linen.

Lady White was still alive when her step-son saw her. The two quite private doctors were sitting by the window of room No. 14, chatting so as to while away the time until she died, and a police surgeon, whose name was Sturgeon, was carrying out what amounted to a pre-mortem examination. He was confident that he would soon be able to make a more thorough examination at the mortuary (but he was wrong in that regard; Lady White did not die until some time before three o'clock on the following morning, when the quite private doctors – who, if they were paid for their attendance by the hour, were pleasantly exhausted – agreed that there was no pulse). Of the notes made by Sturgeon following his examination at the bedside, only a few need to be reported here:

'There was probably more than one blow, struck with a considerable amount of force with some heavy, blunt instrument. The laceration of the scalp extended for nearly eight inches. There was a very extensive fracture of the skull, and the bones had been splintered into several pieces. Unconsciousness would have resulted from the first blow.' Sturgeon noted a heavy bruise on the back of Lady White's left hand. In his opinion – based, it seems, on the fact that he needed to lift the top sheet, blanket and eiderdown so as to observe both hands and forearms – the bruise was not a 'defence wound' from the warding off of a blow.

Inspector Cornish asked Arthur White if he could identify the dying woman. The question, which had to be put as a formality, was more than formal:[1] before answering, Arthur White leaned over the bed, staring at the face, which was 'practically unrecognisable'. He stated that the woman was definitely his step-mother – and then, though he was only a dentist, he was permitted by Dr Sturgeon to examine the wounds; he agreed that she was 'obviously beyond any surgical aid'. Presumably at Cornish's request, he looked in Lady White's purse, which was on the dressing-table, next to her gold fob-watch, which was still going. So far as he could tell, nothing had been taken from the purse; it contained, in addition to the bits and pieces that most women carry in their purses, treasury notes and coins – some of the latter in the pocket of the purse that was for slight philanthropy. He took out a bunch of keys, and used one of them to open her jewellery-box, which he had found in a drawer of the dressing-table; her 'everyday jewellery' was, he said – perhaps revealing that he had an inventorial eye – 'all intact'.

Superintendent Neil – who, though he had put Cornish in charge of the investigation, was the titular head of it – popped in during the early evening. By then, probably on Cornish's orders, a Detective-Sergeant Yard had sent some of the uniformed constables away and got the remainder to clear unauthorised persons from the hall and basement; Detective-Constable Ernest Brown had started taking statements from the domestics – first, Alfred Platt, and second, because of Alfred's reference to the false alarm at half-past one in the morning, Henry Jacoby; other detectives had carried out a 'thorough' search of the basement; and, Mr Eden's entreaty having been brushed aside, another detective had begun finger-printing guests as well as employees.

---

[1] *Eleven years later, Cornish was put in charge of the hunt for Samuel Furnace – who, until a day or so before, had been thought to be the man whom he had murdered. An account of the hunt, which would have taken less time if Cornish had not been in charge of it, appears in, among other books, my anthology,* The Christmas Murders, *Allison & Busby, London, 1986.*

Soon after Neil's departure, Superintendent Wensley – in full evening dress, because he was going on to a function – spent a few minutes at the hotel; he was told, among other things, the gist of the parts of Alfred Platt's statement that dealt with night-security – and, while being driven to the function, jotted in his notebook, 'Went to Spencer's Hotel re murder of Lady White. No doubt committed by someone inside hotel.'

Wensley's doubtlessness was not shared by Cornish – who, a day or so later, spent part of the day in the flat in Earls Court (a stone's throw to the north of Finborough Road) of an elderly widow named Constance Sharp who had been attacked by an intruder whom she described negatively as 'not a working-class man'. The attack had occurred soon after the attack on Lady White and no more than a mile and a half south-west of the Hotel Spencer; the attacker had broken into the flat with a jemmy – 'a heavy, blunt instrument' (but had not used it also as a weapon); he had not stolen anything. Those were the items of information that led Cornish to suspect that one man had committed both crimes. Evaluation of his suspiciousness should take account of the fact that, compared with the presently large number of conspicuous press reports of attacks on elderly widows, there were few such reports in 1922.

On Wednesday, 15 March (the day on which, at 3 a.m., the crime at the Hotel Spencer became a murder), Cornish spent part of the morning reading witness statements; as his mind was set on the idea that the murder had been committed by an outsider, his eyes focused on those passages of the statements of Alfred Platt and Henry Jacoby that dealt with the latter's *apparently* false alarm. In the afternoon, he reported to Superintendent Neil at Scotland Yard – and made such particular reference to the *apparently* false alarm that Neil told him to have Platt and Jacoby collected from the hotel for further questioning.

Delivered, they were interviewed, one after the other, by both Neil and Cornish. The night-porter did not retract or amend anything in his statement; nor did he augment or embellish it. The pantry-boy made no retractions or amendments. But, as if relishing the detectives' interest in him, basking in the belief that he really was a Big I Am, he chattered irrelevantly; he was, they thought, 'pretending to act a part in a sensational film or play': though he had not been given a cue to talk about his background, he did so, saying that he had attended a school at St Albans, Bedfordshire, and that he had worked on his grandmother's smallholding near that town until she died, when he had landed the job at the Hotel Spencer. The two servants, who had been driven to Scotland Yard – the first time that Jacoby had ridden in a motor-car – were left to make their own way back to the hotel.

Neil and Cornish conferred – and consequently, that evening, the latter sent one of his men to the hotel to ask Jacoby the addresses of his school and his grandmother's smallholding. Jacoby gave addresses – and then said that his father lived in Goswell Road, in the City; that he would like another word with Inspector Cornish. Having left a note for Mrs Harvey, explaining that he was giving the police a hand, he accompanied the detective to the station in Marylebone Lane. There, he told Cornish that he had lied (he didn't explain why, and Cornish didn't enquire) when saying that he had lived most of his life at St Albans: actually, his birthplace was in the City, and until shortly before his move to the hotel, he had lived with his father in a house rented by his grandmother in Goswell Road. The note-taking constable, just checking, asked: '"Shortly"?' – and Jacoby nodded, explaining that he had run away from home with £30 that he had stolen from a lodger.

According to Cornish's published memoirs, he at once 'decided to detain Jacoby while further inquiries were made about him'; according to evidence given at Jacoby's trial, he did not. The latter version appears to be accurate: I have found no report of Jacoby's detention in newspapers – all reporting everything worth reporting about the case, and much that wasn't – that appeared between 15 and 19 March; and I have found no mention in those papers of a prolonged absence by Jacoby from the hotel. It is safe to say that several things that the investigators should have done before Sunday the 19th were left undone; that several things they did do before that Sunday were done ineffi-ciently; that a finding from one thing that *was* done efficiently before that Sunday either was not communicated to Cornish or was ignored by him. The finding was that, of all the heavy and blunt tools found in the basement or picked from the baskets of workmen who were decorating a room in the hotel that week, only one, a hammer, looked much-used but as clean as a new pin.

Supposing that Jacoby did not spend the Friday night and most of the next day at the police station in Marylebone Lane, he was collected from the basement of the Hotel Spencer at about 7.45 on the Saturday evening (right in the middle of the dinner rush-hour – but that, the collecting detective would have said, couldn't be helped) and escorted to the station – where (suggestive of the fact that the inconvenient time of his collection could have been helped) he was locked in Inspector Cornish's office, alone and more and more palely nervous, for an hour and a half, till 9.30, when Cornish and other detectives entered and started asking him questions, some of the answers to which were noted in writing. The questioning went on, without a break for Jacoby, until 11.30 on the Sunday morning. During the fourteen hours, Superintendents Wensley and Neil visited the station, each at a different time.

Presumably, once the session was closed, Jacoby was given breakfast – brunch. Certainly, he was given a newspaper: that day's *News of the World* – parted and folded quite ingeniously, so that parts of two pages were visible: the left-hand half of page 9, which was composed of pictures of Lady White and the Hotel Spencer and of a report headed **LONDON HOTEL MURDER/ TITLED LADY'S UNKNOWN ASSAILANT/£1,000 Reward Offered**; and the foot of the front page, which had, within a bold-ruled frame, a bold-typed announcement that the reward 'will be paid by the "News of the World" to any person, other than members of the Police Force, who shall hereafter supply information leading to the arrest and conviction of the murderer of Lady White . . . All information must be sent direct to New Scotland Yard and not to the "News of the World".' Cornish subsequently derided the notion that he or any of his helpers led Jacoby to believe that, though he (Cornish), they, and the rest of the constabulary were not permitted to receive gratuities for civil services rendered, if the murderer of Lady White supplied information leading to his own arrest and conviction, he would be entitled to the reward.

Jacoby was left alone to look at the paper; but it is reasonable to guess that he was covertly observed, partly to ensure that he did not fall asleep while reading or trying to hum 'I Belong to Glasgow', the words and music of which filled the foot of a page of the paper that had not been made prominent.

At seven o'clock in the evening, either he asked to speak to Cornish (which is what Cornish subsequently swore on the Bible happened) or he was told to prepare himself for another questioning session (which is what he subsequently swore on the Bible happened – adding, still under oath, that he became 'partly hysterical').

By eight o'clock, he had made a full confession, and most of what he had said had been written in longhand by a Detective-Constable Somerset on buff-coloured, lined sheets of foolscap, and he, having been told that he could read what had been written if he wanted to, had put his initials on all but the last page and signed that. The statement contained, among other admissions and explanations, these:

'I did it. I hit her on the head with one of the workmen's hammers.'

About half an hour before, he really had got up to go to the lavatory – really had thought that he heard men whispering. After alerting Alfred Platt and searching the basement with him, he had gone back to his room. Sitting on the bed, he had wondered if the men he still believed he had heard were robbers; then he had wondered, what if he himself robbed a guest? – would suspicion fall on the men whom he and the night-porter had failed to find? He had come to the conclusion that there was a better-than-even chance of that.

'It occurred to me to prepare for an emergency, and so I went to the room where the workmen's tools were kept. I opened one of the workmen's baskets. I first picked up a long rasp. Afterwards I decided to take a hammer, in case anyone got in the way.'

(There was a note to the statement at this point, recording that Jacoby said, 'I will draw the hammer for you if you like,' and that one of the detectives gave him a pencil and paper to do so.)

He had put the hammer in his jacket-pocket and crept up a back staircase to the first floor.

'I tried one bedroom door. It was locked. Then I tried another, which had been left unlocked. I went in and saw that there were two beds, and that there was a woman in the bed nearest the window.'

Lady White had awoken. She had let out a small cry.

'Then I got the wind up and hit her on the head with the hammer, striking her at least twice. Then I went out and washed the bloodstained hammer under a tap in the basement. I dried it with a handkerchief and put it back where I found it. Then I went back to bed.

'I don't know how anyone could help giving themselves up after doing a murder. We don't think of the punishment that comes after.'

Having initialled and signed the confession, Jacoby pleaded to be allowed to sleep. Not yet awhile, he was told.

Perhaps he had already had his pockets felt for articles that could be used destructively, and had had his tie, braces or belt, and shoelaces removed.[1] Now he was searched for material evidence of his guilt. Two handkerchiefs were taken from him. They were bloodstained – and if his explanation for that was true, they must have been disgustingly grubby. He explained that the blood was from his nose – injured during a 'friendly' fight with Alfred Platt nearly a fortnight before. Alfred subsequently confirmed that he and Jacoby *had* done 'some practice sparring' that had given Jacoby a nose-bleed – and he mentioned, in passing, that they were both in shirtsleeves at the time.

Alfred's by-the-way remark caused the detective to whom it was made think of something that he or a colleague should have thought of unaided: that although, according to Alfred's statement regarding the early-morning false alarm, Jacoby was then wearing a dark-blue jacket over his pajama-top – and although the implication from Jacoby's confession was that he wore the same jacket while committing the crime – the jacket he had worn uniformly during the past six days was dark grey. Odd, that. Jacoby, asked where his dark-blue jacket was, said that he had hidden it in the basement, and gave such precise directions as to its whereabouts that one of the detectives who had taken

[1] *When Samuel Furnace (mentioned in the previous footnote) was eventually apprehended, he was searched so inadequately that he was left with a bottle of spirits of salts – which, some hours later, he drank, thereby killing himself.*

part in the thorough search of the basement found the garment without too much difficulty. It was heavily stained with blood.

The hammers, eight in all, that had been collected, together with other heavy, blunt tools, were paraded on a table. Jacoby, asked if he recognised the murder-weapon among them, pointed to the one that looked much-used but as clean as a new pin. In fact, it was not that clean: microscopic examination of the head revealed a spot of something, probably blood, in a dent.

It is a pity that there is no reliable information concerning the time that elapsed between Jacoby's final assistance to the police in their inquiries and Cornish's charging of him with the wilful murder of Lady White. That charge was made on the evening of Monday, 20 March. The fact that he, usually so talkative, did not reply may be taken to mean that he either did not comprehend Cornish's recitation or was too tired to speak.

He soon perked up. Next morning, when he appeared at Marylebone Police Court to be remanded in custody, reporters observed that he seemed 'jaunty' – that he 'exhibited a keen interest in the proceedings'. He was taken on a short ride south, to Brixton Prison, and (as was the practice in regard to prisoners remanded on the charge of murder) lodged in a room in the hospital-block. He chattered to anyone who came near – warders, doctors interested in his mental state, convict-trustees acting as waiters, the two partnered solicitors who had volunteered their services. He pleaded to be told what the papers were saying about him. He commented that the prison cuisine was not as good as that at the Hotel Spencer. One day he received a surprise-visit from a man – slim and dark; macassar-oil shining and scenting his moustache as well as his hair – who was also a non-patient inmate of the hospital-block. Jacoby realised at once that the man was a *gentle*man, a toff, and, knowing his place, stood to a sort of attention. The man indicated that Jacoby should stand at ease – stand easy. He drooped one of his manicured hands ahead of him, and Jacoby, hoping that he understood aright, shook it with one of his unkempt hands. The man, assuming that everybody, but everybody, knew who he was, did not otherwise introduce himself. He chuckled before and while saying: 'Here's another for our murderers' club! We only accept those who kill them outright.' He was still chuckling as the warder whom he had eluded caught up with him and led him back to his quarters.

His name was Ronald True.

He was three months away from his thirty-first birthday. He had been born in the district of Manchester called Chorlton-on-Medlock to a sixteen-year-old spinster and – if a birth-certificate made out six weeks after his birth is to be believed – a youth of seventeen who described himself as a 'journalistic artist'. Already, though he had been famous for only a matter of weeks, all persons in the land who could take hints from what the papers were careful not to say were sure that his father was someone else: someone of eminence, inherited or achieved – aristocratic? – well, certainly no lower on the social scale; of the blood royal? – well, that couldn't be ruled out. The most favoured choice was a military man who, never mind that his blunders had caused a slaughter of Tommies on the Western Front in the first year or so of the Great War, had soon afterwards been created a peer of the realm: the fact that he could only have been True's father if True's mother had been in British India nine months before the unhappy event (as he was commanding Hussars in that dominion at the impregnating time) – and there was no evidence that she had travelled virginally from Manchester farther than Blackpool – does not seem to have diminished his odds-on favouriteness.

But anyway, whoever True's father was, his mother's first eleven years of motherhood seem to have been made worrying only by his naughtiness, never by shortage of funds; and from then on, she having at last married, and married into money, she was even better off – and he received an allowance that was not far short of the wages of junior masters at Bedford Grammar School, where he had just been accepted as a pupil (and where he would remain, his term-reports always bad, till the age of eighteen). When he was in Form 3c, he was visited by an aunt, Mrs Grace Angus (who, as his mother's maiden-name was Angus, was either her sister-in-law or – and this, though it may seem improbable, is more likely – a sister who had married a man also surnamed Angus. True had been christened *Angus* Ronald, but the first of those names, which may have been chosen simply to please Angus-surnamed relatives, appears never to have

caught on: there is no indication that he was ever called anything
but Ronald or, to his displeasure, Ronnie). The purpose of Mrs
Angus's visit was to inform young Ronald that his mother was
gravely ill. Before changing the subject to one that he considered
important – the runners and riders in the 2.30 at Newmarket,
perhaps – he showed that there was a generous side to his nature
by remarking: 'Oh, well, if she dies, all her property will be
mine, and I'll give you her two best rings straight away, and you
can have anything you like of her things and jewellery.'

As he was clearly unsuited to any of the professions or voca-
tions that engrossed the generality of Old Bedfordians,[1] he
became a remittance man: at first – and until, after a year, he
could no longer bear the interminable sheep – in New Zealand;
and then in, among other under-developed places, Argentina,
Canada (where he served in the North-West Mounted Police,
but not long enough to be troubled by saddle-rash), and Mexico;
by 1914, when he was twenty-three, he was in Shanghai. If he
had not acquired a taste for morphia earlier, he did so there.
When the war broke out in Europe, he returned home.

Travel does not broaden the mind; if it did, commercial
travellers, long-distance lorry-drivers, and councillors of towns
twinned with foreign ones would be very broad-minded. But it
does broaden some people's vocabularies, though only with
placenames and foreign words; and some other people are
impressed by that. The recruiters for the Royal Flying Corps
who interviewed True can only have been impressed by his
placename-dropping. They were so impressed that – ignoring his
lack of achievement at school and since; failing to notice symp-
toms of his drug-addiction – they gave him a cadetship at
Gosport Flying School with a view to a commission. Having
failed to pass a single examination, though allowed several tries at
some, he was given his wings; dissatisfied with the size of them,
he fashioned others, three times larger, and sewed them on his
tunic. As his cap hurt his head, he usually kept it tucked in a
pocket – putting it on when he needed to salute a superior officer,
and taking it off as soon as he had complied with that showing of
military discipline. He crashed at least three aeroplanes, two of

---

[1] *The most exalted alumnus – Sir Henry Hawkins, Baron Brampton (also
known as The Hanging Judge) – had recently died.*

which were written off; rescued from one of the latter, much of which was strewn about a field at Farnborough, he lay unconscious for two days, and was subsequently treated for severe concussion of the brain. Towards the end of 1916, someone in authority deemed that True's hindrance of the war effort could no longer be afforded, and so he was invalided out of the RFC; he was one of the very few of the very many servicemen with self-inflicted wounds (SIWs for short) to receive honourable discharge.

Shortly before he returned to civilian life, he treated a man whom he had hired as his chauffeur to a variety show at the Coliseum Music Hall in Portsmouth, close to Gosport. He loved the illegitimate theatre, and whenever possible, as it was on this occasion, he occupied a box. Thinking of the treated chauffeur, one is reminded of the question, 'But apart from that, Mrs Lincoln, how did you enjoy the play?' – for the chauffeur was often distracted from the performance, sometimes because of True's terror that an assassin was lurking at the back of the box, and, less frequently and in common with the occupants of the adjoining box, by True's whimpered complaints that he had a dreadful pain in his right hip. The pain may have been a symptom of syphillis – from which, although it was undetected by doctors who examined him soon afterwards, he was certainly suffering. Those doctors were on the staff of a military hospital to which True had been taken for observation – curtailed when a member of his family arranged for him to be transferred to a private nursing-home in Southsea, the holiday-resort part of Portsmouth. A doctor at the nursing-home prescribed morphia to ease the pain. As normal doses had no effect – because of True's long experience of the drug – the doctor prescribed larger doses. True topped those up with morphia and other drugs that he acquired from shady chemists in the town and from the bribed key-holder of the drugs-cabinet at the home.

Already, far too many people deserved punishment for sins of commission or omission in regard to True; but their sins pale towards pettiness in comparison with that of the recruiter at the Government Control Works at Yeovil, Somerset, who interviewed True early in 1917, following his release from the nursing-home, and took him on as a test-pilot. (In the spring of 1922, when the True-Father guessing-game swept the country, some of the players of it who plumped for a military solution cited the acceptance of True, first into the RFC, then as a government test-pilot, which seemed doubly suggestive of string-pulling, as grounds for their guess. Some twenty years later, during the Second World War, my own father, who had served as an airman for the last two years of the First – initially as a member of the RFC, and then, following the amalgamation of the RFC and the Royal Naval Air Service, as a member of the Royal Air Force – gave me a heavily-censored account of the Ronald True case, and insisted that the 'dotty blackguard' [I clearly recall that term] could only have got into the RFC through nepotism; but my father's argument was weakened, though I didn't dare say so, by the fact that he himself had not reached the official minimum age for service in the RFC until it and the RNAS had become the RAF.)

Test-Pilot True's sole contribution to the science of aeronautics was a repetitive confirmation that what goes up in the hands of a maniac is likely to come down much faster, nose-first, and with a bump so damaging that it can never go up again. Perhaps because he crashed such a large number of aeroplanes, and was concussed more often than he was not, neither his crashes nor his concussions were tallied on his record-sheet; or perhaps the absence of the information was due to slight dilatoriness of the part of the records-clerk, he or she having put a day aside to get the True-sheet fairly up to date, only to be told not to bother as True had been dimissed without notice. He must have been given his cards after no more than a month or so, around about when the United States entered the war, because by June 1917 he was in Manhattan, a toast of the town on account of the natives' swallowing of his tale that he, an ace fighter-pilot, had shot down squadrons of Boche aircraft over France, collecting unwanted and since-discarded medals galore, until a bullet fired by the Red Baron, fleeing from him at the time, had proved so nearly mortal that he had been commanded by his chum George, the King, to give up fighting for Him and Country. The person most influentially taken in was a young actress, Frances Roberts. He and she were wed on 5 November. By then, he – perhaps without the aid and abetment of anyone back home – had beguiled the US War Department into accepting him as an instructor at their flying school at Mineola,[1] on Long Island; he had already crashed one aeroplane, causing worse injury to the trainee-passenger than to himself. Before the end of the year, the school was moved to Houston, Texas; he went with it, leaving Frances, engaged for a Broadway show, behind. They were apart till the following summer, when he returned to Manhattan, having meanwhile spent weeks in Houston (no longer because, having met, proposed to, and gone through a form of marriage with a local girl, all in the space of a few days, he ran up so many bills during the honeymoon that he felt impelled to do a midnight-flit, deserting the girl and escaping beyond the jurisdiction of Texas Rangers), months in Mexico City (for much of the time in hospital, being treated for a 'chest complaint'), and a fortnight or so in Havana.

In July 1918, he returned to England; Frances (who, though she may not yet have been sure of it, was pregnant) accompanied him. They were put up by his mother – for six months, which was very nearly the time it took for True to find a job or for somebody to find him one: as an assistant manager of a mine on the Gold Coast, which is now called Ghana. Frances, who was delivered of a baby girl while still recovering from sea-sickness, must also have been suffering from several sorts of shock; and another, of the culture sort, must have been added, if only because the High (and only) Street of the mining settlement of Taquah was more primitive even than the streets of New Haven and certain other American try-out towns where she had performed. Unless she was, liberally, ahead of her time, she cannot have liked being referred to as 'the mammy' by the natives True was supposed to be managing; liberal or not, she was certainly upset when she overheard some of them speaking of True as 'the massa what live with him mammy and is sick by him head'. The fact that part of the westerly-jutting part of Africa, including the Gold Coast, was reputed to be the White Man's

---

[1] *Best known in the geography of crime as the town that was the centre of the diverse investigations into the death of Starr Faithfull, whose body was found on the nearby Long Beach in June 1931. Like the English Evelyn Foster case, about which I have written, the Starr Faithfull case, which I shall soon be writing about, is fascinating partly because of the uncertainty as to whether the death was due to murder, suicide, or accident.*

Grave was used by the owners of the mine as an excuse for
dismissing True: the climate did not suit him, they said (not
bothering to support that assertion with circumstantial evidence
– for instance, that he strolled around the natives' compound,
morn till night, wearing only winceyette pajamas in addition to a
pith-hat and flying-boots), and packed him and Frances – she
now holding the baby – back to England within a few months of
their arrival. Before the departure, True announced that he
intended to start an airline specialising in the carriage of goods
between England and the Gold Coast; the route he mooted was
almost as peculiar as that of Chesterton's rolling English
drunkard, who went to Bannockburn by way of a Brighton pier.
The airline did not get off the ground. Indeed, True never again
did anything bearing the least resemblance to work.

He spent a consecutive six of the twelve months till September
1920 in a sanatorium at Brighton. Frances spent most of those
twelve months professionally – acting, often with an English
accent, in touring productions of plays. There appears to be no
information as to who sat with the baby while Frances was away
from home; nor as to where the home was. Almost certainly, the
home was the property of, or a leasing by, True's mother, and the
baby-sitter an employee of hers.

During his stay in the sanatorium, True was experimented
upon with an assortment of drugs other than morphia, of which
he was given twelve grains each day – a comparatively slight
topping-up of the amounts that he acquired almost as regularly
from chemists in and around Brighton. It may not have been as
an effect of one of the experiments, or of the cocktailing or
curdling of drugs inside him, that he got the idea, which soon
became an obsession, that he was not alone in being Ronald
True. He couldn't help what his namesake was up to: it was bally
unfair, enough to make a decent chap like himself want to cry,
that he was blamed, held responsible, for The Other True's
mistakes and misdemeanours; one of these days, just wait and
see, he would confront his tormentor – and then, mark his words,
there would be the most fearful how-d'ye-do, accounts of which
would be splashed across front pages. The Other True was
clever, almost as clever as he himself was, there was no doubt
about that – but even so, the blighter (who would soon be the
blighter-bit – that was a good one) simply had to have

accomplices. And he was jolly sure who one of them was – his, The Real True's, lady-wife: a better actress offstage than on: a proper little bundle of deceit, all smarm and, excuse the word, fart. Come to think of it, he only had her assurance that he had put her in the family way, that her baby was also his. Perhaps (his mind zigzagged as he tried to work out the new suspicion) the child wasn't hers at all but something produced from those damned monkey-glands that were suddenly all the rage.

He made a will. A hundred quid to the Battersea Dogs' Home, the same to Dr Barnardo's Homes. Sucks-boo to Frances. The child – theirs, hers, whoever's, whatever's – was to be adopted by a woman he named; he hadn't asked her if she was willing to do it, but he was positive that the sweetener of most of his estate would make her agreeable. The executor (he hadn't been approached either) was told that, supposing that by the time his services were required, The Other True was still in the land of the living, strict precautions were to be taken to ensure that he didn't fiddle even a farthing out of what The Real True had left.

When Frances, chancing upon the document, asked True the meaning of parts of it, he said that it was silly of her to expect him to be able to explain things that he had written in a fit of madness. He merely pouted when she said that, in that case, it was sensible to tear it up, and did so.

The discovery and destruction of the will occurred some time after September 1920. That was the month of True's release from the sanatorium at Brighton. Frances, a resting actress then, volunteered to forsake her career on behalf of housewifery and motherhood, and took possession of a part-furnished flat in Portsmouth. (There must have been some reason why the naval town, which True had got to know well in 1916, was chosen.) Frances's self-denial went unappreciated by her husband, who, imaginative with lies as to why he needed to visit London, was more often there than in Portsmouth – and who, when he *was* in Portsmouth, was more often enjoying entertainments intended to satisfy randy sailors than at home. One of his visits to London was so prolonged that Frances, more intrigued than concerned, sent an enquiring telegram to him at an address he had left with her; as his reply, by mail, read like a suicide-note, she felt obliged to travel to London, to establish whether she was a wife or a widow, and, after extensive traipsing and taxi-ing, located him,

only looking like death, in Soho – on the premises of a con-
glomerate organisation that dispensed drugs in and from the
basement, served Italian-style food (sometimes gratuitously to
detectives from the nearby West End Central station) on the
ground floor, and sub-let the rest of the building, in bed-and-a-
bit sized allotments, to pimps. Frances arranged for True to be
despatched back to Portsmouth.

As soon as he recovered (to his usual, which is not to say
normal, state), he paid another visit to London. Of the visits
there that followed, three were extended unpleasurably – one
because he suddenly needed to have his appendix removed, and
two because, at his mother's insistence, he underwent shock-
treatment for drug-addiction in a private clinic. The first period
of treatment was brief – after only a few short sharp shocks,
True, all of a quiver from the last of them and at the prospect of
more, escaped – but the second covered most of November
1921. While it was in progress, Frances, unoptimistic of its
outcome and, anyway, needing a rest, accepted a theatrical
engagement; she advised in-laws that, at least while she was
engaged, a minder for her husband and child was required.
True's aunt, Grace Angus, agreed to serve. And so, when True
left the clinic for the second time, he went to stay with Mrs
Angus, who was already looking after his child, at Folkestone,
on the coast of Kent.

Her nephew, she thought, had become even more strange: it
was dreadful to think such a thing, but sometimes 'his eyes were
those of a certified lunatic'. At first she gently chided him,
carefully neglecting to speak of his worst excesses but saying, for
instance, that a little bird had told her that, in the months
between his escape from the London clinic and his return to it, he
had taken to shop-lifting: that was not only shameful, she said,
but silly, considering that most of the things he had been caught
trying to steal were useless to him. Quite unrepentant, he
bragged that he had never been prosecuted for any crime; but
then, noting from his aunt's expression that she knew different,
muttered that he had only been fined once – during the summer,
when the Portsmouth magistrates had found him guilty of having
obtained morphia by means of forged prescriptions. Keen to
cancel out that single accident, he catalogued the crimes he had
got away with; but then, noting that his aunt was looking dubious

again (at his assertion that, during his last stay in Mexico, he had had a row with a German over a mining claim and had stabbed him to death for two reasons, one being that his fountain-pen had dried up in the torrid heat, leaving him with no means of signing the claim-form unless he gave the pen a transfusion of the argumentative German's blood), he turned the one-sided conversation to his experience of fortune-telling, remarking that three palmists, respectively of Buenos Aires, San Francisco and Shanghai, had assured him that he would die prematurely through some incident involving a young woman. Since the sands of his time were running out, he commented with a chuckle, all he could say was san-fairy-ann! – he really would need to have his head examined if he chucked in the towel and didn't make his short life a gay one.

By the time Christmas came, Mrs Angus needed a rest. Though she – with the child in a pram, with True holding on to it for support rather than as a touching sign of pride in the occupant, for he was again doubtful of the child's provenance – travelled hopefully to where True's mother was spending the festive season, she found no respite there. On the contrary: True's mother, hardly recognising the shambles as her son, implied that it was Mrs Angus's fault that he was hardly recognisable; True, vaguely conscious that the two women were discussing him unflatteringly, took umbrage and muttered that if his mother had been in less of a hurry in becoming one, either he or his defects would never have arisen; and that made his mother weep – copiously when Mrs Angus tried to comfort her; and that started the child crying; and that caused True to scream with vexation; and so on. It was not an enjoyable family-reunion. Long before, in other houses, people were singing Auld Lang Syne, True slammed out of the house, shouting the lie that he was going to Bedford on business. Assuming that his mother, his aunt, his child – any or all of them – ever met him again, it was in a place that could be entered only by appointment.

Frances met him towards the end of January; also at the start of February. Both meetings were in London; both at his request, it seems; on both occasions, he told her that he had come up to town from Bedford. He was affable during the first of the meetings, quite the opposite during the second, which he terminated by suddenly standing up, saying that he was leaving her for good, and leaving. She probably prayed that he had just made one promise that he would not break.

Shortly before or shortly after that meeting, which turned out to be their last in a social setting, he met for the first time, quite by chance, a man named James Adolph Armstrong who had recently been sacked as a used-car salesman – probably because he was the sort of man that no one in his right mind would buy even a used bike from. He was a spiv. But for his inability to hide that fact, he might have achieved his life-long ambition of being a confidence-trickster. True and an acquaintance were having tea at Lyon's Corner House in Leicester Square; Armstrong sidled into the restaurant, was recognised by True's acquaintance as someone he had done a deal with (which doesn't say much for the acquaintance) and was introduced to 'Major True' and invited to share the pot. Even before the 'nippie', acting upon True's finger-click order, had brought a third cup and yet another jug of hot water, Armstrong had evaluated True's clothes and visible accessories, and placed him round about the Daimler mark on a scale rising from Morris to Rolls-Royce. He said what he thought were all the right things. And True, charmed, was reciprocally charming. Their introducer felt left out. Leaving him to pay the bill, they sauntered off together – perhaps to one of the members-only drinking-clubs to which Armstrong, in common with most of the other regular customers, did not belong: the Ham Bone, Rector's, Murray's, or the brand-new 43 – so called because it was at 43 Gerrard Street (the house in which John Dryden had spent his last years), at the back of Leicester Square.

By the following day, at the latest, True and Armstrong were almost inseparable pals. They remained so for about a month. Together, they drank, dined, and went to music halls, picture palaces, boxing arenas, dog tracks – and (though True, because of his bad hip, couldn't dance) dance halls. True didn't mind the expense. Armstrong, rather than being put to any, made a small profit. That came from his sale to True of an automatic pistol and a quantity of fitting cartridges. He roared with laughter when True proposed the formation of a 'murderers' club', the members of which would accept commissions to 'put away' non-members at the rate of 'a bob a nob'. He tittered uncertainly at True's suggestion that they should be partners in an airline in the United States – but was made straight-faced when, a minute later, True telephoned the Cunard Company to arrange for the conveyance of themselves, an aeroplane and a motor-car to New York a.s.a.p. True said nothing more about the scheme. Nor did Armstrong.

There *were* times when the two men were apart: Rarely, and then usually briefly, during the day. Some evenings. Nearly always between small hours and 10 a.m. or so. Armstrong, who was a bachelor, had a bedroom in his mother's house in Cleveland Gardens, near Paddington Station, the terminus of the Great Western Railway. True often slept in expensive hotels – hardly ever in one for two nights running. (Unless he bought or 'lifted' garments when those he was wearing started to stink, and threw those away, he must have had a case of clothing deposited somewhere.) Once or twice, he bedded down in the Savoy Turkish Baths in Jermyn Street. And he occasionally slept with some woman or other.

One of those women was Mrs Elizabeth Wilson, who, unparticular about most things of a formal nature, was most particular about being referred to as Mrs; she insisted upon the use of the title as if fearing that its omission might start a rumour that she was virginal – which, though preposterous, could prove damaging to her social life. On Sunday, 5 February, True accompanied Armstrong to Murray's Club (which was in Beak Street, leading towards Soho from Regent Street), and left without Armstrong but in the company of Mrs Wilson. If not later that day, then during the following eleven, he saw a lot of her; but before the end of that period, she felt that she was seeing far too much of *him* – was telling friends that the Major, whom she had at first considered Funny Ha-Ha, was Funny Peculiar. Instances: If she as much as passed the time of night with another man while he was around, he trembled with rage and went wild-eyed – and on some such occasions produced and threateningly flourished a pistol. Once, in conversation with her, he abruptly changed the subject to murder, saying, 'I will kill somebody one of these days – you watch the papers and see if I don't. I'm perfectly certain I'll get off. I want to try it out.' He telephoned her late one night, apologised for not having rung earlier, and explained that he had been tied up with a family crisis – having called at his mother's house, he had found her lying on the floor, alive despite the fact that her head was battered in, and he, being a loving son, had rushed her to a nursing-home and arranged for a leading surgeon, a *Mr* Wilson, to perform an operation. Next day, Mrs Wilson scoured the papers without spotting the slightest reference to the outrage, and when she saw True in the evening, asked him why that was – and was told, 'I'm keeping it dark; there's to be a big case about it.' Next day, she learned that True's mother was perfectly well, her head unmarred. And, last but not least, there was the strange matter of The Other True.

For some reason, or for none, True never mentioned his invisible *doppelgänger* to Armstrong. He did to Mrs Wilson, though – and she, while pleading with Armstrong to stay close to the Major whenever the latter seemed likely to be heading in her direction, told him what True had told her about The Other True. Understandably muddled, she said she couldn't make up her mind as to which True – her pesterer or his – gave the stronger grounds for fearing that she was in danger. If the Major wasn't exaggerating, then his impending fight to the death with The Other True – guns firing, knives flashing, fists flailing, and so on – could hardly fail to cause damage to innocent persons in the neighbourhood.

Rather as if a 1920s Picasso were given a touch of unreal realism by Magritte, the damned elusive Other True suddenly seemed to turn up – in the person of a Mr Ronald *Trew*, a member of Murray's Club. Hearing of his near-namesake, True insisted that 'Trew' was a deliberate spelling mistake; when people at Murray's insisted to him that Mr Trew was inoffensive, a perfect gentleman, not at all devious, True agreed wholeheartedly, pointing out that all of those qualities were to be expected in an evil master of disguise. The manager of Murray's, keen to keep Mr Trew's custom and anxious to avoid unpleasant scenes, thought of barring True – and might have done so if True had sought admission after 17 February. But True didn't – the reason being that he had cashed a forged cheque at the club, and was apprehensive that if he returned after it had bounced, the club's bouncers would be impolite. He may have signed the cheque 'Trew'; one is left unsure by the manager's subsequent testimony.

True's last visit to the club, on the 17th, was also the last time he saw Mrs Wilson. He and Armstrong had spent the earlier part of the evening watching fights at The Ring, near Waterloo

Station; he paid his bill at the club from five pounds that he had borrowed from Ted Broadribb, the referee at The Ring.[1] Whatever remained of the fiver was all the cash he had. His wallet, plump with treasury notes when he had left his mother's house, some seven weeks before, would now have been as thin as a rake if he had not stuffed it with various visiting-cards, each carrying a different expensive-sounding address. Supposing that the wish-fulfilling delusion that his mother was at death's door had cleared from his mind, the thought of going to her for money was probably countered by his terror that she would grasp the opportunity to get him back into that nursing-home for more shock-treatment. He had to borrow. Or steal. Or swindle. Those were the only alternatives. Other chaps in a similar predicament might stoop to begging their way out of Shit Creek. Not he. His jolly old pride was worth more than rubies, or whatever the saying was.

The fact that True spent the night of Saturday, the 18th, with a prostitute does not necessarily mean that he had borrowed, stolen or swindled cash during the twenty-four hours or so following his final visit to Murray's, his final meeting with Mrs Wilson.

The prostitute's name was Gertrude Yates; but, unhappy with that as a trade-name, she called herself Olive Young. She tried not to think of herself as a prostitute, but as 'a lady with male friends'. She had done very well in the three or four years since she had worked on her feet all day in a West End fur-store: now twenty-five (though claiming that she was twenty-three), she had over £160 in the Post Office Savings Bank, also some real jewellery and a string of Ciro cultured pearls among her custom-alluring trinkets, and was able to afford, not only the weekly rent of forty-three shillings on a nice little flat (admittedly a bit dark, as it was in a basement, but made to look cosy – and inviting – by

---

[1]*Broadribb had been a boxer, sometimes billed as Young Snowball; he subsequently made far more money as a manager – of, among other boxers, Tommy Farr and Freddie Mills, who was briefly a world champion (and who, in the mid-1960s, long after his retirement from boxing, was suspected by some investigators of being the culprit of a series of murders of prostitutes in West London; the best account of the crimes is* Found Naked and Dead *by Brian McConnell, New English Library, 1974; Mills committed suicide).*

the disposal around it of sateen weeping-Pierrot dolls, shiny-pot reminders of day-trips to seaside resorts, sequinned greetings-cards that were too pretty to throw away), but also the daily attendance of a younger woman, Emily Steel, an absolute treasure, to keep the little flat always looking nice. The flat was at the foot of a four-storeyed house numbered 13 (but Olive Young – let us call her that – didn't mind: she was so determinedly unsuperstitious, so conscientious in her efforts to prove it – by, for instance, making detours so as to walk under ladders – that she was, in a way, extraordinarily superstitious). The house was in Finborough Road, which leads south-east from Earls Court to Fulham, with the vast Brompton Cemetery on the right of anyone travelling in that direction.[1]

True thoroughly enjoyed his first night with Olive, and, as he was leaving (Emily Steel had just arrived), remarked that he would like to come again. Olive replied politely; but certain things that he had said and done made her none too sure that she wanted him as one of her regular male friends. And immediately

[1] *It is unlikely that Olive knew this, but one of the upstairs rooms of the house had been the home and business location of a prostitute who was really a Young – her first name was Ruby – till the end of 1907, when she was the star-witness for the prosecution at the trial of her erstwhile lover, Robert Wood, for the murder of 'Phyllis' Dimmock, also a prostitute, in Camden Town. To the great delight of everyone who had not bothered to read the evidence, Wood was acquitted – and the feeling against the girl who had been forced to 'tell on him' was so strong (exemplified by the mass-screaming of a couplet, 'Ruby Young/Should be hung', while she was being smuggled from the Old Bailey in the clothes of one of the courts' charwomen) that she decided not to return to 13 Finborough Road but to find a provincial hiding-place.*

In 1948, the house two doors away was the scene of a murder. George Epson, a 41-year-old engineer, recently widowed, picked up a prostitute, Winifred Mulholland, in Piccadilly Circus, and took her to his first-floor flat at 17 Finborough Road. According to his subsequent statement to the police, she stole nine pounds from him. He hit her with sufficient force to make her stagger back, hitting her head on the mantelpiece with sufficient force to kill her. He kept the corpse in the bedroom for a couple of days, and then – on the night of 5 May – threw it over the balcony into the basement-area, where it was found next morning. He was convicted of murder and sentenced to death; but as the Commons had recently approved a Bill that suspended capital punishment, and the Lords had not yet disapproved of it, he was reprieved.

after his departure, looking in her handbag and finding that a fiver had gone from it, she became certain that he was a nasty customer. Thinking back, she recalled that he had gazed admiringly, perhaps appraisingly, at her jewellery. She checked. No, none of it was missing. Not entirely relieved, she pottered around the flat, checking that all of her sad-faced dolls and seaside souvenirs were there. They were. Though grateful for small mercies, she scowled at her memory of the Major – and then wondered if all plain-clothed majors carried pistols, as he did. Without even realising that she was breaking her code of unsuperstitiousness, she tapped a permed wave of her presently raven hair and thought – may, indeed, have said – 'Touch wood, I'll never entertain *him* again.'

Emily Steel had arrived soon after nine (she was supposed to arrive dead on nine, but though she lived only just up the road, at No. 61, never did). Olive told her of her experience with the Major while sharing the pot of tea that was part of the breakfast that Emily always made for herself as soon as she did arrive. And in the evening – which, as it was of a Sunday, was a time of rest for Olive – she retold the tale to a visiting friend, Doris Dent (who no doubt, while tutting, was preparing to cap the tale with one about a man who had once gypped *her*). Suddenly remembering, Olive told Doris that she, Doris, had *seen* the Major – only briefly, as he had entered the flat the night before just as she, having popped round from *her* flat in Redcliffe Road for a quick word, was on her way to her beat. Oh, *him*, Doris said, as if she remembered him clearly. Perhaps she did – but the thing she remembered most clearly was that he didn't have a hat (which was a quite unusual lack in those days). Now – she went on without pausing for breath – let me tell you about this rotten bugger that pulled a fast one on *me*. . .

During the following twelve days, True made many attempts to arrange another get-together with Olive: he went to the house, he prowled around the West End pub where he had first come across her, he telephoned her. But she respectively refused to answer the door, altered her accustomed custom-collecting route, and when he rang up, either pretended that she was Emily, all alone, or put on a frazzled voice to say that she was all behind like the pig's tail, couldn't talk now, toodle-oo.

When True's mind was not concentrated upon Olive, he –

usually with Armstrong nearby – dashed from one place of
entertainment to another, often in motor-cars that he had hired
on credit or by giving dud cheques; he was slightly less inefficient
as a driver than as a pilot, but still, it is surprising that the
number of road-accidents in London in the second half of February 1922 was about the same as in the first half. Meanwhile, he
bilked sufficient cash to pay for pleasures that he was forced to
pay cash for.

During the daylight hours of the last day of the month, he
pawned a gold watch that had lately been on someone else's
wrist, and in the evening, sitting with Armstrong in the
Hammersmith Palais de Danse (which was the western outpost
of the entertainment empire of Howard 'Bill' Booker, whose
centrally-located establishments included Rector's Club and the
Grafton Galleries – publicised as 'a Heavenly Spot to Fox-
Trot'), he gave Armstrong rather a fright by waving his arms
about and shouting what sounded like 'Sex!-Sex!-Such a surprise!' – an outburst provoked by his recognition of half of a
dancing couple as a man named Sach, an Englishman whom he
had encountered on an aerodrome in America. True's luck was
in: as well as touching Sach for a sovereign, he persuaded him –
and his lately-partnering wife – to extend an invitation to dinner
at their flat in Hyde Park Mansions next day, and while they were
regretting it, each trying to think up an excuse for cancelling the
arrangement, said that if it was OK by them, as he was sure it
was, they being such bricks, the table would be laid for four: he
and his dear old pal Jamie Armstrong, salt of the earth and all
that, would arrive an hour before the suggested time, thirsts at
the ready.

And they did. And they stayed till the small hours of the
morning of 2 March. Then they went their separate ways,
Armstrong to his mother's, True to the Victoria Hotel,
Northumberland Avenue, off Trafalgar Square. After sleeping
and breakfasting, he left without paying – and, crossing the
Avenue, booked into the Grand Hotel, explaining to the recep-
tionist that he had come by cab from Croydon Aerodrome,
having flown his plane there from Paris, and arranging for a
bell-boy or someone of the sort to go to the aerodrome to collect
his luggage: no hurry – any time from tomorrow onwards would
be tickety-boo. In the afternoon, he telephoned a garage in

Chesham Mews, off Belgrave Square, and told the man who answered that he, Major Ronald True, resident at the Grand, required a chauffeured limousine – trouble was, he had just arrived from Gay Paree and, though flush with francs, hadn't a bean of Great British legal tender: would it be satisfactory if he settled up after the events, so to say? The answerer, a chauffeur named Luigi Giuseppe Mazzola, said but of course – he personally would be honoured to transport the Major. His first assignment, that evening, was to drive True to Armstrong's mother's house, and his second, a few hours later – after True had been fed by Mrs Armstrong (and had pocketed her purse while she was washing up, her son drying) – was to drive him and Armstrong round the town, one of the last stops being in Fulham, at the corner of Finborough Road. True got out of the car alone, and hurried up the road. He soon returned, saying that the friends he had hoped to see were out.

It was probably some time earlier that day when True's wife and his mother, and perhaps other members of his family and a legal adviser, conferred to decide what was to be done about him. His mother had last seen him just over two months before; but though he had been out of her sight, communications concerning him had not allowed her to put him out of her mind – for instance, Frances's account of the meeting when he had said that he was leaving her; letters and telephone calls from his bank manager and from sundry creditors, some of whom had supplied goods or services which they, the creditors, felt they had better euphemise; a message from the manager of Murray's Club in regard to a forged cheque. The conference ended. There was unanimous agreement that the subject of it would only get worse if something draconian were not done to make him, if not better, less bad. He had to receive long-term treatment; that could only happen if he were locked up: if that meant having him certified as a lunatic, so be it. First, of course, he had to be traced.

And so Frances, his next-of-kin, went to Scotland Yard. Sorry, she was told – from what she had said (very carefully, steering clear of the least suggestion that her husband had broken any criminal law), it was not up to the police to assist. Not actively, at any rate. But if she wanted the name and address of a reputable private investigator. . . She said that she did. The investigator's name was James Stockley. He was a retired inspector of the Metropolitan Police. She arranged to see him at his office in John Street,[1] Adelphi, on Friday, 3 March. He made notes, gave her receipts for a snap of True and a retaining fee, and promised that 'his number-one operative' (actually, he was speaking modestly of himself, for his was a one-man operation) would institute preliminary inquiries with all possible speed and commence the assignment in earnest first thing on Monday morning.

That would be too late.

There is, on the one hand, too little 'legal' evidence, and, on the other, too much 'unlegal' evidence, regarding True's movements, behaviour and remarks on the Friday, Saturday and Sunday. The men who could, between them, have made a virtually complete diary of those days left a good many gaps, either because barristers did not ask them all that they should have been asked or for less explicable reasons. Those men were James Armstrong, Luigi Mazzola, and (the preamble to his surname has not been mentioned till now) Robert Dare St Aubyn Sach. After they had not said all that they might have done in a witness-box, several uncalled persons offered fillings for more gaps than the number left available, thereby turning the three days into a jigsaw with too many pieces. Both the reticence and the volubility create suspicion about all of the uncorroborated contributions. It is best, I think, to pick and choose from them, limiting the selection from the 'unlegal' batch to one – that of Kate Meyrick, who was London's Irish equivalent of Manhattan's 'Texas' Guinan, the lady who welcomed customers to her El Fey Club with the bellowed greeting, 'Hello, Suckers!' Mrs Meyrick ruled the 43 Club; indeed, she *was* the 43: to go there and find that it was her night off made an even worse disappointment than going to a matinée of *Bulldog Drummond* at the nearby Wyndham's Theatre, having booked up months in advance, only to learn that Gerald du Maurier's unknown understudy was standing in for him that afternoon. So she said in her memoirs,[2] in the early part of the Saturday or

---

[1] *John Adam Street, one block south of the Strand, used to be two streets: Duke Street (running west from York Buildings to Villiers Street) and John Street.*

[2] Secrets of the 43, *John Long, Kate Meyrick, London, 1933.*

Sunday evening (she may have remembered which, but she did not make clear which she was talking about), True was at her club:

> . . . he laughed and joked without cessation, and was the very life and soul of his party. Several people made comments to me on the subject of his conspicuous gaiety, and at one period of the evening he and his friends came into my office to tell me what a wonderful time they were having. 'Let's have plenty more nights like this down here!' True exclaimed. . .

My instinct, trained by long experience of mental cases [years before, she had helped her husband – who, fewer years before, she had left – to run a mental home in Brighton], told me beyond all doubt that there was something essentially 'wrong' with Ronald True; the moment I set eyes on him I said to myself, 'That man is insane,' and even before that night was out my feeling was to receive startling confirmation. . .

> After his visit to my office I kept an eye on him, and soon I noticed a remarkable change in his demeanour. He sat with blazing eyes, giving monosyllabic answers to the friend [it must have been Armstrong] who had brought him as a guest. He cast furtive glances about him, scowled whenever he was addressed, and kept grimacing at people who came anywhere near him. Whenever any of the dancers got in his way he literally snarled at them, and once he was on the very verge of assaulting a man whom he imagined to have made some disparaging remark to him. As a matter of fact the man had not spoken to him at all, but True was only calmed down with the utmost difficulty.
>
> The climax of all this unpleasantness came when some dancer knocked against him in passing. True let out a furious yell and seized the luckless man by the scruff of the neck. The victim was an undersized little fellow; he trembled in that savage grasp and sobbed like a frightened child. Just as True was preparing to smash his fist into the other's face I rushed across, calling to him to stop.
>
> True turned on me like a tiger, and if ever I saw madness burn in a fellow-human's eyes it was then. However, my many dealings with deranged people at Brighton had taught me to stand my ground, so I seized him by the coat-lapels and ordered him not to be such an idiot. Then began a terrible battle of wills. Now was

the test of the hypnotic skill I had acquired with such pains. True was still clutching the terrified young man, but it might be my turn any moment. The strain of the ordeal made me feel sick, I was afraid I might faint.

Suddenly the cowering youth made a desperate effort and tore himself loose from the madman's clutch, leaving his collar and tie behind. This was my chance and I took it. Putting into my gaze every ounce of mental force I could muster, I caught True's eyes and held them. . . At long last – it seemed a veritable eternity! – he became passive. . .

The young man he had attacked was still sobbing and giggling hysterically. Catching the sound, True turned as white as a sheet. With an air of utter bewilderment he gazed round at the scared onlookers. It was quite evident that he had no idea at all of the scene in which he had just figured. Yet he must have realised in a vague, disordered sort of way that he had done wrong, for almost at once he made an incoherent apology and walked straight out of the club, hatless.

No sooner had he vanished through the doorway than I collapsed, while the reaction of the club members, for the most part, took the form of hysterical joking about the occurrence. But the youth who had been in Ronald True's mad clutches was not disposed to laugh. He crossed over to me with a sheepish air and apologised for his own spineless conduct. 'I was never nearer to death, Mrs Meyrick,' he concluded. 'You've saved my life. He meant murder.'

'I know he did,' was my answer, 'but a case of that sort is like clay in the hands of anyone with mental experience.'

According to Sach, he and his wife were with True only twice during the long weekend: on the Friday evening, again at the Hammersmith Palais (Armstrong was there too), and on the Saturday afternoon, starting with lunch at the Strand Corner House and continuing with tea at the Castle Hotel, Richmond, on the south-western outskirts of London (unaccountably, Armstrong spent the afternoon away from True – who, taking advantage of his absence, prevailed upon Mrs Sach to get a fishmonger of her acquaintance to cash a cheque from the purse that he had stolen from Armstrong's mother; Mazzola – who, unless he had diminutive handwriting, must have just about filled both sides of the fare-sheet listing Major True's trips in the limousine, not even a furlong of which was paid for – drove the Major and the Sachs to the Castle, lingered in the car-park for far longer than it can have taken them to drink Darjeeling and eat sardine sandwiches, then drove them back into town, there dropping the Sachs off before taking the Major to the first of several destinations in inner London). In the course of one or both of the above occasions, True told the Sachs about The Other True (once telling them not to look now, but there he was, bold as brass); and told them about *another* man who was tormenting him so – as well as swindling his mother – that he was determined to murder him on Sunday, once he had got into the man's basement-flat in Fulham (a plan of which he drew on the back of a menu; even if Sach had patronised Olive Young, he would still not have thought that the plan was of *her* flat, for True was hopeless at drawing); and told them about *yet another* man – an absolute cad, though he too had been at Bedford Grammar School, who was behaving disgracefully towards a girl called Olive who lived in Bedford (having caught sight of this third man at an adjacent table in the Castle, True followed him out of the room – and, returning a few minutes later, apologised to the Sachs for his unexplained departure before explaining that he had threatened the man with dire consequences if he didn't stay away from Olive, and had spoken to her comfortingly on the telephone).

Late on the Friday (accompanied by Armstrong, after they had been at the Palais, part of the time with the Sachs) and late on the Saturday (unaccompanied by Armstrong), True got Mazzola to drive to the junction of Fulham Road and Finborough Road, alighted from the limousine, hurried up the latter road, and returned soon afterwards. (According to Mazzola, on the Friday night True returned, and then, *with Armstrong*, hurried up Finborough Road again, and returned with Armstrong soon afterwards – but Armstrong never said that that was so. Strangely, he was never asked if it was.)

On the Sunday night – True, Armstrong and Mazzola having spent most of the day at Reading (about as far west from Windsor as Windsor is from the centre of London), where True and Armstrong whiled away part of the time by firing flares from a gun – Mazzola drove True and Armstrong to Fulham, arriving there soon after eleven. True, as usual, hurried up Finborough Road and soon returned. On his order, Mazzola drove to Armstrong's home. True waved goodbye to his friend, then told Mazzola to drive back to Fulham – not to the usual corner but to right outside 13 Finborough Road. Having alighted, he descended the steps to the basement. Soon returning, he dismissed Mazzola, telling him that he was to be back outside No. 13 next morning at eleven. Mazzola drove away.

Olive Young had spent the evening with Doris Dent at the Chinese restaurant in Piccadilly Circus. Parting from Doris (who, one gathers, had decided to stay in the Circus, seeking trade), she boarded an Underground train to Earls Court Station, a few minutes' walk from her nice little flat. She arrived home at about eleven – shortly before True's reconnaisance. Whenever she was out at night, she left a light burning in the entrance hall. Perhaps True knew that. If so, the blackness of the oblong of glass above the door was a sign to him that she was at home. He got rid of Armstrong. He got rid of Mazzola.

It is impossible to explain what made her change her mind and let him in.

But she did.

She let him stay the night.

She may have stirred in her sleep – may even have awoken – when, at seven in the morning, True got up. If she did open her eyes, it is to be hoped that she closed them again, went straight back to sleep, and dreamed a good dream. Not necessarily in this order, True dressed and went to the bathroom (in which, it is almost certain, the WC had a lid muffed in a pink candlewick thing that Olive had bought from Gamage's or Whiteley's), then went to the kitchen and, while making tea, rummaged around and found just what he needed, a stout rolling-pin. He carried the tea-tray, also the rolling-pin, into the bedroom, set the tray on a tiny table, poured two cups of tea – not putting sugar into Olive's, as he couldn't remember if she was sweet-toothed – and after nestling the saucer of her cup into the pillow beside hers, murmured 'day-break, day-wake' or something of the sort, and thumped her head as hard as he could with the rolling-pin. His nestling of the saucer of her cup did not stop the tea from spilling. The cup had toppled, had been jolted away from the saucer, had rolled on to the floor and broken, by the time he delivered the fifth blow with the rolling-pin. There was a piece of Turkish towelling by the bed. He thrust it deep into her gullet, perhaps meaning to throttle, perhaps meaning to gag. There was a cord-belt to a pajama-suit that Olive had not worn since last autumn. He twisted it round the neck of the corpse.

The he drank his tea.

Had a smoke.

And, meanwhile, dabbed at bloodstains on his suit with a hankie that he had moistened with water, still quite hot, from the little jug on the tray. The blessed stains refused to budge. He would have to get himself a new suit. A similar blue one? Or brown for a change? Rather dashing, brown. Anyway, something off the peg. In the good old days, the making-to-measure aces would knock up a three-piece for an esteemed client between brekkers and tiffin, and then say sorry for the delay. No longer so. Further proof, not that any was needed, that England wasn't the land fit for chaps like himself that the political johnnies had promised. He noticed that the dippings of his hankie in the jug – A Present from Herne Bay – had turned the water that was left a funny sort of angostura colour. He squeezed the pink hankie, patted it flat, and arranged it in his breast-pocket so that the part left visible resembled airman's wings. Looking at himself in a mirror, he tidied his hair, thinking that it needed a trim – and suddenly thought, *A hat!* He must remember to buy one when he was buying the suit. One that was a size too large, so that it didn't hurt his head. He hadn't worn one since the year dot. Anyone trying to find him – The Other True . . . the rest of the pesterers . . . their lackies, the rozzers – they would be on the look-out for someone who wasn't wearing a titfer: they wouldn't take a blind bit of notice of someone who was. Brilliant.

He vaguely remembered telling the I-tie chauffeur chap (what *was* his name? – something beginning with M; it would come to him) to do something or other this morning. Something to do with doing something at some time or other. It would come to him. What time did Olive's maid report for duty? Nine-ish? Hadn't Olive said something to him that had prompted him to say something rather droll to her? – words to the effect that punctuality was the politeness of queens. A good one, that. But she, silly bitch, hadn't twigged – had carried on chattering until his head felt as if it was going to burst. It felt that way now.

He had better do a spot of housework.

He hauled the corpse into the bathroom, left it lying on the linoleum-covered floor, swilled his hands, wiped them, came out, closing the door behind him, and made sure the catch had caught. He bumped up the pillows, laid them lengthwise on the bottom sheet, the top of the top one near the bolster, pulled the covers up and almost over the bolster, stood back and squinted at the bed, and decided that, yes, it looked for all the world as if Olive were asleep in it. Taking care not to disturb his composition, he tucked the rolling-pin between the eiderdown and the blanket. He undid the tortoise-shell clasp on her Sunday-best handbag, took out the cash – about eight pounds – and closed it; he scooped up a pile of shillings that had been intended to feed the gas-meter, also a half-crown and some pennies that had been put aside to pay the milk bill; he searched drawers and cupboards, peered in seaside-souvenir pots, felt the stuffing of dolls, and, having gathered together most of the jewellery, put what seemed to him the best items into a jewel-case that he had also picked up, pocketed that, and replaced the other items where he thought he had found them. He made some more tea.

It cannot have taken him till half-past nine to complete those tasks.

About twenty minutes before that time, Emily Steel arrived. She noticed a man's dark coat, gloves, and blue-and-red scarf on the sofa in the sitting-room – and so, sure of what they meant, she was as quiet as a mouse as she made her breakfast of sausages and fried bread and tea (the pot was warm, she noticed), had it, washed up, and started dusting the sitting-room. All of a sudden, a man appeared. Though she had only seen him once before, and then only for a minute or two, she recognised him as Major True, the man her mistress had so often said she never wanted to see again. Taking it for granted that Emily knew who he was, he did not introduce himself. 'Don't disturb Miss Young,' he said, as if he owned the place. 'We were late last night, and she is in deep sleep. I'll send a car round for her at midday.' Emily helped him on with his coat and handed him his scarf and gloves. He tipped her half-a-crown – two tips as one, he said, explaining that comment by reminding her that she had hailed a cab for him the last time he was leaving the flat, when he didn't have a single presentable coin of the realm on his person. She offered the same sort of service. He declined with thanks. Her subsequent assertion that she saw him hailing a cab at the corner of Finborough Road must mean that, a few seconds after he had left, she went out to the basement-area and poked her nose round the railings. Then she finished dusting the sitting-room. Then she tiptoed into the bedroom. Then she opened the door of the bathroom.

As soon as True boarded the cab, he remembered (*a*) the name of the man who in the past few days had saved him a good deal of money on cab-fares, (*b*) the name of the firm that Luigi Mazzola would soon be sacked from, (*c*) where Mazzola would park his limousine in just over an hour if he were not told not to. And so he asked the cabbie to drive to the nearest post office. From there, he telephoned Mazzola, countermandably instructing him to collect Mr Armstrong and deliver him to the Strand Corner House. Hurrying back to the cab, he told the cabbie that he was in a great hurry to get to Coventry Street, between Piccadilly Circus and Leicester Square. Arrived, he told the cabbie to park (which, it now seems unbelievable, was lawful) while he visited Horne Brothers' male-attire shop, opposite the Prince of Wales's Theatre, where the first West End production of *The Gipsy Princess* had just closed after a long run.

Hornes' was one of the few shops, other than those of chemists, where True was both known to and welcomed by the assistants. This morning, one of them hovered while he chose a hat – a bowler costing 18/6d – and passed him on to a colleague when he said airily that he had ruined his suit in a flying accident and needed a ready-made replacement. Having tried on several suits, he chose a brown one, remarking that it was 'not so bad for a reach-me-down', and asked for the bloodstained suit to be parcelled. The assistant given that task preliminarily felt in the pockets. He found the jewel-case. True at once opened it, displaying the contents – 'little mementoes', so he said, of a flying visit to France that had been marred by the accident that had made it necessary for him to splash out five guineas on a new suit. True also bought a collar (10½d) and a tie (12/6d), He handed over seven of the one-pound notes he had stolen from Olive Young's handbag, took the change (3/1½d), and, with a cheery chin-chin to all who had served him, walked out of Hornes' and back to the cab.

Perhaps, when he had told the cabbie to wait, he intended to travel farther from Coventry Street than Wardour Street, a couple of hundred yards north, but having awoken the cabbie, he told him to drive to a barber's shop in the latter street. As there were no one-way 'systems' in the way, it can only have been a minute later when he paid off the cabbie, pleased him with a tip, and sauntered into the shop for a haircut and a shave. He took off his collar and tie before the barber, Marius Dinesens, began – and when Dinesens had done all the slapping, stroking and spraying things that barbers used to do as addenda to a shave, put on the new collar and tie. He had bought a bowler a size larger than his then-unkempt head – and so, with his hair cut short back and sides, the hat was only stayed from falling over his eyes by his ears; he may not have minded, thinking that the more of his countenance that was covered, the better was his disguise. He stuffed the grubby collar and tie in the parcel of the bloodstained suit, and before paying and tipping Dinesens, got his permission to leave the parcel in the shop – just for a few minutes, 'while I pop across the road'. He never came back.

He went to the nearest of the pawnshops that he had patronised lately; at this one he had pledged a cigarette-case and a wrist-watch, both silver, for ten shillings. This morning – it must have been about eleven o'clock by now – he showed the assistant, Herbert Eliett, two women's rings, saying that he would not accept less than seventy pounds for them. Eliett offered forty-five pounds less, and True accepted. And he redeemed the cigarette-case and the watch.

Perhaps because the tip he had given Dinesens had left him penniless, and the adjusted payment from Eliett was all in notes, he did not take a cab to the Strand Corner House but walked there; it was about half a mile south-east of Wardour Street. Mazzola was parked outside. Armstrong was within. And so was Sach – who, it appears, had phoned Armstrong or Mazzola to learn where he might ambush True. His wife or the fishmonger she had persuaded to cash a cheque for True, or both of them, had caused him to worry over that transaction. But as soon as True arrived and was button-holed by Sach, he handed over seven pounds, the amount the fishmonger had given him. His alacrity may have been prompted by a fear that Armstrong might eavesdrop on a clue to the mysterious disappearance of his mother's purse. Sach's departure before True and Armstrong ordered snacks may have been prompted by a fear that, if he lingered, True might insist on treating him and Armstrong to four-course luncheons with wine, and then cadge a couple of the seven pound-notes to pay the bill.

It must have been about noon when True and Armstrong emerged from the Corner House. True wore his bowler – and held on to its brim, both to stop it from being jolted so that he couldn't see where he was going and, as there was a slight breeze, to stop it from being blown off – during the short journey between the restaurant-door and Mazzola's limousine. As soon as he was lolling on the back seat, he removed the hat, sighing with relief as he did so. Armstrong assumed that the hat had made True's head ache; but he does not seem to have wondered why True, mindful of the fact that hats made his head ache, had bought one – or, for that matter, why he had bothered to wear the expectedly irritating bowler while walking from one side of a pavement to the other.

The two pals were driven by the man whose occupation barred him from being a pal of theirs to various places on the western and southern outskirts of London: *inter alia*, Hounslow, Feltham (where they looked at internal combustion engines, Armstrong with interest, True with that knowing expression that meant he was baffled), Croydon (where, before they had tea, True bought a paper: his first choice, the *Sportsman*, being unavailable, he settled for an early edition of the evening *Star*, much of the front page of which was devoted to the first news of the murder of Olive Young; he glanced at the headlines, murmured that there was 'nothing of interest', and tossed the paper in the back of the limousine), and Richmond (where True bought a shirt to go with his new collar and tie, put it on in the shop, and had the assistant make a parcel of the one he had taken off; returning to the limousine, he tucked the parcel under a seat and forgot about it).

He and Armstrong dined (presumably Mazzola turned a glove-compartment into a larder at the start of each day, and survived on biscuits and things until, dismissed, and though by then as much in need of rest as of hot food, he had a proper meal). At about half-past eight, in West London, an area in which there were several theatres, True told Mazzola that as he and Armstrong were going to the second-house at one of them, he,

Mazzola, could take the rest of the night off. True left his coat in the limousine. In a pocket of the coat was the jewel-case containing most of the jewellery he had stolen from Olive Young.

Mazzola drove to his garage. He was surprised to find it crowded – shocked to learn that the crowd was almost wholly composed of detectives impatient for his return. About eleven hours before, two of the detectives (they of B [Chelsea and Fulham] Division) had gone to 13 Finborough Road in response to a telephone call from the landlady, Mrs Trimborn, she having been roused by Emily Steel; they and some of the rest of the detectives had needed only the first few of those hours to establish the identity of the man who had been in the basement-flat when Emily arrived there. By tea-time, following the appearance of an early edition of an evening paper that carried a report of the crime, the leader of the investigation, Chief-Inspector William Brown, had heard over the phone from ex-Inspector James Stockley that, unless he was much mistaken, the man Brown wanted to question was the man he had been hired to trace, and had subsequently met Stockley and 'borrowed' his case-file; and by nine in the evening, the investigators had learned everything they believed they needed to know about the man – excepting where he was.

Mazzola told them that. He, poor, fellow, couldn't make up his mind as to what it was more disturbed by: the fact that his nothing-on-account chauffeuring of Major True seemed unlikely to be recompensed – or the fact that one of the detectives, having let slip that True probably had a gun, insisted that he, Mazzola, being perfectly suited to the task of picking out True in an audience, had to accompany the arresting posse of four inspectors. Adding to Mazzola's misery about the miles and hours that looked like being an excessively bad debt, the insistent detective further insisted that he was to drive the posse in his limousine to where he had just come from. It is reasonable to guess that he was either sullenly silent throughout the return-journey or continuously complaining to four pairs of deaf ears – deaf because their unarmed owners' minds were concentrated, as one, on the thought that the murderer they hoped to arrest was probably mad, probably armed, and possibly prepared to kill again so as to escape arrest.

Any reader who, as I do, savours odd coincidences in and

between tales of murder will feel rather let down by True. As I have mentioned, he, having decided to go with Armstrong to a theatre in West London, had several to choose from. It would be nice if he had decided upon the Granville, Walham Green – and, even allowing for his strangeness, it seems strange that he did not, considered the feast of entertainment offered there: in addition to half a dozen variety acts, there was a showing of a *Pathe Gazette* newsreel – *and*, top of the bill, N. Carter Slaughter & Company in a comedy-playlet entitled *Where's My Baby?* (Not long after the week at the Granville, Slaughter replaced 'N. Carter' with 'Tod'; his subsequent career, during which he often gave larger-than-life portrayals of real-life murderers, is outlined on page 103.) It would be even nicer if True had decided upon the Chiswick Empire, where the sole attraction was *The Savage and the Woman* – for the Savage of that production of 'a drama of the Wild West, with a plot full of thrills, but not blood-curdling ones,' was the American actor Philip Yale Drew, who was then better known as 'Young Buffalo', the sobriquet he had been saddled with as the star of a series of few-reel cowboy films. (In 1929, at the end of the week in which a touring thriller, *The Monster*, was playing at Reading, a tobacconist was murdered in his shop near the theatre, and eventually, when *The Monster* had been to several other towns, Yale Drew, the detective in the play, became the prime suspect in the murder case; lacking decent evidence against him, the leaders of the investigation persuaded the Reading coroner to conduct a 'trial by inquest' of Yale Drew, but the jury returned a 'not proven' verdict.)

For some reason that is hard to fathom – but, whatever, hard to forgive – True spurned both the Granville and the Chiswick Empire in favour of the Hammersmith Palace, which was in King Street, close to the Broadway, and just round the corner from the Hammersmith *Palais*. Perhaps it was the proximity of the theatrical Palace to the terpsichorean Palais that decided him: perhaps he meant to go with Armstrong to the dance hall after the show. The Palace's show for the second time that night, and twice-nightly for the rest of the week, cannot ever have filled more than half of the nearly three thousand seats: the posters advertising it were so loud of words like TREMENDOUS and SENSATIONAL, and so reticent regarding the identity of the component acts, that it must have been little better than one of those amateur-talent programmes that are shown on television nowadays. Since variety bills of the twenties and thirties always included an Irish tenor, usually male, one can be confident that an Irish tenor was on the Palace's bill – and it is fairly safe to say that either the tenor or a singer with some other sort of voice sang the most popular pop song of the day, which was 'You Never Grow Too Old for Mummy's Kisses'. However, assuming that that song was sung, it may have come near the end of the show, when the little lighted frame at the side of the stage, showing the act-number, was well into double figures – and by which time True, who would have had mixed feelings about the Oedipeal sentiments of the lyric, was out of earshot.

Mazzola imagined, understandably nervously in view of the pre-trip tidings that True probably had a gun, that he would have to walk backwards down the aisles, like an empty-handed seller of programmes, chocolates and cigarettes, staring left and right in search of his erstwhile passenger – who, having killed once that day without using the gun, wouldn't hesitate to kill again, using the gun this time – while the posse of obvious detectives, facing him, followed, clarifying the purpose of his backward progress. But, for the first and only time that night, Mazzola had cause to praise God rather than pray to Him. He and the detectives walked through the foyer and, furtively, to the back of the stalls – and he, his eyes attracted by the bright stage, his mind appalled by the overflow of brightness into the auditorium, making it seem, to him, as well lit as the Coliseum in Rome during a matinée, saw, out of the corner of his left eye, a stage-box. Having blinked, just to make sure that he had not been deceived by a mirage of his own making, he felt sure that the occupants of the box – their faces in profile, reverse-silhouettes upon crimson plush – were True and Armstrong. He told the detectives so.

No novelist would dare give four detectives the names of those four detectives. As you know, the chief inspector's name was Brown; the mere inspectors were called Smith, Burton and Hawkins. Leaving Mazzola to recover, they walked to the door on their left, turned right and walked along the corridor, padded up the short flight of stairs, stood for a breath-taking moment by the door to the box, opened it, entered. Burton was in the lead.

According to the official account of what happened next, he, and he alone, made a bee-line for the chair in which True sat, looking the other way, held his arms, and whispered, 'I am a police officer. Come out with me.' The apprehension may not have been as gentle as that sounds; another detective may, by the time Burton had whispered, have helped with the holding – and it would be surprising if another detective had not taken hold of Armstrong, in case he displayed his affection for True in a silly way. Whatever really happened, it happened either quietly or while the orchestra was fortissimo: everyone else in the audience remained engrossed in whatever was happening on the stage. Compared with the most similar incident – the ambushing of John Dillinger, America's Public Enemy Number One, at a cinema in Chicago in 1934, which, through being over-planned by an FBI agent who could not even plan what to do on his days off, resulted in gallons of blood, most of them Dillinger's, being spilt – the capture of True was immaculate.

Out in the corridor, he was searched (and so was Armstrong – who was not detained for long after they and the detectives had been driven to Chelsea police station[1] by Mazzola, who left the station at the same time but did not offer to give Armstrong a lift home). The pistol was taken from True's hip-pocket – the left one, presumably: he would not have wanted it making an uncomfortable bulge against the hip that hurt. He had more cash than he should have had, going by his outlays since his pawning of the two rings; perhaps he had done business with a suburban pawnbroker during the afternoon. Among the other things in his pockets were two Hammersmith Palace ticket-stubs: they applied to seats in the rear-stalls: as soon as the show had begun, he had noticed the empty box, and, with Armstrong following, had trespassed there. Right to the end of his free life, he had cheated.

*　　　*　　　*

[1] *Which was then in Walton Street, which starts at the north-eastern end of Fulham Road and continues to the back of Harrods. According to the shorthand notes of True's trial, Inspector Burton, giving evidence, first said that the station was in Wilton Street, and then that it was in Wilton Road; perhaps the shorthand-writer, having suspected that he had misheard the first time, and being muddled owing to an extraneous noise when the address came up again, decided to give another version, assuming that one or other would be right, and was both times wrong.*

'Here's another for our murderers' club! We only accept those who kill them outright.'

That, you will recall, was True's remark to Henry Jacoby, shortly before a warder took him back to his own quarters in the hospital-block of Brixton Prison.

The remark, odd in itself, is made odder by the fact that, from the moment of his arrest, he claimed that he had not murdered Olive Young. Perhaps, when speaking to Jacoby, he was admitting that he had committed a murder or murders that had passed unnoticed.

The day after his arrest, he had told Inspector Burton:

> . . . I think it only fair to myself to state that a man whose description is as follows – age thirty-one, 6 feet 2 inches, dressed in a dark suit, light grey overcoat, bowler hat – was seen by myself, the chauffeur, and Mr Armstrong, to run down from Finborough Road to Fulham Road, between 10.20 and 10.30 p.m. on Sunday, 5 March. Upon observing me, he immediately went faster. This man knew for a fact that I had an appointment with him at Mrs [sic] Yate's ['Young's'] flat, 13 Finborough Road – one of several which he had already broken. On my calling at the flat at 10.30 p.m. on 5 March, I was met at the door by Mrs Yates, who was in her dressing-gown, and who informed me that he would return at eleven o'clock, and she requested me to do likewise. This I did, and found them both there. A stormy scene ensued, and I left between 12.30 and 1 a.m., Monday, 6 March. Mrs Yates and the man were then in the midst of a violent argument and blows. . .

Donald Carswell, the barrister who introduced and edited *Trial of Ronald True*,[1] reports that, throughout True's stay in the hospital-block,

> he was kept under close observation by the medical officer, Dr [William Norwood] East, and his assistant. . . It was characteristic that he was distinctly popular with his fellow prisoners, being, as always, affable and jocular – but a constant source of trouble and anxiety to the warders and doctors. He slept little, was more

[1] *Hodge, Edinburgh, 1925.*

or less in an excited state, and, in spite of his jocularity, was easily provoked into violence. One of his first acts was to commit a sudden assault on a fellow prisoner, whom he accused, without any justification, of stealing his food. This incident convinced Dr East that sedatives were imperative, for there was every indication that if excitement and insomnia were not abated, another murder would be laid to True's account. . . He was inordinately boastful, incapable of speaking the truth, even when no conceivable purpose could be served by lying, and appeared to have the delusion that people were going about impersonating him. After prolonged observation, Dr East formed the opinion that True was in a state of congenital mental disorder, aggravated by the morphia habit, and that he was certifiably insane. . . The assistant prison doctor came to the same conclusion. The two doctors reported accordingly. These opinions were confirmed and in some respects amplified by the eminent alienists, Dr Percy Smith and Dr Henry Stoddart, who examined True at the request of his relatives. Their examinations, of course, were separate and independent. Their conclusions were practically identical. To both True boasted about his capacities and achievements, and he seemed elated rather than depressed by his position.

The judge at both trials, of Jacoby and of True, was Mr Justice McCardie – who, eleven years later, himself broke a law (which was not abrogated until 1961) by attempting to commit suicide, but was not tried for the misdemeanour because the attempt had succeeded.

Jacoby was prosecuted by Percival Clarke, the eldest son of a greater advocate, and was defended by Lucien Fior, of whom I know nothing other than he had been a barrister of Gray's Inn for less than two years. True was prosecuted by Sir Richard Muir, the Senior Counsel to the Treasury, and was defended by Henry Curtis Bennett, KC, who was among the most expensive of 'actor-barristers', and Roland Oliver, one of the busiest members of the junior bar; the defence had been prepared, and the defenders briefed, by Freke Palmer, the senior partner of the best-known firm of solicitors specialising in the criminal law.[1]

---

[1] *In the following year, Percival Clark prosecuted, and Curtis Bennett and Oliver were 'defence understudies' to Sir Edward Marshall Hall, KC (all*

The public gallery of No. 1 Court, Old Bailey, was always full, but never uncomfortably so, during Jacoby's trial, which lasted two days, till the late afternoon of Friday, 28 April. When, in the absence of the jury, Jacoby's counsel protested that his confession had been 'extracted from him by "third-degree" methods such as are attributed to the American police', Mr Justice McCardie enquired, 'What does "third-degree" mean?' and having been told, decided that certain parts of the confession were not to be mentioned in the jury's presence. Jacoby, giving evidence on his own behalf, insisted that he had not meant to kill Lady White – or anyone, for that matter. While wandering round the first floor of the Hotel Spencer – with a hammer in his pocket – he had thought he heard murmurings in room No. 14: 'I rushed in, saw a form, and lashed out with the hammer. I didn't know it was Lady White. I thought it was someone else who had no right to be there.' The jury retired, came back to ask the judge whether their unanimous belief that Jacoby had intended robbery, not murder, permitted them to find him guilty of manslaughter, which they were told it did not, and, forty minutes after they had first retired, returned with the verdict that Jacoby was guilty of murder; they added a recommendation to mercy 'on the ground of the prisoner's youth and the fact that we do not believe he went into the room intending to kill'. Asked if he had anything to say before sentence was passed, Jacoby replied, 'Nothing at all, sir.' Mr Justice McCardie said that he agreed with the verdict but that he would communicate the recommendation to the Home Secretary, and then passed sentence of death. Several reports of the trial note that Jacoby seemed 'quite unmoved'. He was taken to Pentonville Prison.

On the following Monday, True stood trial in the same court. The proceedings lasted five days. The public gallery was always packed, partly with women; those downstairs places reserved for persons who could not be expected to

---

three having been briefed by Freke Palmer), at the trial of the French Madame Marguerite Fahmy for the shooting to death of her rich, sexually-perverted Egyptian husband outside their suite at the Savoy Hotel. An account of the case appears in Murder in High Places, *Piatkus Books, London, 1986.*

queue were always filled, partly with 'fashionably-dressed ladies'. At the start, True pleaded Not Guilty to the indictment. He said nothing more until near the end. Meanwhile, he was usually seated in the dock, and then usually had a toy duck in his lap; as Sir Henry Hawkins, recently supplanted as the most famous alumnus of Bedford Grammar School, had often had one or other of his pet-terriers, Jack and Joe, with him while presiding in this court and others, True was surely entitled to the company of an inanimate bird. Also meanwhile, Curtis Bennett and Oliver did their best, as for a shorter time did the defence's medical witnesses, to persuade the jury, who could not be expected to believe what True had said, that he was guilty *but insane*. But they did not succeed. The jury, having retired at five past six on the Friday, returned shortly after half-past seven with the one-word verdict. Asked if he had anything to say before sentence was passed, True replied, 'I am innocent, my Lord; that is all.' Mr Justice McCardie passed sentence of death. Several reports of the trial note that True seemed 'quite unmoved'. He was taken to Pentonville Prison.

Jacoby's lawyers appealed. So did True's. Both appeals were dismissed.

On 6 June, the day before Jacoby was scheduled to die, a petition for his reprieve, signed by 'several hundred people' – including two members of the jury that had convicted him – was handed in at the Home Office. Edward Shortt, the Liberal Home Secretary of the Coalition Government – who was also a barrister – announced: 'Nothing can be done. Every representation made in the case has been carefully considered, and I can say nothing more.' Jacoby wrote a letter to his solicitors, Messrs Butcher and Burns, thanking them for doing their best, and continuing:

> Well, I am going to a better land, where I hope I will make good. . . I had a game of cricket tonight, but I lost. Well, I seem to be losing everything just lately, don't I? I have given a note to the governor, thanking him and the other officers for their kindness to me – they are looking after me like anything. I shall be buried in my own clothes, so I shan't have to worry over anything like that. . . – HJ 382. Please excuse this curious signature, as this is what I shall be buried under.

Early next morning, he was confirmed by the Bishop of Stepney, who had come to the prison chapel specially. As a rule, the bell of the nearby St Clement's Church was tolled for hangings, but on this occasion, as another man was awaiting execution, it was not. The ceremony was performed by John Ellis, the last of the several barber-hangmen. At the subsequent inquest, it was stated that Jacoby was dead within ten seconds of his departure from the condemned cell. What was meant, surely, was that fewer than ten seconds elapsed between the start of Jacoby's journey and Ellis's tug on the lever – by the time someone with medical knowledge peeped beneath the scaffold, HJ 382 was fit for further disposal.

A week before, True had received a letter of condolence from the man who, for some months of 1916, had acted as his chauffeur in and around Gosport (far less credulous than Luigi Mazzola, he had never allowed more than an hour or so of credit[1]) – and, breaking off from acknowledging the previous day's delivery of fan-mail, had dashed off a reply which read, in part,

> If I may say so, life is too short – mine will probably not exceed another 14 days – to worry, and as you no doubt know, it is not my nature. Besides, the weather is so hot. It is unfortunate that I shall probably cash my chips in just prior to my birthday – i.e., June 16, and am considering petitioning the King to extend the period to June 17, should it be necessary. Anyway, my motto always has been 'Kismet'. I'm feeling fairly fit in myself, but could be better, also worse. As the French used to say, 'Never worry – things are never so bad that they might not be worse,' and if they are worse that means you are dead and you couldn't worry then. . .
>
> Naturally there's no news to tell you, as, owing to circumstances over which I have no control, I don't get much outside information. It may interest you to know that the winner of the Derby is included in this little lot – Re-echo, Tamar, Diligence, and Lord of Burghley – and with a little judicious management you should be able to have them running for you at a small

---

[1] *Just prior to his appearance as a witness for the prosecution of True, Mazzola's luck had changed. The owner of the garage had rescinded his sacking, having received a cheque from True's mother for at least the amount her son owed.*

investment and still be well covered. . .[1] Give my kindest regard
to your wife, and again thanking you also. Cheerio! old nut, and if
you come to the same place as I'm going to I'll have a drink of nice
cold water ready for you on your arrival.

Though the whole letter gave, or was meant to give, the impression that True was maintaining a stiff upper lip, he must have
scribbled the Sydney-Cartonesque lines of it with tongue in
cheek. He must have known by then that (to amend a comment
by Mark Twain) the reports that he was close to death were
exaggerated.

Soon after sentencing him, Mr Justice McCardie had drawn
the Home Secretary's attention to the evidence given by the
medical witnesses for the defence (the two doctors from Brixton
Prison among them). In dismissing the appeal, Lord Chief
Justice Hewart had said that as Mr Justice McCardie had clearly
and accurately explained the legal definition of insanity to the
jury, and had told them that they were entitled to return the
verdict of Guilty but Insane, it was not in the power of the Court
of Appeal to alter their verdict – but had added that, 'apart
altogether from any question of appeal, there are certain powers
vested in the Home Secretary which, in a proper case, are always
exercised'. Next day, Edward Shortt had done what he had to
do, in accordance with a section of the Criminal Lunatics Act,
1884: he had appointed a commission of medical men, three of
them, to examine True and report on his state of mind.

The Three Wise Men (as they would be called by some
satirical journalists) had been at work for four days when True

---

[1] *The Derby, which was held on the day of Jacoby's execution, was won by the
10–1 shot, Captain Cuttle, ridden by Steve Donoghue, trained by Fred
Darling, and owned by Lord Woolavington (who was the most successful
owner in 1922; ten of his horses, between them, won twenty races with total
prize money of £31.569). Sports-loving readers may like to know that, while
Jacoby and True were on remand, Huddersfield Town beat Preston North
End in the final of the Football Association Cup, which was played at
Stamford Bridge, in Fulham Road (halfway between, and a quarter of a mile
from, the Granville and Finborough Road), and Cambridge won the Boat
Race – from Putney to Mortlake (close to Richmond), via Hammersmith. It
seems likely that if True had made an each-way bet on that contest, his
selection would not have been placed.*

wrote to the sorrowful chauffeur. They had begun dotting the i's
and crossing the t of *insanity*, the word that appeared over and
over again in the draft of opinions they had formed after interviewing and observing him. He probably believed that he was
perfectly sane, but unless he was even crazier than the commissioners believed, he had surely gathered that they were of one
mind in believing that his was so diseased that though he may
have known what he was doing when he murdered Olive Young,
and may have known that what he was doing was wrong, he had
no control over what he did – and therefore should not be put to
death.

The commissioners may have presented their report before
Jacoby was hanged. The Home Secretary's decision to respite
the execution of True and have him removed to Broadmoor
Criminal Lunatic Asylum was announced on the following day.

True is said to have smiled when the Governor of Pentonville
Prison told him that his life had been spared – is said to have
remarked to one of the warders now relieved of 'death-watch
duty', 'I knew I should never be hanged. After all, I've committed no crime.' He was taken to Broadmoor next day. He was
handcuffed during the journey. He wore the suit and tie that he
had bought from Horne Brothers with cash that he had stolen
from the recently-late Olive Young's nice little flat; perhaps the
collar as well, but not the bowler – certainly not.

There were angry editorials or feature-articles, or both, in
most of that morning's newspapers; angrier ones in the evening
papers; even angrier ones next day. And so it went on – delight-
fully   for   Anti-Everything-They-Envied   readers,   who,
determinedly doubtless of whatever they didn't want to doubt,
protested that the Home Secretary, Scourge of the Proletariat
and Protector of the Toffs, had been only too happy to allow the
execution of Jacoby – not only because he was the son of a
working-class man but also because he had (unintentionally,
accidentally) caused the death of a titled woman – but had felt
impelled to rescue True – not only because he was the son of a
woman who had married into the peerage (or was it the Royal
Family?) but also because he had savagely murdered a woman
whose death didn't matter, she being of the unfortunate class.
Come to think of it, perhaps some Men in High Places, one-time
customers of poor Olive, had been pleased to hear of her passing;

come to think of it, perhaps one of those Men, or a conspiracy of Them, had put True up to eradicating her, assuring him of His or Their protection. Most of the Sunday Voices of the People were shrill, the shrillest of them being the *News of the World*, which in the course of one of the five pieces that took up most of a large page, all under the headlines **ONE TAKEN – ONE LEFT** and **Surprising Decisions**, insisted, brooking no argument, that 'it was known that powerful influences were at work in a final endeavour to save True from the gallows', and, in the course of another, made it sound as if, for True, Broadmoor Criminal Lunatic Asylum would be no more unbearable than a Bournemouth five-star hotel:

The reprieved [sic] man's life at Broadmoor will be one of pleasant relaxation, without any of the hardships of a convict penal establishment. In fact, True will be able to live the life of a country gentleman, with the exception that he will be under detention and have as associates other criminal lunatics. Broadmoor is about five miles from Wokingham [near Reading], and situated in beautiful country. . . True will be placed in the asylum infirmary for a probationary period. If he is then judged to be sufficiently mentally fit, and has the means, he will be housed in what is known as the 'Gentlemen's Block'. The inmates of this portion of the institution are allowed all kinds of privileges. They are not obliged to work unless they feel so inclined, but if they elect to take employment of some kind, they are allowed 1½d out of every shilling they earn. There is a very large mechanical shop, and many of the inmates of Broadmoor have worked here and earned considerable sums of money. Other occupations at which they can engage are carpentering and gardening, and for those who prefer more manual work there is road-mending and cleaning in the large grounds. The inmates of the 'Gentlemen's Block' are allowed to mix together, and among the games which are played are billards, cards, chess, draughts. Of outdoor games cricket is very popular with these privileged inmates. Patients of good position are allowed to have other inmates to look after them in the capacity of servants. Their boots are cleaned, beds made, and when meals are permitted in their own rooms these attendants act as waiters. These 'gentlemen' are permitted to make any purchases they desire in the way of food, tobacco, and drink, excepting only intoxicants. In addition to these privileges they are given a little garden. This engages their attention all day if they desire to cultivate botany or grow vegetables. They buy their own seeds, and some extraordinarily fine flowers and vegetables are grown. These may be consumed by the growers or sold for profit.

From Monday, the 'Jacoby/True Scandal' engrossed established correspondence columns – was seen to be a reason for such columns by editors of papers that usually only printed letters of the personally agonised sort. Most of the correspondents complained that there was one law for the rich, another for the poor; others expressed concern that trial by jury was being superseded by 'trial by Harley Street'; others ingeniously used the respite of True on behalf of the campaign for the abolition of capital punishment. Proving their impartiality, one or two editors published one or two letters pointing out that if the cases had not occurred together, neither Jacoby's execution nor True's respite would have occasioned much comment; pointing out that the Home Secretary had had no legal ground for reprieving Jacoby, and that if he had granted a reprieve simply because of Jacoby's youthfulness, then all future murderers who were of much the same age of responsibility would, on the face of it, be entitled to the same dispensation.

Reports that MPs were putting down questions for the Home Secretary prompted several to do so. Donald Carswell notes that when Edward Shortt went to the House to explain his action (apropos of True; he was not asked to explain his inaction apropos of Jacoby),

the general opinion was that he would be humiliated to the dust. He wasn't. He read the House a stiff but lucid lecture on the law of England with respect to insane criminals. When he rose the House was actively hostile. Before he had finished members began to think the least said about True the better, and when he sat down, with that quick generosity and shrewd appreciation of plain facts that characterise the House of Commons, they cheered him heartily. After that not much could be said.

So far as the press was concerned, not enough was said. Few of the papers that had lavishly criticised Edward Shortt allowed more than an inch or so to his answer. Many members of the public never read that what they had read about before was a storm in a tea-cup; some of those that did preferred to pretend that they hadn't; and some of those that did instantly decided that the short end-of-the-matter reports, not the earlier reports of the matter, should be pooh-poohed: they were 'white-wash jobs': they just went to show that you couldn't believe everything you read in the papers.

It appears that the *News of the World*'s prophecies regarding True's life at Broadmoor were not far out. He had a nice time. He revelled in being one of the celebrities of the place – admired by those lesser inmates who were capable of admiration, stared at by those visitors who had come along with the hope of seeing someone worth staring at.

Once the probationary period was over, he asked the staff how he might help. Some task apt to an ex-officer and a gentleman – ideally, something of a social sort that would keep his qualities of leadership in trim. What needed to be run? Well, there were the whist-drives, the *thé-dansants*, the billiards, bowls, boxing, croquet, archery (with rubber-suckered arrows) and ping-pong competitions, the cricket, hockey and both sorts of football teams, the dramatic, literary, art, photographic and choral societies. About the only exclusion from the list of supervisory roles was that of conductor of the orchestra: for the past quarter of a century, the maestro had been Richard Prince, who had made his name as a criminal lunatic by stabbing to death the matinee-idol William Terriss outside the Royal Entrance to the Adelphi Theatre, in the Strand[1] – till True's arrival, Prince had been the undisputed star of the asylum, and he would not take kindly to any attempt by his general competitor to oust him from his conducting platform. But staff worries on that score were dispelled by True, who said he fancied organising outdoor pursuits. And so he was put on a sports sub-committee. Soon

---

[1] *I have written about the case in* Acts of Murder *(Harrap, London, 1986) – which also includes accounts of John Dillinger's life and death (the latter mentioned herein on page 205) and the Reading murder case of 1929 (mentioned herein, on page 203); a far more detailed account of that case is given by Richard Whittington-Egan in* The Ordeal of Philip Yale Drew, *Richard Whittington-Egan, Harrap, 1972.*

afterwards, he appointed himself its chairman; and then he ascended to *the* sports committee, and in a while became its secretary.

Years passed. Outside the walls, there was a General Strike . . . a Stock Market Crash . . . a Depression . . . a less Great War. In the late 1940s (by which time the name of the place had been changed to Broadmoor Institution, and the criminal lunatics were called Broadmoor patients), an author, Ralph Partridge, was allowed within. One of his visits coincided with the patients' annual sports day:

> The prize-giving was a great occasion for the Sports Secretary. Ronald True . . . was largely responsible for the organisation on the field. With his two active and competent Assistant Secretaries he had succeeded in squeezing the original five-hour programme into four hours, and the prizes were being awarded with Broadmoor punctuality at 6.30 precisely. He had kept the sideshows in funds, limped round [his hip still troubled him] to see that all had their tea, and found time to be affable to the visitors. The proceedings had gone without a hitch. And now, as he called out the names of the winners, he was in his element as a wisecracker, making amusing commentary of topical remarks and sly allusions, which found great favour with his mixed audience. When the last prize had been handed out, votes of thanks were passed . . . As the last cheers died down, True dropped a white handkerchief as a signal to the distant Band [more tuneful since 1937, when the tin-eared Prince had been forced, only by death, to relinquish the baton] to strike up God Save the King.[1]

True died in 1951. He was sixty. If Jacoby had been alive, he would have been forty-eight. That point was made by one of the newspapers that noted True's death. All of the noting papers looked back at the 'Jacoby/True Scandal' of 1922, and a couple of them admitted that it wasn't a scandal at all. The rest revived the legend.

It still hasn't withered. I doubt that it will. Legend is more pliable, and therefore more durable, than truth. A month or so

[1]Broadmoor: a History of Criminal Lunacy and Its Problems, *Chatto & Windus, 1953.*

ago, I was in the White Cross pub at Richmond, close to where the Castle Hotel used to be. For the past twenty-four hours, the media (not just the press any more) had been making a fuss over the fact that two men had been convicted of similar speeding-offences by the same magistrate during the same sitting, and while one of the men – rich, related by marriage to a famous family – had been let off a driving-ban, the other – a car-salesman, single – had been disqualified for a month. At a nearby table in the pub, two women were chatting about the juxta-position. One of them was elderly, but I guessed that she had not been born by 1922. She said that times didn't change – that though, admittedly, exceeding the speed-limit on a motorway wasn't to be compared to murder (why, *everyone* except her hubby ignored motorway regulations), she was reminded of something that had happened, oh, a long while ago: a rich and well-connected but peculiar fellow called True did a dreadful murder and was let off scot-free, while a working-class lad, she couldn't remember his name, did a murder not half as dreadful and was hanged. *Well*, she said, we all know what *that* means, don't we? And her companion, who was toying with a Baby-cham, said yes, of course we do.

The publishers would like to thank the following organisations for permission to use their photographs in this book: Mary Evans Picture Library (*The Burkers*), John Frost Historical Newspaper Services (*Michele de Marco Lupo, Norman Thorne's 'living apartment'*), Topham Picture Library (*James Burns*), Syndication International (*Norman Thorne, Henry Jacoby*).